JONATHAN DEMME
INTERVIEWS

CONVERSATIONS WITH FILMMAKERS SERIES
PETER BRUNETTE, GENERAL EDITOR

Courtesy Associated Press

JONATHAN DEMME
INTERVIEWS

EDITED BY ROBERT E. KAPSIS

UNIVERSITY PRESS OF MISSISSIPPI / JACKSON

www.upress.state.ms.us

The University Press of Mississippi is a member of the Association of American University Presses.

Copyright © 2009 by University Press of Mississippi

All rights reserved

First printing 2009

Library of Congress Cataloging-in-Publication Data

Jonathan Demme : interviews / edited by Robert E. Kapsis.
    p. cm. — (Conversations with filmmakers series)
  Includes index.
  ISBN 978-1-60473-117-0 (cloth) — ISBN 978-1-60473-118-7
1. Demme, Jonathan, 1944– —Interviews. 2. Motion picture producers and directors—United States—Interviews. I. Kapsis, Robert E.
  PN1998.3.D393J66 2008
  791.43'0233092—dc22

                                      2008025227

British Library Cataloging-in-Publication Data available

CONTENTS

Introduction *vii*

Chronology *xxi*

Filmography *xxv*

Demme's Monde: A B-Movie Maker Makes the Grade 3
   TOM ALLEN

Demme Monde 6
   CARLOS CLARENS

Director Continues Small-Town Romance 14
   JOANNA CONNORS

Jonathan Demme: On the Line 17
   MICHAEL SRAGOW

Start Making Sense: An Interview with Jonathan Demme 25
   MICHAEL DARE

Could This Also Be the Start of Something Big? 30
   HARRY HAUN

Something Wilder 32
   J. HOBERMAN

Kael and Demme: Meeting of Two American Film Heavies 39
   ROB NELSON

Interview with Jonathan Demme 42
   MICHAEL HENRY AND HUBERT NIOGRET

Identity Check 58
GAVIN SMITH

Demme's Monde 71
AMY TAUBIN

Still Burning 76
AMY TAUBIN

Demme's Philadelphia Story 78
ANN KOLSON

The *Rolling Stone* Interview: Jonathan Demme 84
ANTHONY DECURTIS

The *Guardian*/NFT Interview: Jonathan Demme 96
ADRIAN WOOTTON

Breaking the Rules for *Beloved* 115
ERIC HARRISON

A Conversation with Director Jonathan Demme 120
CHARLIE ROSE

A Young Director Tells a Veteran How He Did It 138
ROB SCHMIDT AND JONATHAN DEMME

The Onion A.V. Club Interview: Jonathan Demme 141
SCOTT TOBIAS

An Interview with Jonathan Demme 147
THEAGRONOMIST.COM

Film-makers on Film: Jonathan Demme on Jared Hess's *Napoleon Dynamite* 151
SHEILA JOHNSTON

Mind Control 154
DAVID THOMPSON

Interview: Singer Neil Young and Director Jonathan Demme 161
TERRY GROSS

Index 177

INTRODUCTION

JONATHAN DEMME is an underappreciated American filmmaker who came of age in the 1970s. Other directors who hit their stride during the seventies but who have received greater overall recognition include Martin Scorsese, Clint Eastwood, Woody Allen, Steven Spielberg, George Lucas, Brian De Palma, Robert Altman, and Francis Coppola. Demme's "youthful infatuation with movies, music, and multiculturalism," writes film critic David Edelstein, has made him "a hipster hero to a generation of filmmakers and film-lovers—a sort of rock 'n' roll Jean Renoir" (*New York Times*, October 27, 2002). But outside this small band of film aficionados, most of whom are film critics, Demme has gone largely unnoticed. While a number of Demme's films have made a strong impression on ordinary filmgoers (e.g., *The Silence of the Lambs*, 1991, and *Philadelphia*, 1993), few are aware that he directed them. His name, in other words, hardly resonates with most filmgoers. It is my hope that this volume of Demme interviews will succeed in introducing this important American director to a larger audience.

Most of the interviews included here focus on Demme's artistry, his filmmaking philosophy, and especially on how his social and political concerns have influenced the subject matter he has been drawn to as a filmmaker. These interviews, spanning the more than three decades of Demme's directorial career, suggest why he has failed to find a larger following outside the film community. The sheer variety of his output, which began with low-budget exploitation pictures and now ranges from Oscar-winning fiction films (*The Silence of the Lambs*, 1991), to impassioned documentaries with a progressive political leaning (*The Agronomist*, 2004), to groundbreaking rock performance films (*Stop Making Sense*, 1984), has made Demme a difficult filmmaker to categorize and fully appreciate.

Demme first broke into the film world during the late 1960s as a critic and publicist. Between 1970 and 1976, he learned the filmmaker's craft working for Roger Corman on several B movies as screenwriter, producer, and finally director. His first three directorial credits came on *Caged Heat* (1974) and *Crazy Mama* (1975), both for Corman's New World Pictures, and *Fighting Mad* (1976), produced by Corman for Twentieth-Century Fox. As "the quirkiest graduate from the Corman College of Quick and Punchy Movies" (as critic Carlos Clarens would call him), Demme learned valuable lessons from his mentor, such as how to work cheap. In a *New York Times* profile by Janet Maslin (May 13, 1979; not included in this collection), Demme declared, "I try not to waste money. . . . To me $165,000 is a huge weight; I'd feel as bad about squandering somebody's $165,000 as squandering their $5 million." (For an extended discussion of Demme's B-movie period, see the commentary track by Demme and Corman in the 2002 DVD release of *Crazy Mama*, which also features a recent interview of Demme by Corman that could not be included here.)

The first two interviews in this collection, by Tom Allen and Carlos Clarens, shed light on Demme's early period and his beginnings as a director of films for major American studios. Allen's profile appeared in the *Village Voice* in 1977, a few months after Demme's first major studio film, *Handle with Care* (originally titled *Citizens Band*) had flopped on release. Now that the film was about to be given a second chance by being screened at the prestigious New York Film Festival, Allen proclaimed that "Jonathan Demme, like his movie, is ripe for discovery," calling him "the most promising newcomer from the Roger ('I'm crazy about him') Corman camp since Monte Hellman and Francis Ford Coppola." Demme tells Allen that in making *Handle with Care* for Paramount, he had complete freedom in the casting and choice of other personnel. One of Demme's strongest character traits—his generosity as a filmmaker—surfaces in this profile, when he singles out for praise the "unique" work of his cinematographer, production designer, scriptwriter, and titles designer.

Early in Carlos Clarens's informative and insightful interview from 1980, Demme reveals that one of the things that had attracted him to *Handle with Care* was "the absence of arbitrary violence" in a rural film about redneck America. "There was no heavy police presence, no gun fights or car crashes. I thought, 'How marvelous. A rural film that doesn't resort to exploitation devices.'" Demme had followed *Handle with Care* with the Hitchcock-inspired thriller *Last Embrace* (1979), which was not a success; Demme felt that the studio (United Artists) had rushed the film into production before script problems were worked out. But the Film Society of Lincoln Center selected his next film, *Melvin and Howard*, to open the 1980 New York Film Festival, and Clarens's interview appeared in *Film Comment*, the prestigious organ of the Film Society, at the time of the Festival.

Melvin and Howard, an upbeat and compassionate comedy about small-town Americana, would go on to win two Academy Awards and three New York Film Critics Circle Awards, including one for Demme as Best Director. Demme's discussion of the film here is highlighted by his description of his use of crane shots at the moment when Melvin becomes a national hero of sorts after learning that he is one of the beneficiaries of Howard Hughes's will. "It was a desire to create an epic feeling, the one epic moment in the person's life. A crane is a very expressive tool, especially if you're after a certain effect. . . . It's like a special paint brush for a big stroke." Demme also emphasizes the importance of the film's final sequence. "When [Melvin and Howard] first meet in the story," says Demme, "they fight and bicker for the first five minutes . . . but gradually they reach an accord: Howard Hughes forgets that he's the richest man in America, Melvin forgets that he's the poorest man in America, and a friendship is struck. And to have Howard take the wheel and Melvin go to sleep in the final sequence articulates a dimension of trust that resulted from that encounter."

In 1981 the Walker Art Center in Minneapolis honored Demme with the first complete two-week retrospective of his films. The retrospective included an advance screening of his latest work, *Who Am I This Time?* (1982), a one-hour TV drama adapted from a Kurt Vonnegut Jr. short story for the PBS *American Playhouse* series. An interview by Joanna Connors was published in the *Minneapolis Star* around the time of this event and focuses on Demme's vision of small-town America, especially as revealed in *Who Am I This Time?*, but also in *Handle With Care* (1977) and *Melvin and Howard* (1980). Demme tells Connors, "Well, I'm in love with America, and I spend a lot of time driving around it. . . . One of my favorite things to do is just get in a car and drive around to places I've never been before. Not many people do that, especially people who live in big cities. Especially people connected with movies. And so they develop this impression of small-town people as hicks, which they aren't at all. People who live in small towns happen to know that they have a lot going for them. I love the small towns."

The Michael Sragow interview for *American Film* (1983) appeared shortly before the release of Demme's next film, the World War II drama *Swing Shift*. We learn here that a number of writers had been involved in developing the film's screenplay and that the difference between the "highly political" original script by Nancy Dowd and the final screenplay was quite dramatic. "From what I saw on paper," says Demme, "she wrote an *exposé* of what was done to women working in the defense industries during World War II." Demme's movie, by contrast, "is a *salute* to the women, and I think that's a crucial distinction." We learn that the documentary *The Life and Times of Rosie the Riveter* was "a big source of thematic inspiration" for Demme. "It documented that the U.S. war machine tried to manipulate women into work at the beginning, despite all the real dangers, and, then, at the end, coerced them into returning to the kitchen; that there was still sexism on the job, and so on. But the biggest thing I got from *Rosie the Riveter* was a sense of triumph." For Demme, the key moment in the film is "when the women are partying, after they've all been fired, and one of them says, 'Boy, they laughed at us the first day we came to work.' And another woman says, 'Yeah, but we showed them.' To me that is what the whole thing is about."

Demme's comments about *Swing Shift* are unusually upbeat considering what we now know about this film's ill-fated production history. In a 1998 interview for the *Guardian*, Demme told Adrian Wootton that a bitter dispute, sparked by the film's star, Goldie Hawn, erupted between himself and the studio (Warner Bros.) after the film's completion. After extensive rewrites, which he was obliged to shoot, had changed the shape of the film, Demme walked away from the project.

After the *Swing Shift* debacle, Demme returned to New York (his home base since 1978) and began what many regard as the most creative and prolific period of his career. Between 1984 and 1988, he directed two feature films (*Something Wild*, 1986; *Married to the Mob*, 1988), a two-hour rock performance film (*Stop Making Sense*, 1984), a film version of performance artist Spalding Grey's monologue about his experiences in Southeast Asia (*Swimming to Cambodia*, 1987), a one-hour documentary for British television about Haitian culture and politics (*Haiti: Dreams of Democracy*, 1987), and several short rock videos. Accordingly, I sought interviews from the 1984–1988 period that captured the intensity and diversity of Demme's creative outpourings during this time. Between 1984 and 1988, as Gavin Smith would observe, Demme gradually took on a new persona, "still quirky, still doing his own thing, but now the words most frequently attached to him by critics are 'hip,' 'urban,' 'multiethnic,' 'wacky,' 'kitchy,' '*subversive.*' Somebody somewhere must have called him a Downtown, as in hip, filmmaker—after all, his office is in NoHo, no-man's-land between the Village, SoHo, and Little Italy. Yup, that's Demme, always on the edges" (see "Identity Check," 1991, in this volume).

Demme's choice of media, collaborators, and subject matter all contributed to his emerging reputation as a hip downtown filmmaker. *Stop Making Sense*, the Talking Heads "rockumentary," is a key film from this period. In a

1988 *Premiere* profile, J. Hoberman called *Stop Making Sense* "a turning point in [Demme's] career—not just a 'return to the joy of moviemaking'" (after his humiliating experiences working on *Swing Shift*) "but also a return to his roots. 'Music was my first love, movies came second,' Demme told one interviewer." Indeed, one of his many jobs in New York during the late sixties had included writing rock criticism for the Boston-based underground weekly *Fusion*. In Jonathan Dare's 1984 *LA Weekly* interview devoted entirely to *Stop Making Sense*, Demme is emphatic about the film's uniqueness. *Stop Making Sense* is a performance film—not a concert film like Martin Scorsese's *The Last Waltz*. "A concert film," says Demme, "may intend, like *The Last Waltz* did so effectively, to give you a sense of what it was like to be at an event the focal point of which was the music. In *Stop Making Sense*, I'd just as soon it didn't occur to people that they're watching a concert, but rather a band performing without the distancing factor of it being an event that happened once. That's why there's no audience in the film until the very end. I thought it was important if the film was to be as effective for filmgoers as it was for me watching the concert. I wanted to capture the energy and the flow and that unrelenting progression of music."

Stop Making Sense was the first of Demme's several collaborations with New York–based avant-garde musician David Byrne, who also contributed to the soundtrack of Demme's nightmarish comedy *Something Wild* (1986) and did the score for Demme's gangster movie comedy *Married to the Mob* (1988). Byrne's contribution to these films is noted by Hoberman and in other interviews from this period. Other avant-garde musicians that Demme collaborated with in these years include Laurie Anderson, who composed the soundtrack for Demme's 1987 experimental performance film *Swimming to Cambodia*.

As pointed out in Hoberman's 1988 profile, the overriding theme of Demme's fiction films (including the two from this period, *Something Wild* and *Married to the Mob*)—"America's optimism, the drive toward personal reinvention"—is also Demme's story. "*Married to the Mob*," writes Hoberman, "recapitulates the story of Demme's own journey from Long Island to Florida to Lower Manhattan." Other interviewers around this time also suggest a correspondence between the man and his work. A *People Magazine* profile by Joshua Hammer (May 25, 1987; not included in this collection), describes Demme "bustling down Broadway" in Midtown Manhattan, "his rainbow-striped African scarf flapping in the breeze, his arms spilling over with Haitian paintings, reggae albums, notebooks filled with jottings and Demme pensées. In his high school baseball jacket, baggy khakis, and tennis sneakers, he looks like a prophet of New York hip, cruising to the ganja-inspired rhythms of ghetto blasters and record-store loudspeakers." Or, as Hoberman puts it, Demme "dresses the way his movies feel."

The *Positif* interview by Michael Henry and Hubert Niogret, published in 1989, returns to many of the same stories and issues covered in earlier interviews, but with fascinating elaborations and embellishments that are generally more substantive and informational than simply anecdotal. One of the highlights of the interview is a candid discussion about Demme's fascination with Middle America and American kitsch. "Middle America is where I grew up," says Demme, "[a]nd I was treated well there as a person. To me it seems a warm place to grow up. . . . The word kitsch . . . I think . . . involves images that recall home to us, things we use to decorate our homes, which partake of kitsch. It's also related to how you dress, the way you 'decorate' yourself, things that express a certain image of yourself, of what you are or aren't."

Also noteworthy about this interview is its coverage of a number of Demme's lesser known experimental projects, such as his controversial documentary *Haiti: Dreams of Democracy*. We learn that PBS had refused to distribute the film in the U.S. and the reasons behind that decision. Demme had wanted the film to be "the voice of Haiti," so he was careful not to "impose a point of view" on the material, seeking instead to "give a shape to all [the] energy" he found there. Because the film is "a discontinuous compilation of conscience, and not at all the documentary linear approach they're used to," says Demme, PBS refused it. (It was eventually shown in the U.S. on Bravo.)

If the *Positif* interview has a unifying theme, it is "how exemplary the process of collaboration can be." As in earlier interviews, Demme is generous in praising his many collaborators over the years, especially B-movie mogul Roger Corman, cinematographer Tak Fujimoto, composer David Byrne, and monologist Spalding Gray. Indeed, during his discussion of kitsch, Demme praises the role of the production designer (with his or her "great imagination" and "great sense of observation") in finding material "that you find interesting to look at and which is going to help the story along."

In the fall of 1988, Demme and *New Yorker* film critic Pauline Kael came to the Walker Art Center in Minneapolis to discuss the art of filmmaking and Demme's artistry in particular. Rob Nelson covered the event for the *Badger Herald*. Kael had been an early champion of Demme's work, and early on in Nelson's piece, we learn that Demme was a devoted reader of Kael. "If you're a filmmaker, you read what Pauline Kael says about you, and you read it in a certain way. I've had my mind changed on several occasions by her. She has a point of view, an artistry that's extraordinary for a film enthusiast [to read]. When the *New Yorker* comes out and you see that, by God, she likes your movie, it's a spectacular feeling, and you read it over and over. When she doesn't like your movie, you read [her review] only once."

The evening began with Kael explaining her enthusiasm for Demme's work: "What I love about Jonathan Demme is that he searches for the poetry in the tacky, the everyday. I value that much more highly than the so-called tasteful movies people make. It takes more courage to be as unhighfalutin and democratic as he. And movies are, or were intended to be ever since they were first shown, a democratic art form." In the course of the evening, Kael showed selected clips of Demme's films and commented on them. The showing of the high school reunion scene from *Something Wild*, reports Nelson, triggered an interesting exchange between Kael and Demme about "the Demme trademark of a mesmerizingly chaotic *mis-en-scène*."

> Kael: "I love the cluttered, messy screen in your movies. They're wonderfully busy."
> Demme: "I think that's one of the things I learned from Roger Corman. . . . When I first started working with him he took me to lunch, sat me down and said, 'Okay, Jonathan, we've got an hour. The most important thing to remember is that this is a visual medium, first and foremost. The eye is the primary organ, and if you can't keep the eye stimulated you're not going to keep the brain stimulated.'"

Kael also gets Demme to mention other directors and films that he admires, such as Martin Scorsese, his favorite contemporary director. Commenting on the violent second half of *Something Wild* that was off-putting to some in the audience, Kael makes a connection between Scorsese and Demme: "Part of what is wonderful about Scorsese's earlier work like *Mean Streets* and *Taxi Driver* is that it does upset you and it doesn't apologize. I don't think the violence *in Something Wild* is gratuitous, and I think it's absolutely crucial to the movie. Without that second half the movie would make no sense." We also learn that "if pressed," Demme would name the 1967 documentary *Far from Vietnam* his favorite film. "To me," says Demme, "that film is proof that movies can effect positive change, even if it's only in one person."

In 1991 Demme directed the serial killer/feminist thriller *The Silence of the Lambs*. It was his first big commercial success, earning more than 130 million dollars. It was also a huge critical success and the recipient of numerous awards, including Academy Awards for Best Picture and Best Director. The 1991 *Film Comment* interview by Gavin Smith makes the case that within the context of Demme's career, *The Silence of the Lambs* is no aberration but a "distillation of everything Demme's done up to now," especially his interest in featuring assertive women characters who want another life, to achieve something better, like Angela in *Married to the Mob* or Clarise in *The Silence of the Lambs*. "Ever since my days of working with Roger Corman, and perhaps before that," says Demme, "I've been a sucker for a woman's picture. A film with a woman protagonist at the forefront.... It has to do with the fact that just in everyday life, in this male-dominated society, women are operating under some handicaps. For women to achieve what they want is harder than for men to achieve what they want. That brings a touch of the underdog to them and I respond to that." In *The Silence of the Lambs*, Demme wanted to put audiences in Clarice's shoes. "That meant shooting a lot of subjective camera in every sequence she was in," says Demme. "[Y]ou always had to see what Clarice was seeing." The one exception is the sequence in the killer Gumb's basement when Demme, with a Hitchcock-type touch, shifts from Clarice's point of view to that of Gumb—stalking her through his night vision goggles. "I relish that," says Demme, "on a technique-of-making-a-movie level: the idea that we'll be predominantly in the shoes of the protagonist throughout, and then when she's deprived of her sight, we'll be in the shoes of the killer. And perhaps that abandonment of Clarice's point of view will make the situation even more distressing on a certain dialectic level."

By contrast, in Amy Taubin's *Village Voice* interview with Demme, also from 1991, she argues that *The Silence of the Lambs* is unprecedented in Demme's career, in particular that Demme's heightened "understanding of female experience" distinguishes this film from all his previous work. His sensitivity to female experience is revealed in a discussion of the final exchange between Clarice and Crawford, her boss at the FBI, that takes place after her graduation from the FBI Academy. "After Crawford says that line to Clarice, 'Your father would have been proud of you,'" Demme reminds the reader, the film "cuts to a close-up of Jodie, who gives him what I think is the most complicated smile in the history of cinema. I don't want his statement to be taken literally. I see Clarice as a woman who has to unencumber herself from those velvet shackles."

Taubin also interviewed Demme shortly after the release of his next film, *Cousin Bobby* (1992), a documentary (produced by Spanish TV) about his cousin, Reverend Robert Castle, a radical clergyman in Harlem who during the 1960s became involved in the civil rights struggle, especially through his contacts with members of the Black Panther Party. The interview sheds light on Demme's own political leanings. "*Cousin Bobby*," writes Taubin, "concludes with a montage of what Demme describes as 'American race war footage from the '60s.' As KRS-One raps a 'WakeUp' to history African American style, we see cities burning: Detroit, Boston, Watts..." "I share Bob's feelings and I marvel at his devotion," says Demme, "but I'm not an activist and I hate sounding as if I thought I was. I'm a taxpayer who hates the way my government is behaving. My response to the riots is as a filmmaker, and luckily, I have a chance to channel my rage."

In 1993 Demme produced and directed *Philadelphia*, Hollywood's first major movie about AIDS. The film earned over 40 million dollars and won two Academy Awards and two Golden Globes, for Tom Hanks's performance in the leading role and Bruce Springsteen's song "Streets of Philadelphia." It also generated fierce criticism, especially among gay activists, who complained that the film contained no explicit sex scenes involving the gay couple. Anthony DeCurtis's "*Rolling Stone* Interview: Jonathan Demme" (1994) focuses mainly on *Philadelphia*—how Demme became involved in the project, what he hoped to accomplish by making the film, etc. However, the real subject of this interview is Demme's emergence as a socially responsible filmmaker. This becomes dramatically evident in a discussion of what motivated him to make *Philadelphia*. Since several critics had speculated that Demme had made the film to appease the gay community, which had perceived his previous film, *The Silence of the Lambs*, as homophobic, Demme is quick to dismiss this speculation as ridiculous. "Who on earth would get the shit kicked out of them," asks Demme, "and then turn around and do something nice for the people who kicked the shit out of them?" In fact, we learn that Demme "was already working on *Philadelphia* before *Lambs* came out." One of Demme's friends, Juan Botas, had contracted AIDS, and "the desire to do a film on AIDS," says Demme, "was born of Juan's sickness."

The interview also reveals that Demme very consciously made *Philadelphia* with an eye toward changing public opinion about the AIDS crisis. "We looked for a story for a long time, and we decided it would be pointless to make a film for people with AIDS. Or for their loved ones.... We wanted to reach people who *don't* know people with AIDS, who look down on people with AIDS." Increasingly, after 1994, Demme would become more involved in making low-budget documentaries than big-budget feature films like *Philadelphia* or *The Silence of the Lambs*. Demme tells DeCurtis that "the great thing about documentaries is that if you're interested in social issues, you don't need a $20-million budget to put them on the screen." To illustrate this point, Demme mentions *One Foot on a Banana Peel*, a documentary by his friend Juan Botas that he produced for less than $30,000. "It's wonderful," says Demme. "It sheds light on the experience of having AIDS in a very different way than *Philadelphia* does." The *Rolling Stone* interview ends with Demme admitting his growing preference for making films that address serious social issues over pure entertainment films. "I'm probably not as open to full-tilt entertainments, 'Never mind the message, let's just have a ball' kind of films, as I might have been five, certainly ten years ago. I'd rather read books and be a lazy person than just make a movie anymore."

The next three interviews in this collection are from 1998—the year that *Beloved*, Demme's adaptation of Toni Morrison's Pulitzer Prize–winning novel, opened in theaters. *Beloved* was his first feature since *Philadelphia* in 1993. During this five-year period, Demme served as producer or executive producer on a number of fiction films and documentaries (for example, *Household Saints*, 1993; *Devil in a Blue Dress*, 1995; *That Thing You Do!*, 1996; *Mandela*, 1996), and directed two performance films: *The Complex Sessions* (1995), a thirty-minute music video for the album *Sleep with Angels* by Neil Young and Crazy Horse, and *Storefront Hitchcock*, a full-length film featuring English singer/songwriter Robyn Hitchcock, released in the same year as *Beloved*.

The Charlie Rose interview included here originally aired on PBS just as *Beloved* was opening in theaters. It provides compelling evidence of Demme's great passion for film in general and films about the black experience in particular. We learn that the project to translate *Beloved* into a film originated with Oprah Winfrey, who picked Demme to direct it. Demme describes a recent conversation with Oprah, in which he told her that, regardless of how the film might fare, "I wanted her to know that I was completely happy and thrilled with it and I was really happy to hear her come back and say that she wouldn't change a thing in it."

Besides providing specific information about the making of *Beloved*, the Rose interview delves into Demme's broader concern with race issues. Given the centrality of race to the American experience, how can one explain the relative absence of African American stories in the movies? "It's such a big part of our . . . life here in America," says Demme. "How come it's not represented more in the movies?" We learn that, earlier in his career, Demme had wanted to direct *Boyz n the Hood*, but its screenwriter, John Singleton, decided to direct it himself. "And I reference that," says Demme, "because [after Spike Lee] put the news out there that African Americans could make fantastic movies that could also make money . . . John Singleton kicked the door open a lot wider as well, and suddenly it seemed there was at last a really thrilling wave of African American directors—men and women—making . . . everything from mindless, delightful comedies to serious stuff . . . penetrating studies of what's going on today." Demme goes on to discuss the role that film can play in helping us understand how race has divided us as a nation. "I don't think that *Beloved* can have an impact on the way the country views race or views our shameful, tragically ignored past of slavery," cautions

Demme. "But I do think—and I know that the movie can change you a little bit . . . individuals can have their thoughts changed about things from movies, and . . . that's why we need movies that aspire to turning on light bulbs . . . and the trick is to make 'em really entertaining in the doing."

Eric Harrison's *Los Angeles Times* piece ("Breaking the Rules for *Beloved*," 1998) focuses on the difficulties of making a film based on a novel that "combines elements of several genres into a work that refuses to be pinned down." "There are probably at least a dozen levels that the book operates on," says Demme, but that was "part of the excitement . . . the challenge [of making the film]." The interview describes the unconventional approaches Demme adopted to translate the novel into a film that would remain true to the novel. "We felt that to back off in any manner from what the book was trying to achieve thematically and narratively would blow it," says Demme. "We felt that the book, being the exquisitely made piece of literature that it is, we really had to honor it."

Adrian Wootton's *Guardian* interview from 1998 focuses primarily on Demme's other fearlessly offbeat film released that year, the performance film *Storefront Hitchcock*. One of the highlights of the interview is a discussion of the importance of setting in Demme's performance films, from *Stop Making Sense* and *The Complex Sessions* to the current one featuring songwriter-guitarist Robyn Hitchcock. "With David Byrne and Talking Heads," says Demme, "you had a whole stage full of musicians to cut to, so you were obliged to cut to a certain extent. . . . With Robyn it was basically 'there he is' . . . and it's just one guy and one guitar. . . . We didn't want to do it in just one room, in an enclosed space, because the eye might get too familiar with the surroundings." So Demme came up with the idea, inspired by a Hungarian theater group called Squat Theatre, to set the Hitchcock performance "in a storefront space" where there would be a drape that from time to time opened to reveal the street. "So when we were trying to think of how we'd make the Robyn show have more going for it visually," Demme recalls, "we thought 'Ah! Homage to the Squat Theatre.'"

Since 1999 Demme has directed only two mainstream Hollywood films, both remakes of classic American films from the early 1960s—*The Truth about Charlie* (2002), a remake of Stanley Donen's 1963 romantic thriller *Charade*, and *The Manchurian Candidate* (2004), adapted from John Frankenheimer's 1962 cold war thriller. Demme tells Scott Tobias of *The Onion*'s A.V. Club (2002) that *The Truth about Charlie* presented him with "an opportunity . . . to acknowledge the incredibly important part that French movies have played in [his] movie-going life." Indeed, the film is really his homage to the French New Wave and to his parents who "God bless 'em, took me to French movies when I was a little kid." Later in college during the early sixties, he "discovered New Wave films and devoured years and years of the stuff." In the 1989 *Positif* interview described earlier in this introduction, Demme recalls seeing François Truffaut's *Shoot the Piano Player* in college and being blown away by the experience. "I love this movie and I love the fact that I love this movie. I still think it's an exceptional film. Seeing it and appreciating it allowed me to look at films differently. . . . Suddenly, I could appreciate a film like that, in black and white, coming from France, with subtitles. Just as [Charles] Aznavour says, 'May my mother die if I'm not telling the truth'—there's a cut and a woman drops dead. That was for me an essential moment. It was the first time I realized what montage was. This film really opened my eyes to the work of filmmakers. Afterwards, I could admire people who make films the way I admired people who write books. I had never been aware of that until then, when those images struck the screen." Altogether appropriate then is Charles Aznavour's cameo in *The Truth about Charlie*—part of the film's homage to the French New Wave.

In David Thompson's 2004 *Sight and Sound* interview, we learn that what attracted Demme to remake *The Manchurian Candidate* was not simply his affection for the original but rather the "idea of replacing communism as the great global threat to mankind with what," according to Demme, "is arguably the biggest threat to humanity today: the multinational corporations who profit from war." Demme acknowledges that *The Manchurian Candidate* is, above all, a psychological thriller. But it is also, says Demme, a "good time-capsule movie" about today and "if it provides some food for thought as well, that's terrific."

In addition to his feature film assignments (another, *Rachel Getting Married*, will be released in 2008), Demme has continued working on various music projects, and in 2006 he directed the acclaimed performance film, *Neil Young: Heart of Gold*, highlighting the career of singer/songwriter Neil Young. Demme and Young discuss the challenges of making this film with Terry Gross on National Public Radio's *Fresh Air* (2006). The major challenge, according to Demme, was to capture the strong emotional bonds existing between Young and the other brilliant musicians performing with him and "making that [bonding] part of the texture of the film."

In recent years, Demme's name has frequently appeared in credits as a producer of both fiction films and documentaries on widely varying topics. He also directed three of these documentaries—*The Agronomist* (2003), about Haitian journalist and freedom fighter Jean L. Dominique; *Right to Return: New Home Movies from the Lower 9th Ward* (2007), a TV miniseries about New Orleans in the aftermath of Hurricane Katrina; and *Jimmy Carter Man from*

Plains (2007), a verité-style look at the thirty-ninth president that received three awards at the Venice Film Festival. I have included an interview about *The Agronomist* from the film's official website. This informative interview covers a number of topics relevant to *The Agronomist*—how Demme became interested in Haiti and acquainted with Jean Dominique; when he decided to shoot a documentary about Dominique's life; the sources of the images used in the film; and what Demme found most striking about Dominque's attitudes and beliefs. What emerges from this interview is not only Demme's passion for the man but also his great love of Haiti—its culture, its people.

Regarding his penchant for alternating between documentaries and fiction films, Demme told David Carr in a recent *New York Times* interview (October 21, 2007; not included here), "I like the strange dichotomy.... In fiction you are trying to make it seem as real as possible, and in documentary you are seeking to make it as dramatic as possible."

In addition to making films on subjects that he is passionate about, Demme has also found time to champion the careers of up-and-coming filmmakers who have excited him. I end the introduction with a discussion of two unusual selections from 2000 and 2004. In Sheila Johnston's 2004 interview for the *London Telegraph*, Demme talks about twenty-four-year-old Jared Hess's first feature film, *Napoleon Dynamite*. The 2000 piece appeared in the *Los Angeles Times* and is actually a conversation between Demme and thirty-four-year-old director Rob Schmidt, whose latest film, *Crime + Punishment in Suburbia*, Demme had enjoyed, having seen it recently at the Sundance Film Festival. Both of these selections remind us of Demme's generosity of spirit, a quality that surfaces again and again in interviews from all phases of his career. For example, Demme tells Sheila Johnston what he especially admired about *Napoleon Dynamite*: "What I loved as an audience member and was in awe of as a filmmaker," says Demme, "was its endless originality.... For anyone who wishes to do something offbeat, there could be no greater challenge than *Napoleon Dynamite*, made on a shoestring. I hope I find in the next year or two that, yes, I too still have the courage and ability to make a movie like that."

As with all books in the *Conversations with Filmmakers* series, the interviews are reproduced as they originally appeared and have not been edited in any significant way (typographical errors and the like have been silently corrected). Indeed, the repetitions found here reflect Demme's recurring concerns, such as his love of music, and the stories retold, as pointed out in my discussion of the 1989 *Positif* interview, usually receive interesting elaborations that are almost always more informational than anecdotal.

I would like to thank Peter Brunette, general editor of the *Conversations with Filmmakers* series, for offering me this project, my third in the series (the others were on Woody Allen and Clint Eastwood), and Walter Biggins, my editor at the University Press of Mississippi, for his guidance and encouragement. Susan Kapsis was always available for editorial counsel. I would also like to thank Queens College and the Professional Staff Congress-City University of New York (PSC-CUNY) Research Award Program for providing much-needed financial support. Finally, special thanks are due to Kathie Coblentz, my multitalented editorial consultant and translator, for her invaluable contributions.

REK

CHRONOLOGY

Unless otherwise noted, films are listed according to release year, though the production year may differ. Details of Academy Awards and nominations and Golden Globes and nominations may be found in the Filmography. Other major awards (but not nominations) are listed here.

1944–58   Jonathan Demme is born in Baldwin, Long Island, New York, 22 February 1944. Grows up in neighboring Rockville Center.
1951–58   Father works as a publicist for an airline. Parents travel frequently, especially in the Caribbean. Demme recalls a memorable trip his parents took to Haiti and a family vacation in Puerto Rico and the Virgin Islands when he was seven. At an early age, his parents also expose him to quality foreign films like *Mr. Hulot's Holiday* and *Black Orpheus* and many films by Fritz Lang. By age eleven or twelve, he travels alone to see popular American films all around Long Island.
1959   Father accepts a publicity job at the Fontainebleau Hotel and family moves to Miami.
1964–65   Enrolls in the University of Florida at Gainesville to study veterinary medicine; here he is first exposed to the films of Ingmar Bergman and François Truffaut and other New Wave directors. Writes movie reviews for the student paper. Does poorly in science courses and drops out of school after a year, but soon resumes reviewing films for a local suburban weekly (*Coral Gables Times*).
1964   Demme's father, who by now has become head of publicity at the Fontainebleau Hotel, introduces his son to movie mogul Joseph E. Levine. Demme is offered a position in Avco Embassy's publicity department after Levine reads Demme's enthusiastic review of one of his studio's films (*Zulu*).

1965–67 Completes military service. Moves back to New York. Works as a publicist at Avco Embassy, Pathé Contemporary, and United Artists. Writes movie reviews for *Film Daily* and rock criticism for the Boston-based underground weekly *Fusion*. Makes his first movie, a short called *Good Morning, Steve*.

1968–69 Moves to London to work as a sales representative for a company that produces commercials; continues as rock correspondent for *Fusion*. Meets Roger Corman, who hires him to work as a unit publicist on one of his films (*Von Richthofen and Brown*) being shot in Ireland.

1970–76 Learns the filmmaker trade working for Roger Corman on several B-movies. Moves to the West Coast. Marries film producer Evelyn Purcell.

1971 Writes (with Joe Viola) and produces the motorcycle movie *Angels Hard as They Come*.

1972 Writes (with Joe Viola) and produces *The Hot Box*. Gets experience as a second-unit director on the film.

1974 Writes and directs *Caged Heat*—a women's prison film that New York's Museum of Modern Art will later acknowledge with a special screening.

1975 Directs *Crazy Mama*.

1976 Writes and directs *Fighting Mad* for Twentieth-Century Fox.

1977 Directs the redneck comedy *Handle with Care* (previously titled *Citizens Band*)—his first major studio film. It premieres at the New York Film Festival and receives a rave review from *New Yorker* critic Pauline Kael. Though it goes on to win the National Society of Film Critics Award for Best Film, it flops at the box office.

1978–79 Moves back to New York. Directs *The Last Embrace*—his homage to Alfred Hitchcock's *Vertigo*.

1980 Directs *Melvin and Howard*, his upbeat and compassionate comedy about small-town Americana. It opens the New York Film Festival, wins two Academy Awards, a Golden Globe for Mary Steenburgen's performance in a supporting role, a National Society of Film Critics Award for Best Film and the New York Film Critics Award for Best Director. Ends his ten-year marriage.

1981 The Walker Art Center in Minneapolis honors Demme with a complete two-week retrospective of his films.

1982 Directs a one-hour TV drama, *Who Am I This Time?*, adapted from the Kurt Vonnegut Jr. short story, for the PBS *American Playhouse* series.

1984	Directs the World War II drama *Swing Shift*, a film that is taken away from him in a bitter dispute with Warner Bros. and the film's star, Goldie Hawn. Writes and directs *Stop Making Sense*, the Talking Heads performance film and the first of his several collaborations with avant-garde musician David Byrne; it wins the National Society of Film Critics Award for Best Documentary.
1985–89	Directs several rock videos.
1986	Directs the nightmarish comedy *Something Wild*. David Byrne, Laurie Anderson, and John Cale contribute to the film's soundtrack. Visits Haiti for the first time.
1987	Directs *Swimming to Cambodia*—a film version of performance artist Spalding Gray's one-man two-evening stage performance about his experiences in Southeast Asia, with music by Laurie Anderson. Marries artist Joanne Howard.
1988	Directs the gangster movie comedy *Married to the Mob* with a score by David Byrne. Writes, produces (with Jo Menell), and directs *Haiti: Dreams of Democracy*, a one-hour documentary for television. His daughter Ramona is born (two more children will follow).
1989	Produces a collection of popular Haitian music, *Konbit*.
1990	Produces *Miami Blues*, a thriller directed by George Armitage.
1991	Directs the feminist thriller *Silence of the Lambs*. It is a huge critical and commercial success, winning five Academy Awards; a Golden Globe for Jodie Foster's performance in the leading role; the Directors Guild of America Award for Outstanding Directorial Achievement in Motion Pictures; the Writers Guild of America Award for Best Screenplay Based on Material from Another Medium; and two British Academy of Film and Television Arts Awards.
1992	Directs *Cousin Bobby*, a documentary about his cousin, Reverend Robert Castle, a radical clergyman in Harlem.
1993	Produces and directs *Philadelphia*, Hollywood's first major movie about AIDS discrimination. It wins two Academy Awards and two Golden Globes, for Tom Hanks's performance in the leading role and Bruce Springsteen's song "Streets of Philadelphia."
1993–2001	Directs several short music videos, including three with Bruce Springsteen ["Streets of Philadelphia" (1993), "Murder Incorporated" (1995), and "If I Should Fall Behind" (2000)].
1994	Produces *One Foot on a Banana Peel, the Other Foot in the Grave*, a documentary about a group of AIDS patients, directed by Juan Botas and Lucas Platt.

1995	Directs *The Complex Sessions*, a thirty-minute video for the album *Sleeps with Angels* by Neil Young and Crazy Horse.
1996	Produces *That Thing You Do*, the directorial debut of *Philadelphia* star Tom Hanks. Produces three documentaries about Haitian torture victims (*Courage & Pain*), Double-Dutch rope skipping (*Into the Rope*), and Nelson Mandela (*Mandela*).
1997	An exhibition of more than one hundred paintings from Demme's own collection of Haitian Art opens at the Equitable Gallery in Manhattan.
1998	Directs *Storefront Hitchcock*, a performance film featuring English singer/songwriter Robyn Hitchcock. Directs *Beloved*, based on the Pulitzer Prize–winning novel by Toni Morrison that tells the saga of a former slave.
2000	Member of jury at the Cannes Film Festival.
2002	Writes, produces, and directs *The Truth about Charlie*, a remake of Stanley Donen's classic 1963 romantic thriller *Charade*. Produces *Adaptation*, directed by Spike Jonze, which wins an Academy Award for Chris Cooper's supporting performance and two Golden Globes for Cooper's and Meryl Streep's supporting performances.
2003	Produces and directs *The Agronomist*, a documentary about Haitian journalist and freedom fighter Jean L. Dominique. It receives the Independent Feature Project (IFP) Award for Best Documentary.
2004	Produces and directs *The Manchurian Candidate*, a remake of John Frankenheimer's 1962 cold war classic.
2006	Produces and directs *Neil Young: Heart of Gold*, a performance film highlighting the career of singer/songwriter Neil Young.
2007	Produces and directs *Right to Return: New Home Movies from the Lower 9th Ward*, a TV miniseries about New Orleans in the aftermath of Hurricane Katrina. Writes, produces, and directs *Jimmy Carter Man from Plains*, a documentary about the former president. It premieres at the Venice and Toronto Film Festivals. The Guggenheim Symposium honors Demme for his work as a documentary filmmaker.
2008	Directs the contemporary drama/comedy *Rachel Getting Married*, based on Jenny Lumet's original screenplay. Produces and directs *Neil Young Trunk Show*, a new performance film to be released on 2009.

FILMOGRAPHY

Unless otherwise noted, date is for earliest known U.S. release, and names are given as credited.

As Director

1974
CAGED HEAT (Artists Entertainment Complex, Renegade Women Productions/New World Pictures)
Executive producer: S. W. Gelfman
Producer: Evelyn Purcell
Director: **Jonathan Demme**
Screenplay: **Jonathan Demme**
Cinematography: Tak Fujimoto (DeLuxe)
Editing: Johanna Demetrakas, Carolyn Hicks, Michal Goldman
Art direction: Eric Thiermann
Music: John Cale
Cast: Juanita Brown (Maggie), Roberta Collins (Belle Tyson), Erica Gavin (Jacqueline Wilson), Ella Reid (Pandora), Barbara Steele (Supt. McQueen)
83 minutes

1975
CRAZY MAMA (New World Pictures)
Producer: Julie Corman
Associate producer: Peter Cornberg
Director: **Jonathan Demme**
Screenplay: Robert Thom
Story: Frances Doel
Cinematography: Bruce Logan (Metrocolor)
Editing: Lewis Teague, Allan Holzman

Art direction: Peter Jamison
Music coordinator: Marshall Leib
Songs: Boudleaux Bryant, J. P. Richardson, and others
Additional music: Snotty Scotty and the Hankies
Cast: Cloris Leachman (Melba Stokes), Stuart Whitman (Jim Bob Tucker), Ann Sothern (Sheba Stokes), Linda Purl (Cheryl), Donny Most (Shawn), Bryan Englund (Snake), Merie Earle (Bertha)
83 minutes

1976
FIGHTING MAD (Santa Fe Productions/Twentieth Century-Fox)
Producer: Roger Corman
Co-producer: Evelyn Purcell
Director: **Jonathan Demme**
Screenplay: **Jonathan Demme**
Cinematography: Michael Watkins (DeLuxe)
Editing: Anthony Magro
Music: Bruce Langhorne
Cast: Peter Fonda (Tom Hunter), Lynn Lowry (Lorene Maddox), John Doucette (Jeff Hunter), Philip Carey (Pierce Crabtree), Harry Northup (Sheriff Len Skerritt), Scott Glenn (Charlie Hunter)
87 minutes

1977
HANDLE WITH CARE (originally CITIZENS BAND) (Fields Company/Paramount Pictures)
Executive producer: Shep Fields
Producer: Freddie Fields
Associate producer: Paul Brickman
Director: **Jonathan Demme**
Screenplay: Paul Brickman
Cinematography: Jordan Cronenweth (Color: Movielab)
Editing: John F. Link, II
Production design: Bill Malley
Music: Bill Conti
Cast: Paul Le Mat (Spider/Blaine Lovejoy), Candy Clark (Electra/Pam), Ann Wedgeworth (Dallas Angel/Joyce Rissley), Marcia Rodd (Portland Angel/Connie Rissley), Charles Napier (Chrome Angel/Harold Rissley), Alix Elias (Hot Coffee/Debbie), Bruce McGill (Blood/Dean Lovejoy), Roberts Blossom

(Papa Thermodyne/Floyd Lovejoy)
98 minutes

1978
COLUMBO: MURDER UNDER GLASS (TV) (Universal TV/NBC)
Producer: Richard Alan Simmons
Associate producer: Anthony Kiser
Director: **Jonathan Demme**
Screenplay: Robert Van Scoyk
Cinematography: Duke Callaghan (Color)
Editing: Gene Ranney
Art direction: Howard E. Johnson
Music: Jonathan Tunick
Cast: Peter Falk (Lt. Columbo), Louis Jourdan (Paul Gerard), Shera Danese (Eve Plummer), Richard Dysart (Max Duvall), Mako (Kanji Ousu)
73 minutes

1979
LAST EMBRACE (Taylor-Wigutow Productions/United Artists)
Producers: Michael Taylor, Dan Wigutow
Associate producer: John Nicolella
Director: **Jonathan Demme**
Screenplay: David Shaber
Novel: Murray Teigh Bloom (*The 13th Man*)
Cinematography: Tak Fujimoto (Technicolor)
Editing: Barry Malkin
Production design: Charles Rosen
Art direction: James A. Taylor
Music: Miklos Rozsa
Cast: Roy Scheider (Harry Hannan), Janet Margolin (Ellie Fabian), John Glover (Richard Peabody), Sam Levene (Sam Urdell), Charles Napier (Dave Quittle), Christopher Walken (Eckart), **Jonathan Demme** (Man on Train) (uncredited)
102 minutes

1980
MELVIN AND HOWARD (Universal Pictures)
Producers: Art Linson, Don Phillips
Associate producer: Terry Nelson

Director: **Jonathan Demme**
Screenplay: Bo Goldman
Cinematography: Tak Fujimoto (Technicolor)
Editing: Craig McKay
Production design: Toby Rafelson
Art direction: Richard Sawyer
Music: Bruce Langhorne
Cast: Paul Le Mat (Melvin Dummar), Jason Robards (Howard Hughes), Mary Steenburgen (Lynda Dummar), Elizabeth Cheshire (Darcy Dummar), Chip Taylor (Clark Taylor)
95 minutes
Academy Awards: Actress in a Supporting Role, Mary Steenburgen; Writing, Screenplay Written Directly for the Screen, Bo Goldman
Academy Award nomination: Actor in a Supporting Role, Jason Robards
Golden Globe: Best Performance by an Actress in a Supporting Role in a Motion Picture, Mary Steenburgen
Golden Globe nominations: Best Motion Picture—Musical or Comedy; Best Performance by an Actor in a Motion Picture—Musical or Comedy, Paul Le Mat; Best Performance by an Actor in a Supporting Role in a Motion Picture, Jason Robards

1982
AMERICAN PLAYHOUSE (series): WHO AM I THIS TIME? (TV) (Rubicon Film Productions/PBS)
Executive producer: Morton Neal Miller
Producer: Morton Neal Miller
Director: **Jonathan Demme**
Screenplay: Morton Neal Miller
Story: Kurt Vonnegut Jr.
Cinematography: Paul Vom Brack (Color)
Editing: Marc Leif
Music: John Cale
Cast: Susan Sarandon (Helene Shaw), Christopher Walken (Harry Nash), Robert Ridgely (George Johnson), Dorothy Patterson (Doris)
53 minutes

1984
SWING SHIFT (Lantana Productions, Hawn/Sylbert Movie Company, Jerry Bick Productions/Warner Bros.)
Executive producers: Alex Winitsky, Arlene Sellers

Producer: Jerry Bick
Associate producer: Charles Mulvehill
Director: **Jonathan Demme**
Screenplay: Nancy Dowd (credited as Rob Morton); Bo Goldman, Ron Nyswaner (uncredited)
Cinematography: Tak Fujimoto (Technicolor)
Editing: Craig McKay; additional editing: Gib Jaffe
Production design: Peter Jamison
Art direction: Bo Welch
Music: Patrick Williams
Cast: Goldie Hawn (Kay Walsh), Kurt Russell (Mike "Lucky" Lockhart), Christine Lahti (Hazel Zanussi), Fred Ward (Archibald "Biscuits" Touie), Ed Harris (Jack Walsh)
100 minutes
Academy Award nomination: Actress in a Supporting Role, Christine Lahti
Golden Globe nomination: Best Performance by an Actress in a Supporting Role in a Motion Picture, Christine Lahti

1984
STOP MAKING SENSE (Performance film) (Talking Heads Films, Arnold Stiefel Company/ Island Alive, Cinecom)
Executive producer: Gary Kurfirst
Producer: Gary Goetzman
Director: **Jonathan Demme**
Conceived for the stage by: David Byrne
Cinematography: Jordan Cronenweth (Technicolor)
Editing: Lisa Day; additional editing: Barbara Pokras
Music: David Byrne and Talking Heads; song "Take Me to the River" by Al Green and Mabon Hodges
With: Talking Heads: David Byrne, Bernie Worrell, Alex Weir, Steve Scales, Lynn Mabry, Edna Holt, Tina Weymouth, Jerry Harrison, Chris Frantz
88 minutes

1986
ALIVE FROM OFF CENTER (series): Segment ACCUMULATION WITH TALKING PLUS WATERMOTOR (TV/Performance film) (KCET-TV, KTCA-TV, Trisha Brown Company, UCLA/PBS)
Executive producer: Melinda Ward (for *Alive from Off Center*)
Producers: Carol Markin, Edward Saxon
Director: **Jonathan Demme**

Cinematography: Jacek Laskus (Color)
Editing: Pam Wise
With: Trisha Brown (choreography and performance)
11:30 minutes

1986
SOMETHING WILD (Religioso Primitiva/Orion Pictures)
Executive producer: Edward Saxon
Producers: **Jonathan Demme**, Kenneth Utt
Associate producers: Bill Miller, Ron Bozman
Director: **Jonathan Demme**
Screenplay: E. Max Frye
Cinematography: Tak Fujimoto (Color: DuArt)
Editing: Craig McKay
Production design: Norma Moriceau
Art direction: Steve Lineweaver
Music: John Cale, Laurie Anderson; songs by David Byrne, UB40, New Order, Fine Young Cannibals, and other artists
Cast: Jeff Daniels (Charles Driggs), Melanie Griffith (Audrey Hankel), Ray Liotta (Ray Sinclair), Margaret Colin (Irene), Jack Gilpin (Larry Dillman)
113 minutes
Golden Globe nominations: Best Actor—Motion Picture Musical or Comedy, Jeff Daniels; Best Actress—Motion Picture Musical or Comedy, Melanie Griffith; Best Supporting Actor—Motion Picture, Ray Liotta

1987
SWIMMING TO CAMBODIA (Performance film) (The Swimming Company/Cinecom Pictures)
Executive producers: Lewis Allen, Peter Newman
Co-executive producers: Amir Malin, Ira Deutchman
Producer: R. A. Shafransky
Associate producer: Edward Saxon
Director: **Jonathan Demme**
Screenplay: Spalding Gray, based on his monologue
Cinematography: John Bailey (Color)
Editing: Carol Littleton
Production design: Sandy McLeod
Music: Laurie Anderson
With: Spalding Gray
85 minutes

FILMOGRAPHY   xxxi

1987
(U.K. TV; first aired in the U.S., 1988)
HAITI: DREAMS OF DEMOCRACY (Documentary/TV) (Clinica Estetico, Channel Four, Transvision-Haiti/Cinema Guild Inc.)
Executive producer: Edward Saxon
Producers: **Jonathan Demme**, Jo Menell
Associate producer: Sandy McLeod
Co-producer: Craig McKay
Directors: **Jonathan Demme**, Jo Menell
Cinematography: Jean Fabius, Dyanna Taylor (Color)
Editing: Kathy Schermerhorn
Music: Manno Charlemagne, Group Foula, Les Frères Parent, and other artists
With: Abouja, Orès Jean-Baptiste, André Pierre, Wilfred Lavaud, Lucien Phararon, Philippe Dodard
52 minutes

1987
TRYING TIMES (series): Episode A FAMILY TREE (TV) (VisionArts Communications, KCET/PBS)
Executive producer: Phylis Geller
Producer: Jon S. Denny
Associate producer: Stephanie Anderson
Director: **Jonathan Demme**
Screenplay: Beth Henley, Budge Threlkeld
Cinematography: Tony C. Jannelli
Editing: Ruth Foster, Craig McKay (series credit)
Production design: Sandy McLeod
Music: Eric Allaman (series credit)
Cast: Rosanna Arquette (Kara Dimley), John Stockwell (Maxwell Fletcher), Hope Lange (Frances Fletcher), David Byrne (Byron), Robert Ridgely (Marlin Fletcher)
30 minutes

1988
MARRIED TO THE MOB (Mysterious Arts/Orion Pictures)
Executive producers: Joel Simon, Bill Todman Jr.
Producers: Kenneth Utt, Edward Saxon; Michael A. Cherubino (uncredited)
Associate producer: Ron Bozman
Director: **Jonathan Demme**
Screenplay: Barry Strugatz, Mark R. Burns

Cinematography: Tak Fujimoto (Color: DuArt)
Editing: Craig McKay
Production design: Kristi Zea
Art direction: Maher Ahmad
Music: David Byrne
Cast: Michelle Pfeiffer (Angela de Marco), Matthew Modine (Mike Downey), Dean Stockwell (Tony "The Tiger" Russo), Mercedes Ruehl (Connie Russo), Alec Baldwin ("Cucumber" Frank de Marco)
103 minutes
Academy Award nomination: Actor in a Supporting Role, Dean Stockwell

1991
THE SILENCE OF THE LAMBS (Strong Heart/Demme Productions/Orion Pictures)
Executive producer: Gary Goetzman
Producers: Edward Saxon, Kenneth Utt, Ron Bozman
Associate producer: Grace Blake
Director: **Jonathan Demme**
Screenplay: Ted Tally
Novel: Thomas Harris
Cinematography: Tak Fujimoto (Technicolor)
Editing: Craig McKay
Production design: Kristi Zea
Art direction: Tim Galvin
Music: Howard Shore
Cast: Jodie Foster (Clarice Starling), Anthony Hopkins (Dr. Hannibal Lecter), Scott Glenn (Jack Crawford), Ted Levine (Jame "Buffalo Bill" Gumb), Anthony Heald (Dr. Frederick Chilton)
118 minutes
Academy Awards: Actor in a Leading Role, Anthony Hopkins; Actress in a Leading Role, Jodie Foster; Director, **Jonathan Demme**; Writing, Screenplay Based on Material Previously Produced or Published, Ted Tally; Best Picture, Edward Saxon, Kenneth Utt, Ron Bozman, Producers
Academy Award Nominations: Film Editing, Craig McKay; Sound, Tom Fleischman, Christopher Newman
Golden Globe: Best Performance by an Actress in a Motion Picture—Drama, Jodie Foster
Golden Globe Nominations: Best Director—Motion Picture, **Jonathan Demme**; Best Motion Picture—Drama; Best Performance by an Actor in

a Motion Picture—Drama, Anthony Hopkins; Best Screenplay—Motion Picture, Ted Tally

1992
COUSIN BOBBY (Documentary) (Tesauro S.A./Cinevista)
Producer: Edward Saxon
Associate producers: Valerie Thomas, Lucas Platt
Director: **Jonathan Demme**
Cinematography: Ernest Dickerson, Craig Haagensen, Tony Jannelli, Jacek Laskus, Declan Quinn (Color)
Editing: David Greenwald; Li-Shin Yu, associate editor
Music: Anton Sanko; song "Blackman in Effect" by KRS-One, from *Edutainment*
With: Robert W. Castle, **Jonathan Demme**
70 minutes

1993
PHILADELPHIA (Clinica Estetico/TriStar Pictures)
Executive producers: Gary Goetzman, Kenneth Utt, Ron Bozman
Producers: Edward Saxon, **Jonathan Demme**
Associate producer: Kristi Zea
Director: **Jonathan Demme**
Screenplay: Ron Nyswaner
Cinematography: Tak Fujimoto (DuArt, Technicolor)
Editing: Craig McKay
Production design: Kristi Zea
Art direction: Tim Galvin
Music: Howard Shore; original songs: Bruce Springsteen, Neil Young
Cast: Tom Hanks (Andrew Beckett), Denzel Washington (Joe Miller), Jason Robards (Charles Wheeler), Mary Steenburgen (Belinda Conine), Antonio Banderas (Miguel Alvarez), Ron Vawter (Bob Seidman), Joanne Woodward (Sarah Beckett)
119 minutes
Academy Awards: Actor in a Leading Role, Tom Hanks; Original Song, Bruce Springsteen, for "Streets of Philadelphia"
Academy Award nominations: Makeup, Carl Fullerton, Alan D'Angerio; Original Song, Neil Young, for "Philadelphia"; Writing, Screenplay Written Directly for the Screen, Ron Nyswaner
Golden Globes: Best Performance by an Actor in a Motion Picture—Drama,

Tom Hanks; Best Original Song—Motion Picture, Bruce Springsteen, for "Streets of Philadelphia"
Golden Globe nomination: Best Screenplay—Motion Picture, Ron Nyswaner

1997
SUBWAY STORIES: TALES FROM THE UNDERGROUND (TV) (Clinica Estetico, Ten in a Car Productions, HBO NYC Productions/HBO)
Executive producers: **Jonathan Demme**, Rosie Perez, Edward Saxon
Producers: Richard Guay, Valerie Thomas
Associate producer: Victoria Westhead
Directors: **Jonathan Demme**, Craig McKay, Bob Balaban, Patricia Benoit, Seth Rosenfeld, Lucas Platt, Alison Maclean, Julie Dash, Abel Ferrara, Ted Demme
Screenplay: Adam Brooks, John Guare, Lynn Grossman, Angela Todd, Seth Rosenfeld, Albert Innaurato, Danny Hoch, Julie Dash, Marla Hanson, Joe Viola
Cinematography: Tom Hurwitz, Anthony Jannelli, Ken Kelsch, Adam Kimmel
Supervising editor: Andy Keir
Production design: Edward Check
Music: Mecca Bodega
80 minutes (entire show; 10 segments)
Segment 1, SUBWAY CAR FROM HELL
Director: **Jonathan Demme**
Screenplay: Adam Brooks
Editing: Andy Keir
Cinematography: Anthony Jannelli (Color)
Cast: Bill Irwin (Himself), Kris Parker/KRS-One (Vendor)
4:26 minutes (continued in closing credits sequence, 9 minutes)

1998
STOREFRONT HITCHCOCK (Performance film) (Clinica Estetico, Orion Pictures/MGM)
Executive producers: Gary Goetzman, Edward Saxon
Producer: Peter Saraf
Associate producer: Steven Shareshian
Director: **Jonathan Demme**
Cinematography: Anthony Jannelli (Color: DuArt)
Editing: Andy Keir

Music: Robyn Hitchcock
With: Robyn Hitchcock (guitar, harmonica, vocals), Deni Bonet (violin), Tim Keegan (guitar, backing vocals)
77 minutes

1998
BELOVED (Touchstone Pictures, Harpo Films, Clinica Estetico/Buena Vista Pictures)
Executive producer: Ron Bozman
Producers: Edward Saxon, **Jonathan Demme**, Gary Goetzman, Oprah Winfrey, Kate Forte
Associate producer: Steven Shareshian
Director: **Jonathan Demme**
Screenplay: Akosua Busia, Richard LaGravenese, Adam Brooks
Novel: Toni Morrison
Cinematography: Tak Fujimoto (Technicolor)
Editing: Carol Littleton, Andy Keir
Production design: Kristi Zea
Art direction: Tim Galvin
Music: Rachel Portman
Cast: Oprah Winfrey (Sethe), Danny Glover (Paul D), Thandie Newton (Beloved), Kimberly Elise (Denver), Beah Richards (Baby Suggs), Lisa Gay Hamilton (Younger Sethe)
172 minutes
Academy Award nomination: Costume Design

2002
THE TRUTH ABOUT CHARLIE (Clinica Estetico, Magnet Entertainment/Universal Pictures)
Executive producer: Ilona Herzberg
Producers: **Jonathan Demme**, Peter Saraf, Edward Saxon
Co-producers: Neda Armian, Mishka Cheyko
Director: **Jonathan Demme**
Screenplay: **Jonathan Demme**, Steve Schmidt, Peter Stone (credited as Peter Joshua), Jessica Bendinger
Screenplay for *Charade* (1963): Peter Stone
Cinematography: Tak Fujimoto (DeLuxe; Panavision)
Editing: Carol Littleton; co-editor: Suzanne Spangler
Production design: Hugo Luczyc-Wyhowski
Art direction: Ford Wheeler, Delphine Mabed, Bertrand Clerq-Roques

Music: Rachel Portman
Cast: Mark Wahlberg (Joshua Peters/Alexander Dyle/Lewis Bartholomew), Thandie Newton (Regina Lambert), Tim Robbins (Lewis Bartholomew/Carson J. Dyle), Joong-Hoon Park (Il-Sang Lee), Ted Levine (Emil Zadapec), Lisa Gay Hamilton (Lola Jansco), Christine Boisson (Commandant Dominique)
104 minutes

2003
(festival screenings; released in the U.S., 2004)
THE AGRONOMIST (Documentary) (Clinica Estetico/ThinkFilm, Palisades Pictures)
Executive producer: Daniel Wolff
Producers: **Jonathan Demme**, Peter Saraf, Bevin McNamara
Associate producers: Edwidge Danticat, Lizi Gelber
Director: **Jonathan Demme**
Cinematography: Aboudja, **Jonathan Demme**, Peter Saraf, Bevin McNamara (Color: DuArt)
Editing: Lizi Gelber, Bevin McNamara
Music: Wyclef Jean, Jerry "Wonda" Duplessis
With: Jean Dominique, Michèle Montas
90 minutes

2004
THE MANCHURIAN CANDIDATE (Clinica Estetico, Scott Rudin Productions/Paramount Pictures)
Executive producer: Scott Aversano
Producers: Tina Sinatra, Scott Rudin, **Jonathan Demme**, Ilona Herzberg
Associate producers: Peter Kohn, Polly Mallinson
Director: **Jonathan Demme**
Screenplay: Daniel Pyne, Dean Georgaris
Novel: Richard Condon; 1962 screenplay: George Axelrod
Cinematography: Tak Fujimoto (DeLuxe)
Editing: Carol Littleton, Craig McKay; additional editing: Martin Levenstein
Production design: Kristi Zea
Art direction: Teresa Carriker-Thayer
Music: Rachel Portman; featuring Wyclef Jean
Cast: Denzel Washington (Ben Marco), Meryl Streep (Eleanor Shaw), Liev Schreiber (Raymond Shaw), Jon Voight (Senator Thomas Jordan), Kimberly Elise (Rosie), Bruno Ganz (Richard Delp), Simon McBurney (Atticus Noyle)

129 minutes
Golden Globe nomination: Best Performance by an Actress in a Supporting Role in a Motion Picture, Meryl Streep

2006
NEIL YOUNG: HEART OF GOLD (Performance film) (Clinica Estetico, Shakey Pictures, Playtone/Paramount Classics, Shangri-La Entertainment)
Executive producers: Bernard Shakey (i.e. Neil Young), Elliot Rabinowitz, Gary Goetzman
Producers: **Jonathan Demme**, Ilona Herzberg
Co-producer: Paul Deason
Associate producer: Mia Lee
Director: **Jonathan Demme**
Cinematography: Ellen Kuras (DeLuxe)
Editing: Andy Keir
Production design: Michael Zansky
Music: Neil Young; song "Four Strong Winds" by Ian Tyson
With: Neil Young, Emmylou Harris, Ben Keith, Spooner Oldham, Rick Rosas, Pegi Young, Grant Boatwright, and others, performing nine songs from the album *Prairie Wind* and selections from *Harvest*, *Harvest Moon* and others
103 minutes

2007
RIGHT TO RETURN: NEW HOME MOVIES FROM THE LOWER 9TH WARD (Documentary/TV miniseries) (Clinica Estetico)
Executive producers: Neda Armian, Lisa Hepner
Producers: **Jonathan Demme**, Abdul Franklin, Daniel Wolff
Associate producers: Jamal El-Amin, Lauren Lillie, Sarah Quinn
Director: **Jonathan Demme**
Editing: Abdul Franklin
100 minutes

2007
JIMMY CARTER MAN FROM PLAINS (Documentary) (Clinica Estetico, Participant Productions/Sony Pictures Classics)
Executive producers: Ron Bozman, Jeff Skoll, Diane Weyermann
Producers: **Jonathan Demme**, Neda Armian
Director: **Jonathan Demme**

Writer: **Jonathan Demme**
Cinematography: Declan Quinn (Color)
Editing: Kate Amend
Music: Djamel Ben Yelles, Alejandro Escovedo
With: Jimmy Carter, Rosalynn Carter
120 minutes

2008
RACHEL GETTING MARRIED (Clinica Estetico/Sony Pictures Classics)
Executive producers: Carol Cuddy, Ilona Herzberg
Producers: Neda Armian, Marc Platt
Associate producer: Innbo Shim
Director: **Jonathan Demme**
Screenplay: Jenny Lumet
Cinematography: Declan Quinn (Color)
Editing: Tim Squyres
Production design: Ford Wheeler
Art direction: Kim Jennings
Music: Zafer Ta, Donald Harrison Jr.
Cast: Anne Hathaway (Kym), Debra Winger (Abby), Bill Irwin (Paul), Rosemarie DeWitt (Rachel), Anna Deavere Smith (Carol)

Music Videos (Selection)

1985
THE PERFECT KISS (Factory Records)
Producer: Michael H. Shamberg
Director: **Jonathan Demme**
Cinematography: Henri Alekan (Color)
Editing: Tony Lawson
Music: New Order
With: New Order (Bernard Sumner, Peter Hook, Stephen Morris, Gillian Gilbert)
10:30 minutes

1990
RED, HOT + BLUE (TV Special), segment: IN THE STILL OF THE NIGHT
Producer: Loretta Farb
Director: **Jonathan Demme**
Cinematography: Jacek Laskus (Color)

Editing: Adam Bernstein
Music: Cole Porter
With: The Neville Brothers
3:21 minutes

1993
STREETS OF PHILADELPHIA
Directors: **Jonathan Demme**, Ted Demme
Cinematography: Adam Kimmel (Color)
Music: Bruce Springsteen
With: Bruce Springsteen
3 minutes

1994
THE COMPLEX SESSIONS (Clinica Estetico/Warner Reprise Video)
Executive producer: Peter Saraf
Producer: Gary Goetzman
Director: **Jonathan Demme**
Cinematography: Tak Fujimoto (Color)
Editing: Andy Keir
Music: Neil Young
With: Neil Young and Crazy Horse (Frank Sampedro, Billy Talbot, Ralph Molina), performing four songs from the album *Sleeps with Angels*
27 minutes

1995
MURDER INCORPORATED
Director: **Jonathan Demme**
Editing: Craig McKay
Music: Bruce Springsteen
With: Bruce Springsteen, The E Street Band
5:47 minutes

2000
IF I SHOULD FALL BEHIND
Director: **Jonathan Demme**
Music: Bruce Springsteen
With: Bruce Springsteen, The E Street Band; vocals: Bruce Springsteen, Steve Van Zandt, Nils Lofgren, Patti Scialfa, Clarence Clemons
6 minutes

In addition, Jonathan Demme has directed music videos for Suburban Lawns ("Gidget Goes to Hell"; featured on *Saturday Night Live*, 1980); Talking Heads ("Once in a Lifetime," 1984); Tom Tom Club ("Genius of Love," 1984); Artists United Against Apartheid ("Sun City," 1985); Chrissie Hynde and UB40 ("I Got You Babe," 1985); Sandra Bernhard ("Everybody's Young," 1985); Fine Young Cannibals ("Ever Fallen in Love," 1986); Les Frères Parent ("Chemin Victoire," "Veye Yo!" 1987); Suzanne Vega ("Solitude Standing," 1987); The Neville Brothers ("Sister Rosa," 1987); Les Frères Parent and The Neville Brothers ("Konbit," 1988); The Feelies ("Away," 1988); KRS-One ("Heal," 1990); Steve Earle ("Rich Man's War," 2004).

As Producer, Directed by Others

1971
ANGELS HARD AS THEY COME (New World Pictures)
Executive producer: Roger Corman (uncredited)
Producer: **Jonathan Demme**
Director: Joe Viola
Screenplay: **Jonathan Demme**, Joe Viola
Cinematography: Stephen Katz (Metrocolor)
Supervising editor: Joe Ravetz
Art direction: Jack Fisk
Music: Richard Hieronymos
Cast: Scott Glenn (Long John), Charles Dierkop (General), James Iglehart (Monk), Gilda Texter (Astrid), Gary Busey (Henry)
90 minutes

1972
THE HOT BOX (New World Pictures)
Executive producer: Roger Corman (uncredited)
Producer: **Jonathan Demme**
Associate producer: Evelyn Purcell
Director: Joe Viola
Second unit director: **Jonathan Demme**
Screenplay: Joe Viola, **Jonathan Demme**
Cinematography: Felipe J. Sacdalan (Metrocolor)
Editing: Ben Barcelon, Nonoy Santillan, Richard S. Brummer, Barbara Pokras

Art direction: Ben Otico
Music: Restie Umali
Cast: Carmen Argenziano (Flavio, the guerrilla), Andrea Cagan (Bunny Kincaid), Margaret Markov (Lynn Forrest), Rickey Richardson (Ellie St. George), Laurie Rose (Sue Pennwright), Charles Dierkop (Garcia/Major Dubay)
85 minutes

1990
MIAMI BLUES (Tristes Tropiques/Columbia TriStar Films, Orion Pictures)
Executive producers: Edward Saxon, Fred Ward
Producers: **Jonathan Demme**, Gary Goetzman
Co-producers: Kenneth Utt, Ron Bozman
Associate producer: William Horberg
Director: George Armitage
Screenplay: George Armitage
Novel: Charles Willeford
Cinematography: Tak Fujimoto (DeLuxe)
Editing: Craig McKay
Production design: Maher Ahmad
Music: Gary Chang
Cast: Alec Baldwin (Fred Frenger), Jennifer Jason Leigh (Susie Waggoner), Fred Ward (Sgt. Hoke Moseley), Charles Napier (Sgt. Bill Henderson), Nora Dunn (Ellita Sanchez)
97 minutes

1991
WOMEN & MEN 2: THREE SHORT STORIES (TV), segment: A DOMESTIC DILEMMA (HBO Showcase/HBO)
Executive producers: David Brown, William S. Gilmore
Producer: **Jonathan Demme**
Co-producers: Edward Saxon, Ron Bozman
Director: Kristi Zea
Screenplay: Robert Breslo
Story: Carson McCullers
Cinematography: Tony Jannelli (Color)
Editing: William Scharf
Production design: Leslie Pope
Music: Suzanne Vega, Anton Sanko

Cast: Ray Liotta (Martin), Andie MacDowell (Emily), Michael Galeota (Andy), Eva Donia Silver-Smith (Marianne)
24 minutes

1993
HOUSEHOLD SAINTS (Jones Entertainment, Novena Films, Peter Newman Productions/Fine Line Features)
Executive producer: **Jonathan Demme**
Producers: Richard Guay, Peter Newman
Director: Nancy Savoca
Screenplay: Richard Guay, Nancy Savoca
Novel: Francine Prose
Cinematography: Bobby Bukowski (Color)
Editing: Elizabeth Kling
Production design: Kalina Ivanov
Art direction: Charles Lagola
Music: Stephen Endelman
Cast: Tracey Ullman (Catherine Falconetti), Vincent D'Onofrio (Joseph Santangelo), Lili Taylor (Teresa Carmela Santangelo), Judith Malina (Carmela Santangelo), Michael Rispoli (Nicky Falconetti)
124 minutes

1994
ONE FOOT ON A BANANA PEEL, THE OTHER FOOT IN THE GRAVE: SECRETS FROM THE DOLLY MADISON ROOM (Documentary) (Clinica Estetico, Joanne Howard)
Executive producer: Edward Saxon
Producers: **Jonathan Demme**, Peter Saraf
Directors: Juan Botas, Lucas Platt
Cinematography: Victoria Leacock, Juan Botas (Color)
Editing: Lucas Platt
Music: Anton Sanko
With: Dr. Paul Bellman, Juan Botas, Daniel Chapman, and others; **Jonathan Demme**, narrator
79 minutes

1994
ROY COHN/JACK SMITH (Good Machine, Pomodori Foundation, The Laboratory for Icon & Idiom/Strand Releasing)
Executive producer: **Jonathan Demme**

Producers: Ted Hope, James Schamus, Marianne Weems
Director: Jill Godmilow
Screenplay: Gary Indiana, Jack Smith, from plays *Roy Cohn* by Indiana, *What's Underground About Marshmallows* by Smith
Cinematography: Ellen Kuras (Color)
Editing: Merril Stern
Music: Michael Sahl
Cast: Ron Vawter (Roy Cohn/Jack Smith), Coco McPherson (Chica)
90 minutes

1995
DEVIL IN A BLUE DRESS (Clinica Estetico, Mundy Lane Entertainment/ TriStar Pictures)
Executive producers: **Jonathan Demme**, Edward Saxon
Producers: Jesse Beaton, Gary Goetzman
Associate producers: Walter Mosley, Donna Gigliotti, Thomas A. Imperato
Director: Carl Franklin
Screenplay: Carl Franklin
Novel: Walter Mosley
Cinematography: Tak Fujimoto (Technicolor)
Editing: Carole Kravetz
Production design: Gary Frutkoff
Art direction: Dan Webster
Music: Elmer Bernstein
Cast: Denzel Washington (Ezekiel "Easy" Rawlins), Tom Sizemore (DeWitt Albright), Jennifer Beals (Daphne Monet), Don Cheadle (Mouse Alexander), Terry Kinney (Todd Carter)
102 minutes

1996
THAT THING YOU DO! (Clinica Estetico, Clavius Base/Twentieth Century-Fox)
Producers: Gary Goetzman, **Jonathan Demme**, Edward Saxon
Associate producer: Terry Odem
Director: Tom Hanks
Screenplay: Tom Hanks
Cinematography: Tak Fujimoto (DeLuxe)
Editing: Richard Chew
Production design: Victor Kempster
Art direction: Dan Webster

Music: Howard Shore; original songs by Adam Schlesinger, Tom Hanks, and others
Cast: Tom Everett Scott (Guy Patterson), Liv Tyler (Faye Dolan), Johnathon Schaech (Jimmy Mattingly), Steve Zahn (Lenny Haise), Ethan Embry (The Bass Player/T. B. Player), Tom Hanks (Mr. White), **Jonathan Demme** (Major Motion Picture Director)
108 minutes
Academy Award nomination: Original Song, Adam Schlesinger, for "That Thing You Do"
Golden Globe nomination: Best Original Song—Motion Picture, Adam Schlesinger, for "That Thing You Do"

1996
MANDELA (Documentary) (Clinica Estetico/Island Pictures)
Executive producers: Chris Blackwell, Dan Genetti
Producers: **Jonathan Demme**, Edward Saxon, Jo Menell
Co-producer: Peter Saraf
Associate producers: Richard Stengel, Amina Frense
Directors: Jo Menell, Angus Gibson
Cinematography: Dewald Aukema, Peter Tischhauser (Color)
Editing: Andy Keir; additional editing: Mona Davis
Music: Cedric Gradus Samson, Hugh Masekela
With: Nelson Mandela, Mabel Mandela, Mandla Mandela, Nomzamo Winnie Mandela; narrator: Patrick Shai
118 minutes
Academy Award nomination: Documentary (Feature), Jo Menell, Angus Gibson

1996
COURAGE & PAIN (Documentary) (Clinica Estetico)
Producers: Diana Choi, **Jonathan Demme**, Peter Saraf
Director: Patricia Benoit
Cinematography: Patrick Capone
Editing: Andy Keir

1996
INTO THE ROPE (also known as NYACK JUMPERS) (Documentary) (Clinica Estetico)
Producers: **Jonathan Demme**, Peter Saraf
Director: Lucas Platt

Music: Anton Sanko
With: The Nyack Jumpers

1998
SHADRACH (Millennium Films, Nu Image Films, Tidewater Pictures Inc./ Columbia Pictures)
Executive producers: **Jonathan Demme**, Steven Shareshian, Avi Lerner, Danny Dimbort, Trevor Short, Elie Samaha
Producers: John Thompson, Boaz Davidson, Bridget Terry
Line producer: Ric Rondell
Director: Susanna Styron
Screenplay: Susanna Styron, Bridget Terry
Story: William Styron
Cinematography: Hiro Narita (Color: DuArt)
Editing: Colleen Sharp
Production design: Burton Rencher
Music: Van Dyke Parks
Cast: Harvey Keitel (Vernon), Andie MacDowell (Trixie), Scott Terra (Paul), John Franklin Sawyer (Shadrach), Martin Sheen (Narrator)
89 minutes

1998
THE UTTMOST (Documentary) (Clinica Estetico)
Producers: **Jonathan Demme**, Richard Guay
Cinematography: Patrick Capone (Color)
Editing: Andy Keir
With: Kenny Utt, Angie Utt, **Jonathan Demme**, Jodie Foster, William Friedkin, Anthony Hopkins, Michelle Pfeiffer, Roy Scheider

1999
(festival screenings; released in the U.S., 2000)
THE OPPORTUNISTS (Eureka Pictures, Clinica Estetico, Kalkaska, Flashpoint, Prosperity Pictures/First Look International)
Executive producers: David Forrest, Beau Rogers, Peter Saraf, **Jonathan Demme**, Edward Saxon
Producers: John Lyons, Tim Perell
Co-producers: Martin Fink, Richard E. Johnson
Line producer: William Perkins
Director: Myles Connell
Screenplay: Myles Connell

Cinematography: Teodoro Maniaci (Color)
Editing: Andy Keir
Production design: Debbie DeVilla
Art direction: Niclas Berry
Music: Kurt Hoffman
Cast: Christopher Walken (Vic Kelly), Peter McDonald (Michael Lawler), Cyndi Lauper (Sally Mahon), Donal Logue (Pat Duffy), Vera Farmiga (Miriam Kelly), Jose Zuniga (Jesus Del Toro), Jerry Grayson (Tom Ransome)
90 minutes

2001
MAANGAMIZI: THE ANCIENT ONE (Forest Creatures Entertainment, Gris-Gris Films Inc./Gris-Gris Films Inc.)
Executive producers: **Jonathan Demme**, Mary Joan Cunning, Steven Shareshian
Producers: Queenae Taylor Mulvihill, Martin Mhando, Ron Mulvihill
Co-producers: Dave Rosshirt, Leonard Merrill Kurz
Associate producers: Fatma Alloo, Kelly Askew, Marc Leveri, John Roper, Casta Tungaraza
Directors: Ron Mulvihill, Martin Mhando
Screenplay: Queenae Taylor Mulvihill
Cinematography: Willie E. Dawkins (Color)
Editing: James Ling
Music: Cyril Neville
Cast: BarbaraO (Dr. Asira), Amandina Lihamba (Samehe), Samahani Kejeri (Simba Mbili), Waigwa Wachira (Dr. Odhiambo)
110 minutes

2002
ADAPTATION (Magnet, Clinica Estetico/Columbia Pictures, Intermedia Films)
Executive producers: Charlie Kaufman, Peter Saraf
Producers: Edward Saxon, Vincent Landay, **Jonathan Demme**
Director: Spike Jonze
Screenplay: Charlie Kaufman (credited also as "Donald Kaufman")
Book: Susan Orlean (*The Orchid Thief*)
Cinematography: Lance Acord (Color)
Editing: Eric Zumbrunnen; additional editing: Larry Law
Production design: K. K. Barrett
Art direction: Peter Andrus
Music: Carter Burwell

Cast: Nicolas Cage (Charlie Kaufman/Donald Kaufman), Meryl Streep (Susan Orlean), Chris Cooper (John Laroche), Tilda Swinton (Valerie), Cara Seymour (Amelia), Brian Cox (Robert McKee)
114 minutes
Academy Award: Actor in a Supporting Role, Chris Cooper
Academy Award nominations: Actor in a Leading Role, Nicolas Cage; Actress in a Supporting Role, Meryl Streep; Writing, Adapted Screenplay, Charlie Kaufman, "Donald Kaufman"
Golden Globes: Best Performance by an Actor in a Supporting Role in a Motion Picture, Chris Cooper; Best Performance by an Actress in a Supporting Role in a Motion Picture, Meryl Streep
Golden Globe nominations: Best Director—Motion Picture, Spike Jonze; Best Motion Picture—Musical or Comedy; Best Performance by an Actor in a Motion Picture—Musical or Comedy, Nicolas Cage; Best Screenplay—Motion Picture, Charlie Kaufman, "Donald Kaufman"

2003
BEAH: A BLACK WOMAN SPEAKS (Documentary) (Clinica Estetico, LisaGay Inc., Songhay System/HBO, Women Make Movies)
Producers: Lisa Gay Hamilton, **Jonathan Demme**, Joe Viola, Neda Armian
Director: Lisa Gay Hamilton
Cinematography: Sovonto Green (Color)
Editing: Kate Amend
Music: Bernice Johnson Reagon, Toshi Reagon, Geri Allen
With: Beah Richards, Ossie Davis, Ruby Dee, and others
90 minutes

As Writer Only

1973
BLACK MAMA, WHITE MAMA (Four Associates Ltd./American International Pictures, Inc.)
Executive producer: David J. Cohen
Producers: John Ashley, Eddie Romero
Director: Eddie Romero
Screenplay: H. R. Christian
Story: Joseph Viola and **Jonathan Demme**
Cinematography: Justo Paulino (Color: Movielab)
Production design: Roberto Formoso

Music: Harry Betts
Cast: Pam Grier (Lee Daniels), Margaret Markov (Karen Brent), Sid Haig (Ruben), Lynn Borden (Matron Densmore), Vic Diaz (Vic Cheng)
87 minutes

As Actor Only

1977
THE INCREDIBLE MELTING MAN (Quartet Productions/American International Pictures)
Executive producer: Max J. Rosenberg
Producer: Samuel W. Gelfman
Associate producers: Peter Cornberg, Robert L. Fenton
Director: William Sachs
Screenplay: William Sachs
Cinematography: Willy Curtis (Color: Movielab)
Editing: James Beshears
Art Director: Michel Levesque
Music: Arlon Ober
Cast: Alex Rebar (Steve West/Melting Man), Burr DeBenning (Dr. Ted Nelson), Myron Healey (General Michael Perry), Michael Aldredge (Sheriff Blake), Ann Sweeny (Judy Nelson), **Jonathan Demme** (Matt)
84 minutes

1985
INTO THE NIGHT (Into the Night Productions/Universal Pictures)
Executive producer: Dan Allingham
Producers: George Folsey Jr., Ron Koslow
Associate producer: David Sosna
Co-associate producer: Leslie Belzberg
Director: John Landis
Screenplay: Ron Koslow
Cinematography: Robert Paynter (Technicolor)
Editing: Malcolm Campbell
Production design: John Lloyd
Music: Ira Newborn; featuring B.B. King
Cast: Jeff Goldblum (Ed Okin), Michelle Pfeiffer (Diana), Richard Farnsworth (Jack Caper), Irene Papas (Shaheen Parvisi), Paul Mazursky (Bud Herman), **Jonathan Demme** (Federal Agent)
115 minutes

2000
OZ (series): Episode GRAY MATTER (TV) (Rysher Entertainment, The Levinson/Fontana Company/HBO)
Executive producers: Barry Levinson, Tom Fontana, Jim Finnerty
Supervising Producer: Bridget Potter
Associate Producers: Mark A. Baker, Irene Burns
Director: Brian Cox
Screenplay: Tom Fontana
Cinematography: Alex Zakrzewski
Editing: Ken Eluto
Production design: Gary Weist
Music: David Darlington, Stephen Rosen
Art direction: Katherine Spencer
Cast: Harold Perrineau (Augustus Hill), Ernie Hudson (Warden Leo Glynn), Reg E. Cathey (Martin Querns), Lee Tergesen (Beecher), **Jonathan Demme** (PSA Director)
60 minutes

Miscellaneous Credits

1970
(U.K.; U.S., 1971)
EYEWITNESS (released in the U.S. as SUDDEN TERROR) (Associated British Picture Corporation, Irving Allen Limited/MGM-EMI)
Executive producer: Irving Allen
Producer: Paul Maslansky
Director: John Hough
Screenplay: Ronald Harwood, Bryan Forbes (uncredited)
Novel: John Harris (as Mark Hebden)
Cinematography: David Holmes (Technicolor)
Editing: Geoffrey Foot
Production design: Herbert Westbrook
Music: Fairfield Parlour (formerly Kaleidoscope); additional music: Van der Graaf Generator; David Whitaker
Music coordinated by: **Jonathan Demme**
Cast: Mark Lester (Ziggy), Lionel Jeffries (Grandpa), Susan George (Pippa), Peter Vaughan (Paul Grazzini), Tony Bonner (Tom Jones), Jeremy Kemp (Inspector Galleria)
91 minutes

FILMOGRAPHY

1973
FLY ME (New World Pictures)
Cirio H. Santiago
Director: Cirio H. Santiago
Second unit director: **Jonathan Demme**
Screenplay: Miller Drake
Cinematography: Philip Sacdalan (Metrocolor)
Editing: Barbara Pokras, George Santos
Art direction: Ben Otico
Cast: Lenore Kasdorf (Andrea), Lyllah Torena (Sherry), Richard Young (Doctor), Naomi Stevens (Mother), Dick Miller (Taxi driver)
72 minutes

1973
(U.K.; U.S., 1974)
SECRETS OF A DOOR TO DOOR SALESMAN (released in the U.S. as NAUGHTY WIVES) (Oppidan Film Productions)
Producer: David Grant
Associate producer: Malcolm Fancey
Director: Wolf Rilla
Director of opening sequence: **Jonathan Demme**
Screenplay: Joseph McGrath, Denis Norden (credited as Roy Nicholas)
Cinematography: Mark McDonald (Eastmancolor)
Editing: Peter Horrey
Art direction: Tony Curtis
Music: John Shakespeare, Derek Warne
Cast: Brendan Price (David Clyde), Graham Stark (Charlie Vincent), Chic Murray (Policeman), Bernard Spear (Jake Tripper), Felicity Devonshire (Susanne)
80 minutes

JONATHAN DEMME

INTERVIEWS

Demme's Monde: A B-Movie Maker Makes the Grade

TOM ALLEN/1977

IT COULDN'T HAPPEN to a nicer movie. This year's token American studio film at the 15th New York Film Festival is a major people booster called *Handle with Care*. Jonathan Demme's Paramount movie, which will be shown Friday, September 30, spotlights unabashed, enthusiastic American popularism as a foil for French subtleties, Germanic tracts, Italian manifestos, and a potpourri of international angst.

This is no time to go into the chillingly low pleasure index of the festival, which traditionally has not pandered to slaphappy, cinematic gratifications. The glum worldview of the festival's favored directors is by now a given fact. Against it the programming of *Handle with Care* will be like a Pepsi high in the midst of a wormwood low.

The enviable contrast cannot help but accentuate the bubbling optimism of the Demme film and should get it attention, if only from the yahoo camp as their anti-festival pleasure fix. And attention is what the film needs.

Handle with Care, which was previously released on a regional basis in May as *Citizens Band* and then withdrawn when it failed to attract an audience, is one of many semi-independent, small films with an identity problem. Director Jonathan Demme, reached by phone in his California home, is happy about Paramount's making a second attempt at retooling the image of the movie in the untested New York market and the studio's cooperation with the festival. If nothing else, the festival status will allow the film a quick leap to a single Manhattan art house, the Little Carnegie, where it can get a chance to build its own following.

From the *Village Voice* (October 3, 1977).

Demme is quick to insist that *Handle with Care* is "a comedy about people rather than an exploration of a new machine." Besides, he guesses that CBers are just as prone to stay home and fiddle with their dials as TV addicts are with their sets, and blazoning the name *Citizens Band* is not that likely to attract a new audience. Otherwise, the two of us gave up attempting a definitive tag for the film's new genre: the mechanical *American Graffiti* or electronic *Handle with Care* moving movie, the car-wash-and-gum-ball-rally film—all transparent plot hooks that update the *Grand Hotel* tradition and portray an actively entwined community.

Jonathan Demme, like his movie, is ripe for discovery. He is the most promising newcomer from the Roger ("I'm crazy about him") Corman camp since Monte Hellman and Francis Ford Coppola, and I would say the first real big-league graduate from the present New World Corman period as opposed to the old, more fertile, Filmgroup and American International Pictures period.

Demme, who is in his early thirties, reveals his ascent into filmmaking as one of many pragmatic twists of fate. His first break, unorthodox as these things tend to be, occurred on a Florida houseboat belonging to Joseph E. Levine, when the pugnacious showman read Demme's glowing *Coral Gables Times* review of *Zulu* back in 1964 and offered him a post in Avco Embassy's publicity department.

The next interval in Demme's career included piecemeal jobs in Manhattan. There was reviewing for *Film Daily*. Mailing out-of-town copy to Boston's *Fusion*. Selling films in Pathé Contemporary's theatrical wing. Directing a short feature called *Good Morning, Steve*. And finally, doing time in the United Artists publicity bullpen, along with such restless souls as Mort Engleberg (now a film producer), Steve Panama (now a California expert in trailers), Mike Kaplan (now president of Robert Altman's Lions Gate Films), and Evelyn Purcell (now a filmmaker and Demme's wife).

After a short period in England making commercials, Demme spent the '70s learning the filmmaking trade under Roger Corman's tutelage, first producing such steamy little numbers as *Angels Hard As They Come* and *Hot Box*, and then directing such maddeningly elusive and somewhat cultish films as *Caged Heat* and *Crazy Mama*, which were more likely to emerge briefly on 42nd Street's subterranean circuit than the Museum of Modern Art. Nevertheless, MOMA has acknowledged his existence with a special showing of *Caged Heat*.

Corman's guiding hand extended to Demme's first studio film, *Fighting Mad*, a 1976 Fox release with Peter Fonda; but *Handle with Care* can rightly be considered as Demme's first solo. It's a tricky film and will be reviewed at a later date. But it can be noted that the movie takes great risks in its offbeat casting and in its change-of-pace moods. For one thing, it is at once both more boisterous in feeling and more subtle in characterization than its remote soul mate *American Graffiti* by George Lucas, the great mechanical candyman of the '70s.

Demme is pleased that he had total freedom in the casting and was backed by producer Shep Fields in his choice of crew and artists. Apparently, Demme spent his time well while in the Corman warren, experimenting and talent-shopping. He has individual praise for the "unique work" of cinematographer Jordan Cronenweth, production designer Bill Malley, scriptwriter Paul Brickman, and Pablo Ferro as "the best designer of film titles in the country today."

As the dichotomy between overpackaged productions and the more personalized independent film widens, *Handle with Care* comes in as the strongest small film of 1977. It needs help only because, as Demme says, it does not fit into any immediately recognizable, lucrative formula and is free of "big chase scenes and the action ingredients of most popular recent films." Its second chance at the national market by way of a Manhattan release will be due to its prestigious send-off at the New York Film Festival. Nevertheless, the movie stands as a portrait of the most ingratiating band of citizens that are likely to be met on the American screen this year.

Demme Monde

CARLOS CLARENS / 1980

JONATHAN DEMME, not to be confused with Jacques Demy, shares nonetheless two of the most winsome qualities of his Gallic near-namesake: a penchant for fluid, elaborate camera movements which often ensnare some runaway character back to the relaxed narrative, and a fair-play conviction that each of these tangential characters is worth a movie all to him/herself. It is this obsessional concern with character rather than plot that allows Demme (and the viewer) to string along with some rootless people through their minor crises in tacky motels, trailer camps, and crossroad towns in backwater America.

There are usually two stories in a Demme picture, a duality which unless happily resolved leads to such a disorienting failure as *Last Embrace*. When properly licked, the result is the exhilarating redneck diptych of *Citizens Band* and *Melvin and Howard*. Demme's style and fresh eye for some of the least spectacular locations in the Southwest were already well in evidence in *Crazy Mama*, which he directed for Roger Corman: in fact, Demme is the quirkiest graduate from the Corman College of Quick and Punchy Movies. In 1977, *Citizens Band* broke new ground in the subgenre by omitting entirely the ugly violence that usually attends redneck dramaturgy and discovering instead a humor and sensibility as foreign to citified viewers as those exhibited in an Eric Rohmer talk-fest, and just as welcome.

Best of all, Demme's people are capable of improbably offbeat arrangements with life and each other. In *Citizens Band*, the two wives of a bigamist trucker (who also keeps a mobile mistress on the side) realize their touchy situation as they board the same bus. "Does this mean we're related?" wonders Wife One (Marcia Rodd) to Wife Two (Ann Wedgeworth) having just discovered they share the same husband. (By the way, the ladies also shared a Best Supporting Actress Award from the New York Society of Film Critics.) The trucker—played by Charles Napier, the Fearless Fosdick of Soft Core and one of Demme's regulars—has what it takes to make them both happy, and he braves out the inevitable confrontation with common sense: "Basically I think we have a communication problem here." There is a feeling here for bonds of affection unfettered by legalities, and for people willing to make absurd concessions not to lose each other—Demme's most personal theme, one surmises, and already adumbrated in the *menage à trois* of *Crazy Mama*.

The twin-story structure is even better articulated in *Melvin and Howard*, which is the richest slice of Americana since small towns became redneck hell-holes in the sixties. The main tale belongs to recent history: it deals with the semi-mythical encounter (and subsequent effects) between an injured old-timer (Jason Robards) who may or may not be Howard Hughes, and a jack-of-all-trades who could be none other than Melvin Dummar (Paul Le Mat). This recedes to the background as the plot concentrates on Melvin's domestic and vocational problems. His wife Linda (Mary Steenburgen) leaves him for another man, taking their child with her; Melvin has to rescue her, against her will, from a topless bar in Reno. They divorce, remarry, have another child. Linda wins a prize in a TV game show, and finally walks out on Melvin, who then marries a tough Mormon chick (Pamela Reed) and settles in Utah. All of a sudden, he finds himself named as a beneficiary in Hughes's famous Mormon will. The old prospector he picked up one night in the desert and forced to sing "Bye Bye Blackbird" for his transportation (not to mention Melvin's own "Santa's Souped-up Sleigh" which, alas, will never make the charts) has the posthumous power to change Melvin's life. Or has he?

Q: *The film that first attracted critical attention to your work is a very unstable one. The title was changed from* Citizens Band *to* Handle With Care; *the name of the producer, Freddie Fields, was missing in the first release prints; and for a time it was shown without the final sequence, a freeway wedding conducted through CB radio. I believe it was only after the picture had played at the New York Film Festival in 1977 and got good notices that Fields had his name restored. And that it was only after Pauline Kael in the* New Yorker *and Richard Goldstein in the* Village Voice *complained about the missing ending that it was reinstated. Let's flashback a little.*

A: Freddie Fields was shown an article in the *Village Voice* by Paul Brickman. The idea intrigued Freddie so he commissioned Paul to write a screenplay about CB radios and the people who're obsessed with them. They finally had a script that Freddie liked but which Paramount felt ambivalent about. It was sent to practically every director in town, and it was always turned down. I finally received a copy and became involved. I worked with Paul in a rewrite that was accepted by the Paramount hierarchy, which at the time included David Picker and Richard Sylbert, both of whom liked it a lot, and they put the film into production. By the time we finished shooting there was now a new regime that did not like the movie and couldn't understand why it was made in the first place.

Q: *It's curious that Brickman also wrote* The Bad News Bears in Breaking Training *around that time and which now seems much more disappointing.*
A: Prior to *Citizens Band*, Paul had written a script for 20th Century-Fox that was highly regarded but never filmed. Ask me how we worked together.

Q: *How did you work together?*
A: Paul and I didn't work together at all well. First of all, he was horrified that a Roger Corman director was being attached to his screenplay. I was so taken by the script that I had a natural inclination to want to get along, but this was not possible because of Paul's views on me. Unfortunately, after two days of shooting on location it became necessary for me to insist that Paul leave town—because after the takes, as passionate writers will, he would go to actors and interrogate them as to why they acted the scene this or that way. And then the actors would come to me and say, "I'm getting confused, the writer is asking about such and such." So he had to leave the production, which did not enhance our relationship at all.

Q: *There are two main story lines in* Citizens Band, *but they never really mesh together. All they have in common is the locale.*
A: I felt that one problem with the final picture is that the screenplay was unwilling to explore alternatives, that Paul was unable to refocus. One story is perfect as far as I'm concerned: the characters of the bigamist trucker and his mistress and wives are set up in a wonderful way, they go through changes. But the other story, which theoretically concerns the hero, didn't have nearly the same depth. Brickman was unwilling to come up with new material, the actors and myself were unable to fill in the missing chunks while we were shooting, and as a result the film is weighed in favor of the subtext.

Q: *People assumed, when* Citizens Band *came out, that it was laid in Texas, which is funny because it's never stated in the dialogue and the locations were in California. Redneck America could very well be a country of the mind.*
A: One of the things that attracted me to it in the first place was the absence of arbitrary violence. There was no heavy police presence, no gunfights

or car crashes. I thought, "How marvelous! A rural film with rural characters that doesn't resort to exploitation devices." Which I think turned out to be to the picture's detriment. It would have done much better had we thrown in a couple of fabulous car chases or a couple of good fight scenes. A more exploitable trailer could have been cut for it. As it was, it was a film without a hook.

Q: *It seemed as if you couldn't give it away, good notices and all.*
A: Only one other picture I can think of was shown for free at the time of its original release: Ermanno Olmi's *The Sound of Trumpets* [*Il Posto*], which Don Rugoff liked so much he decided not to charge admission for a day or two. In that case, as with *Citizens Band* later, paying customers stayed away in droves.

Q: *Do you think that it could be the rural locale and characters that kept city viewers away?*
A: That might have been the case—except that it bombed in the suburbs and rural areas with equal impact. There are, to my way of thinking, two peripheral reasons for the film not doing well. One was that the advertising and publicity material wasn't ready when it opened in 700 theaters: there was a black one-sheet with the name of *Citizens Band* unsupported by any sort of interpretative art. Also, there were no stills available to the theaters. Another reason, other than the lack of promotional material for the opening, was a tremendous hostility toward the picture from Paramount, which spread from the promotion people to the sales department to the regional exchanges to the exhibitors. But I think that the bottom-line reason for its commercial failure was that it was about CB radios and the people who use them, which was not a subject of sufficient interest to attract moviegoers.

Q: *But you're no stranger to violence in your own films. Look at* Crazy Mama.
A: Although I enjoy violence in movies, I don't like doing it that much anymore. There was quite a bit of violence in the first three films I directed. I can enjoy it when I see it, but it's not what interests me when directing.

Q: Last Embrace, *which followed* Citizens Band, *has four or five violent sequences. It's a schizoid film, which starts out as the story of a government operative who, in the course of his violent line of work, suffers a nervous breakdown—violence finally intrudes in his personal life when his wife is accidentally killed—and then it picks up a heroine with a psychotic approach to life who goes on a killing spree.*
A: I was sent the script by the producers, Mike Taylor and Dan Wigutow, who had worked for United Artists in various executive capacities and who

had decided to go into independent production. They had bought a book, *The Thirteenth Man* by Murray Bloom, and hired David Shaber to write a script. There was an idea for a movie in the novel, that was all, and David took it and virtually wrote an original screenplay from it. It seemed like a modern *film noir*. David and I worked on a couple of rewrites together and were getting to the point where it was beginning to work and we were licking the problems inherent in the idea. Then, suddenly, we found ourselves going into production. We would have liked to work on the script for another month, but Roy Scheider was available and UA thought it was a viable project.

Q: *The new regime had to keep the production flow, after the top five executives left to form Orion.*
A: We shot the film hoping to lick the remaining story problems and we didn't. I was sorry to see David take a lot of abuse in the reviews for his "incoherent" script, because that was a shared blame. What turned me on about the script was the historical revelation—new to me but one with a basis in fact—that New York at the turn of the century was an active center of white slavery, masterminded by religious groups and camouflaged by socially concerned organizations. It was a revelation like that in *Chinatown*, where you're gaining a startling historical insight as the theme of a detective thriller. But the impact of such a revelation in *Last Embrace* is not to be found in the finished picture. People didn't come out astounded at this historical fact, which in the film comes across as mere plot information without the whack it should have.

Q: *The* film noir *in the forties usually had a preposterous premise but it was presented with such style and it moved so swift that the viewer got caught up in it. The premise in* Last Embrace *is even more farfetched and extreme.*
A: There were scenes in the script which were never shot, due to shooting schedules and commitments for locations, and which would have tied up the CIA subplot with the story of the Jewish brothels. At the time, they were judged not worth the expense of going back and shooting them. The film suffers from their absence.

Q: *The Princeton Tower sequence was mostly shot in studio, and this hyperrealistic set, added to the Miklos Rozsa score, makes it the only one of your films in the Hitchcock vein, a rite of passage nowadays among young American directors.*
A: I hadn't thought of Rozsa until I saw *Providence* and heard the exquisite score. We sent him the script and he answered that he couldn't commit on the basis of it, that he had to see the rough cut. When he did, he agreed. It was a joyful collaboration that I hope to repeat some day. We had a picture

taken together and I asked Miklos to smile for the camera. When he refused, I asked him why. "Jonathan," he said, "have you ever seen a picture of Beethoven smiling?"

In all *Last Embrace* was a delightful experience, much more so than making *Citizens Band*. We were all on the same wavelength. I had a chance to work again with Tak Fujimoto, a cinematographer I started out with. He was not in the union and therefore unable to work with me on *Fighting Mad*, *Citizens Band*, and the *Columbo* episode, which were studio pictures bound by I.A. contracts. Tak also photographed *Melvin and Howard*, of course.

Q: *It seems unusual, to say the least, that a film project on the Melvin Dummar-Howard Hughes story would have been undertaken before the hearing in which the "Mormon" will was thrown out of court. I wonder what the film would have been like, had the will been acknowledged as legitimate.*
A: I wonder, too. Yet the script had been in the works long before. I remember waking up and reading DUMMAR WILL THROWN OUT OF COURT, and thinking "Oh, my God, does this mean the film is dead?" But it didn't even become a dispute point. It didn't bother anybody in the least.

It was the producer, Don Phillips, who had the original idea to make a film based on the extraordinary events in Melvin Dummar's life. Don and his sometime partner, Art Linson, approached Universal, and Universal was intrigued enough to back the development and allow Bo Goldman to write a script. Mike Nichols also became involved in the project, but apparently could not cast the film to his satisfaction; after three rewrites he ceased to be involved. At that point, Universal sent me the script.

Q: *There is a certain similarity between the locales and the characters in both* Citizens Band *and* Melvin and Howard.
A: When Bo became involved, he met Melvin, traveled with him all over the locations where the events happened, talked to his co-workers at the magnesium plant and at the dairy, spent time with Melvin's ex-wife and his second wife and his parents. Bo did a tremendous amount of research on that level, which to me helps account for the fact that the characters in his script are so rich.

I eventually met Melvin myself. When we were shooting, Melvin was a driver for Coors beer: in order to play a small role in the Reno sequence [the counterman at the bus station], he had to get leave from Coors. He is now the West Coast representative for an Alaskan king crab wholesaler. He would like very much to be an actor and have his songs become popular. He actually wrote the songs that you hear Paul Le Mat sing in the movie. I think they're pretty good.

Q: *For once, the credits don't carry the disclaimer that all characters in the film are fictitious. Was there any flack from Suma, the Hughes corporation?*

A: We had no interference whatsoever, but I've been told that there was a spy in one of our crowd scenes who would report to Suma about the movie. *Melvin and Howard* placed Suma in a potentially awkward situation because it shows how much Suma stood to lose in the event that the "Mormon" will was proven to be the true will. It was implicit in the "Mormon" will that Suma be dissolved, and that all of Suma's holdings be divided among the sixteen named beneficiaries, which is why the case was finally thrown out of court. The other beneficiaries—the Boy Scouts of America, the Church of Jesus Christ of Latter Day Saints, etc.—all hired lawyers to defend the will at the beginning of the hearings, but Suma doubled and tripled the efforts to invalidate the "Mormon" will. Slowly but surely, all the beneficiaries dropped out of the case, since they recognized that Suma was fighting for its life and would use every penny in their bank accounts to fight the will in the courts forever.

Q: *One realizes that the high point in Melvin Dummar's life came earlier in the story: in the meeting with the old-timer in the desert, and possibly in the first flush of excitement when the contents of the "Mormon" will are made public and Melvin finds himself a national hero of sorts. It's such a breathless sequence in the film that no recognition of Melvin as legal heir could match it: a series of elating crane shots that stop with a zoom on Melvin hiding on a tree from the crowd of well-wishers, spongers, and just plain curiosity freaks.*

A: It was a desire to create an epic feeling, the one epic moment in the person's life. A crane is a very expressive tool, especially if you're after a certain effect. I met the late Delmer Daves in Los Angeles about six years ago: he told me he had designed his own personal crane which *A Summer Place* paid for. After that, he always had the camera on the crane, crane shot or not. "Get a crane, stick your camera on it, do your close-ups with it." It's like a special paint brush for a big stroke. The crane takes up a certain amount of physical space, but all it really needs is an artist to move it, and we had George Schrader as dolly grip. In fact, with a great guy on the crane, you're freer than you'd be with the dolly. Spontaneous adjustments are more possible.

Q: *I find the final sequence in* Melvin and Howard *extremely bold, moving, and open-ended. Perish the thought that a director should try to spell out the meaning of his film, but do you have any personal conviction as to why the scene had to be done in that certain way? Why do Melvin and Howard switch roles, with Howard taking the wheel this time?*

A: I think it's valuable that they should switch. It has something to do with the fact that when they first meet in the story they fight and bicker for the first five minutes. They are very antagonistic but gradually they reach an accord: Howard Hughes forgets that he's the richest man in America, Melvin forgets that he's the poorest man in America, and a friendship is struck. And to have Howard take the wheel and Melvin go to sleep in the final sequence articulates a dimension of trust that resulted from that encounter.

Of course, the scene gains from having been shot at "magic hour"—the half-hour between the moment when the tip of the sun vanishes and before it gets dark, which gives a very special kind of side light, the light that Tak Fujimoto wanted to shoot any of the daylight scenes in which Hughes appeared. So, Jason Robards had to go through two-and-a-half hours of makeup to shoot for half an hour, and never a grumble. He was fabulous. This was the last stuff we shot for the movie, and everybody was exhausted from locations in Los Angeles, Salt Lake City, Reno, and Las Vegas. Jason came like a breath of fresh air.

Q: *Maybe the great reward for Melvin is that he will replay in his mind—with infinite variations, for the rest of his life—that encounter with Howard Hughes.*

A: Actually, I wanted to play the final sequence—in which Howard Hughes returns as a remembrance—in two different ways. One would be done in the truck as a straight flashback, and the other would be vaguely experimental: the memory of what happened in the pick-up truck would now occur in a different vehicle, in a new car that Melvin drives. It could become "unlabelable," a subjective flashback. To my surprise, Paul Le Mat refused to act the scene in two different vehicles: his reasoning was that, as an actor of integrity, having enacted the scene in one vehicle it would be dishonest of him to perform it in another. I didn't understand that thinking at the time, and I still don't. It was a great disappointment for me, because even though we would have wound up using the version in the truck, nevertheless it would have been great fun to try it the other way.

But that's the good thing about movies: if you don't get a chance to use it in one, if the idea has any merit you can use it at some point in a subsequent movie.

Director Continues Small-Town Romance

JOANNA CONNORS / 1981

DIRECTOR JONATHAN DEMME lives and works in New York City, and sometimes commutes to work in Hollywood. But he is in love, probably forever, with small-town America.

His films show it: *Melvin and Howard*, set in the desert reaches of Utah and Nevada, chronicled the brave pursuit of the American dream by Melvin and Lynda Dummar, a couple perpetually down on their luck, perpetually hopeful. Melvin was the gas-station attendant who was named in the Howard Hughes "Mormon will." Demme's *Citizens Band* (*Handle With Care*) again went into the heart of rural America, focusing on the secret fantasies expressed by an entire Southwestern community over its network of CB radios.

Tonight Demme will be in Minneapolis, almost a small town in Hollywood parlance, to show his latest work at Walker Art Center: a PBS production called *Who Am I This Time*? Based on a Kurt Vonnegut short story (from the *Welcome to the Monkey House* collection), the television film takes place—where else?—in small-town America. It's expected to air in January; the Walker showing tonight is the first and probably the only time Demme will see it with an audience.

He's looking forward to that, and he said in an interview this week from his New York office that he's also deriving great pleasure from the Walker's complete, two-week retrospective of his films, another first for him.

The retrospective continues at the Walker through November 18, and gives audiences a chance to see both Demme's glories and his roots: exploitation films with titles like *Caged Heat* and *Fighting Mad* and *Crazy Mama*. The

---

From the *Minneapolis Star* (November 6, 1981). © 1981 *Star-Tribune*. Reprinted with permission.

glories include *Last Embrace, Citizens Band,* and *Melvin and Howard.* Those are the films made after Demme graduated to "A" films and began having a say about who worked in and on them. They're also the films that have established Demme as one of the most exciting directors to come along in years.

Before you see Demme's films, forget all those other Hollywood visions of small towns: claustrophobia-inducing, bitter little places populated with ignorant rednecks. *God's Little Acre* territory.

Demme's little acres are, above all else, places of wonderful affection.

The deadening landscape is all there, of course: the trailer courts and drive-in churches and Polynesian supper clubs. His characters watch television constantly—game shows mostly. They yearn for split-level ramblers and Mediterranean living room suites, and they drive pick-ups that are destined to be repossessed.

It would be easy to make fun of this world. Demme doesn't. He approaches his characters with respect mixed with gentle humor, an unusual quality these days in movies. What happened to set him apart this way from mainstream Hollywood?

"Well, I'm in love with America, and I spend a lot of time driving around it," Demme explained. "One of my favorite things to do is just get in a car and drive around to places I've never been before. Not many people do that, especially people who live in big cities. Especially people connected with movies. And so they develop this impression of small-town people as hicks, which they aren't at all. People who live in small towns happen to know that they have a lot going for them. I love the small towns."

Demme credits much of the grace in his films to the screenplays. "I'm drawn to screenplays that display affection for the characters. It's a rare commodity in movies now, and it's tough for me to find scripts that I want to work on. *Melvin and Howard* was an especially good screenplay. [It won the 1980 Academy Award for best original screenplay.] After making that, it's been even harder for me to find something to follow it up."

What he found, finally, was *Swing Shift,* the story of a woman who begins working in an airplane factory after her husband goes off to the Pacific theater during World War II. Goldie Hawn will star, and Demme, now doing preproduction work, hopes to begin shooting next summer. That would mean a release date of spring 1983.

That seems a long time to wait for another Demme film. In the meantime audiences can see only the PBS production and the commercial spots Demme made for Norman Lear's organization, People for the American Way. Demme will screen the television spots tonight at the Walker, along with *Speed of Light,* a Demme "discovery" by Texas filmmaker Brian Hansen.

The television commercials were part of a campaign Lear created for the political group he founded as an answer to the Moral Majority. Demme said he isn't part of the group, but that he agrees with its aims. The commercials are intended to show that one of America's strengths is freedom of political opinion and action.

Demme went out on the street in Manhattan and Los Angeles, and into the studio with celebrities such as Goldie Hawn and Muhammad Ali, and asked three questions: What is your favorite way to eat eggs? What is your favorite and least favorite sport? And what is your favorite and least favorite music?

"The big discovery of making the spots was finding out what strong points of view people have on how to make eggs," Demme said. "It was very funny."

Demme got into the PBS production just ten days before shooting started—that, in fact, was one of the things that attracted him to the project.

"I liked the fast involvement," he said. "There was the appeal of shooting on a very, very low budget and still maintaining a high level of quality, which I think we did. We cut it in two weeks, very quickly."

Two other points appealed to Demme: Susan Sarandon was already signed to play the female lead; and he's a "fanatical admirer" of Kurt Vonnegut's work.

Demme likes the bits-and-pieces quality to his career now: making a film, then jumping into a television project, then quickly putting together a few commercials, then going into production on another film. But he emphasizes that this measure of independence, coupled with his New York base, does not constitute a rejection of Hollywood.

"I lived in L.A. in the mid-'70s, and I was very much a part of Hollywood," he said. "I like the Hollywood system, and I like making films. But there are fewer and fewer films being made these days, and when you figure that you spend a year, or a year and a half or more of your life on one project. . . . Well, I have to have the strongest feelings about a film I'm going to put that much time into. That's where my independence comes in. I won't make just anything.

"I think it's healthy for me to do these independent projects when they come up. It's a very positive cross-fertilization. I learned a lot in Hollywood, and I can bring that knowledge to my independent projects.

"At the same time, by keeping that independent spirit alive, I might bring something of that to the Hollywood films I make."

Jonathan Demme: On the Line

MICHAEL SRAGOW / 1984

RIGHT NOW, Jonathan Demme is one of the secret weapons of American cinema. Although his best two movies to date, *Citizens Band* (AKA *Handle with Care*, 1977) and *Melvin and Howard* (1980), were hailed for bringing the heartiness and sensitivity of a homegrown Jean Renoir into latter-day American film comedy, they failed to score at the box office. Conceived as a classy exploitation film at the height of the CB craze, *Citizens Band* offered a witty, affectionate view of radio freaks who create alter egos over the airwaves. But it didn't win over the mass audience. Released again under the title *Handle with Care*, it didn't do any better, despite a warm reception at the New York Film Festival. *Melvin and Howard*, another festival favorite, was praised wherever it played for its poetic, comic vision of the American dream as embodied by Melvin Dummar (Paul Le Mat), the gas station manager named as one of Howard Hughes's heirs in the disputed "Mormon will." Unfortunately, the film never received a broad national release, even after Mary Steenburgen (who played Melvin's first wife) and writer Bo Goldman won Academy Awards.

All this malign neglect may vanish when Demme's next movie, *Swing Shift*, opens in February. It features Demme's biggest name cast so far—Goldie Hawn, Kurt Russell, Christine Lahti, and Fred Ward and Ed Harris from *The Right Stuff*—in a story of women finding love and strength on the homefront assembly line during World War II. Demme is confident that the movie will be everything an audience could want: sexy, humorous, and touching.

When Dwight McDonald wrote that François Truffaut "has a peculiar knack for presenting a *mise-en-scène* that is neither bigger than life (Welles,

Resnais) nor smaller than life (Bresson, Olmi) but exactly life-size . . . he also raises the commonplace to poetry," he might also have been describing Demme.

In this interview, Demme discusses his start as a Roger Corman protégé, his botched suspense movie, *Last Embrace* (1979), and his recent artistic success.

QUESTION: *According to legend, you got your start in the movie industry when your father showed Joseph E. Levine a favorable review of his film* Zulu *that you'd written for the* Coral Gable Times.

JONATHAN DEMME: That's no legend. I was born on Long Island, but my family moved to Miami when I was still a little kid; I went to the University of Florida at Gainesville, hoping to become a veterinarian, but I couldn't hack the science courses I needed. I started writing movie reviews for the college paper, and, as you know, when you start seeing movies for free, there's no going back. After I dropped out, I started reviewing for a local suburban weekly, and I *did* review *Zulu*, and my father *did* show it to Joe Levine, and he *did* give me a job, and the rest is "show-biz history." Levine liked the fact that I had widely praised *Zulu*; he also liked the fact that he was doing a showmanlike thing by giving me a job at Avco Embassy's publicity department in New York.

When I moved to Manhattan in the mid-sixties, I was doing all sorts of things: movie and music reviews, publicity, selling films for Pathé Contemporary's theatrical wing. I made my first movie, a short called *Good Morning, Steve*—a story so simple you barely noticed it: just a way of making a movie. Around that time, Al Viola, the brother of my close friend and collaborator, Joe Viola, set up an office in London to try to get American filmmakers involved in British films—which were very hot at the time. Although we never got a foothold there, that's when I got the call to meet Roger Corman, who was making *Von Richthofen and Brown* in Ireland and needed a unit publicist. I had it in the back of my mind that Corman would be a good man to know if I had an idea for a movie, but he was the one who asked *me* if I had any ideas.

After I did the publicity, Corman said, "Why don't you write a biker movie for my new company?" (He was just starting up New World Pictures.) Joe Viola and I worked on it and arranged to drop off the script at the London Hilton. As we were walking away, Roger called us back; he said, "Joe, you've directed commercials; why don't you direct the movie for me? And Jonathan, you've produced commercials; why don't you produce the movie?" That became *Angels Hard As They Come*.

We knew that you had to use elements from "classier" movies to make successful exploitation movies. I'd just seen *The Savage Seven,* the biker movie that Richard Rush based on *The Seven Samurai,* so Joe and I decided we'd make a biker movie based on *Rashomon.*

QUESTION: *So* Angels Hard As They Come *really was about "the nature of guilt?"*
DEMME: Oh, yeah. You needed reasons like that to justify making the movie.

QUESTION: *Were you influenced by other directors during those days?*
DEMME: I love a lot of directors, but the only role model I had in the Corman days—sort of a group hero for me and George Armitage and Joe Viola—was Raoul Walsh. We'd growl at each other and say, "Just give us an assignment and we'll make something of it. We're professionals!"

I've always loved cheapo movies. And Corman uses one of my favorite formulas—action, nudity, and a little social comment. What more can you ask for in a film?

QUESTION: *Is it an inside joke that Corman plays the head of the MacBride Aircraft Company in* Swing Shift?
DEMME: I wanted Roger to play MacBride because I knew that Roger took parts in movies and I thought he would be great for the part. But I also love that guy, and it was a chance to hang out with him. Of course, it became an inside joke that he was playing a stern slave driver running an airplane factory. That's often how he is when he's making movies!

QUESTION: *Did you ever chafe under Corman the producer?*
DEMME: Paul Bartel is the only guy I can think of who chafed, because Paul probably had much more of a fully realized vision of what he wanted to see on film than the rest of us. We knew what the hell *Corman* wanted and that we'd better deliver it. Roger does kick you out of the nest at a certain point anyway. There are always other new guys coming up.

The most important thing Roger did for me was sit down with me right before I directed *Caged Heat* and run down just how to do a job of moviemaking. He hit everything: Have something interesting in the foreground of the shot; have something interesting happening in the background of the shot; try to find good motivation to move the camera, because it's more stimulating to the eyes; if you're shooting the scene in a small room where you can't move the camera, try to get different angles, because cuts equal movement; respect the characters and try to like them, and translate that into the audience liking and respecting the characters. To me, those are the fundamentals. I don't know if Roger had a similar lunch with Coppola, but look at *The Godfather*. It's a classical Roger Corman movie. All the Corman moves are there—a little sex, a little violence, a little social comment. Also, "make the audience like the characters even if they're mafiosi."

Roger beat me over the head about not getting enough warmth into the characters. He hated my second movie, *Crazy Mama*, hated it to the degree that he almost didn't let me direct *Fighting Mad*. Before *Crazy Mama*, I'd worked for four months on the screenplay for *Fighting Mad*, which was *supposed* to be my second film. Roger wanted a movie in the *Walking Tall* vein and suggested strip mining as a background. The whole subject was galvanizing—I wrote a righteous, kick-ass movie, and we were going to do it for something like $600,000. But Shirley Clarke, who was going to direct *Crazy Mama*, fell out with Roger ten days before shooting, and Roger said to me, "The bad news is *Fighting Mad* gets postponed; the good news is you've got *Crazy Mama* to direct." I had to cast four or five parts, rewrite the script (the actors hated it), and start shooting in ten days.

QUESTION: *You haven't written anything since* Fighting Mad. *Do you still see yourself as a writer-director?*
DEMME: Writing was a way of getting to direct, and I soon realized I was a much better director than I was a writer. I worked very hard at both things and was, at best, an average writer.

QUESTION: *Did you exert a strong influence on Paul Brickman's screenplay for* Citizens Band*?*
DEMME: The producer, Freddie Fields, asked me to direct the screenplay; I supervised the rewrite and Paramount agreed to make it. Paul Brickman had an etched-in-concrete idea about what the movie should be like. Apparently, that was very different from how the movie turned out. He disliked it very much; even when the picture won a certain amount of notoriety, he never went, "Oh, great." He's a very good writer; we just had a lousy relationship.

On our second day of shooting, on location, one of the actors told me that Paul came up to him after a scene and said, "Did you read those lines the way you did because that's the way you wanted to do it or because that's the way Jonathan told you to do it—because that's not at all the way I saw it." The moment I heard that I walked over to the production manager and said, "If you want me working tomorrow, that dude's got to be out of town." And he was on the six o'clock flight that night. The hilarious thing is, the theme of the movie was communication.

QUESTION: *When you are presented with a script like* Citizens Band, *which has a strong original conception, how does it become your movie?*
DEMME: I consider myself an *interpretative* director. If I get turned on by a script, it's my job to make the viewers of the movie feel the way I felt as a reader of the script. If there is a scene in the screenplay that I don't feel I can make work, I'll tell the writer. He'll either say, "OK, we can lose it," or he will explain why the scene is important, so that I'll understand the value of it and be able to direct it well. It's always a dialogue.

QUESTION: *When did you realize* Citizens Band *was in trouble at the box office?*
DEMME: The day it opened, in a seven-hundred-theater regional break. Nobody went. It hadn't been tested at all. The studio, the producers, *everybody* was so convinced that it was going to be an unqualified success because of the CB mania of the day that their attitude was: "Get it together and get it out there and get ready to count the receipts." And nobody went.

QUESTION: *Was it hard to find work after* Citizens Band?
DEMME: I couldn't get arrested. I did do an episode of *Columbo*, because Peter Falk liked *Citizens Band*, but that was it. Finally, two producers who'd seen *Citizens Band*, Mike Taylor and Dan Wigutow, sent me the screenplay to *Last Embrace*, which they were then developing at UA. I thought the story had the potential to be a contemporary film noir, and I thought that Roy Scheider could be the Humphrey Bogart of the seventies. The screenwriter, David Shaber, and I had a terrific time working together, and if we'd been able to do one more draft, I think we would have had something hot. But it got the green light too soon.

QUESTION: *Did you see* Last Embrace *as your chance to pay homage to Hitchcock?*
DEMME: Every movie I make is a chance to show what I have learned from Hitchcock. In terms of style, I'll admit it—I can't match the master. But I employ his techniques constantly. Take the subjective camera—Hitchcock perfected that and I use it a lot. I love putting the audience in my characters' shoes; if you choose your moments well, it's powerful.

QUESTION: *You once said, "*Melvin and Howard *dropped into my hands out of heaven."*
DEMME: One of my favorite little ironies is that before Thom Mount at Universal put me on the movie, I was already meeting with him about some other project, and when I asked him how he was, he said, "I am great! I read

perhaps the finest screenplay I've ever read in my life this morning. It's called *Melvin and Howard*." Mike Nichols had prepared the script with Bo Goldman; I signed on to the movie only after Nichols left. I give the Goldman-Nichols collaboration a lot of credit.

QUESTION: *Bo Goldman told me that at your first meeting he said he wanted his affection for the people to come through, and you said, "Not affection—but respect."*
DEMME: That may be more of my Corman influence; Roger always wanted both. I thought it would be easy for audiences to like the characters in Bo's script, but the tricky part would be to make an audience identify with them and not look down on them. We had to understand the characters' motivations. I told Bo that Melvin's first wife had to come right out and say, "We're *poor*, Melvin." We had to get across what an influence that can have on a person's life.

QUESTION: *Goldman also said that he was much more nervous than you were about the lack of any obvious story.*
DEMME: Whether he intended to or not, when Bo wrote *Melvin and Howard* he went on an amazingly poetic flight of imagination. To open a movie with an eighteen-page dialogue scene, two people riding along in a truck at night? Outrageous idea! It breaks every rule known to man, and yet the emotion he poured into that scene makes it wonderful. What's incredible is that Mary Steenburgen got it right away and that Jason Robards got it, too. Paul Le Mat got it, but he had reservations. It turned out that Paul thought Melvin was a terrific character, but a bit of an asshole. And Bo had some stuff in the script that Paul felt he couldn't do, because he thought it was too foolish, such as sniffing his wife's panties when she was gone or carrying his clothes bag on his back when he entered the strip joint she was working. It was an effort to get him to do any of that kind of stuff, but I thought it was funny and touching.

QUESTION: *As a director who considers himself extremely dependent on the script, how did it feel, on* Swing Shift, *to work with a succession of screenwriters for the first time?*
DEMME: I never really worked with the original writer, Nancy Dowd. I met with her, but then she and the producer, Jerry Bick, had a falling out. When Bo Goldman came on, the deal the studio and the producers were trying to work out with me didn't work out, so I wasn't directly involved in the writing of Bo's script. When *I* came on, Bo was no longer available. Then I got Ron Nyswaner involved, and, together with Goldie Hawn, we unified.

Working with Ron on *Swing Shift* was a very pragmatic process of finding scenes from Bo's and Nancy Dowd's drafts that worked and then fitting them into an organic whole. Nancy's drafts were highly political, and the movie isn't. Who knows what her vision fulfilled would have been? From what I saw on paper, she wrote an *exposé* of what was done to women working in the defense industries during World War II. This movie is a *salute* to the women, and I think that's a crucial distinction.

The Life and Times of Rosie the Riveter was a big source of thematic inspiration for us. It documented that the U.S. war machine tried to manipulate women into work at the beginning, despite all the real dangers, and then, at the end, coerced them into returning to the kitchen; that there was still sexism on the job; and so on. But the biggest thing I got from *Rosie the Riveter* was a sense of triumph.

Every movie has a key line for me. In *Melvin and Howard* it is when Melvin tells his lawyer, "I'm never gonna receive that money; I know that. But Howard Hughes sang Melvin Dummar's song." In *Swing Shift* there's a moment when the women are partying, after they've all been fired, and one of them says, "Boy, they laughed at us the first day we came to work." And another woman says, "Yeah, but we showed them." To me, that is what the whole thing is about.

QUESTION: *What will people get from* Swing Shift *that they couldn't get from* Rosie the Riveter?
DEMME: It is more of an entertainment. We tried to treat our characters as real, complicated people, not as forties movie characters. We had no "conventions" to go by except the conventions of the historical time. There is no genre of stateside wartime movies. There just is none. I started looking at *Since You Went Away*, and the social strata were so elevated and sanitized that it was a waste of time. We did a tremendous amount of research and just went for the reality.

QUESTION: *Isn't there a possible problem posed by merely glancing at some of the social issues? Isn't there a danger that they'll simply seem tacked-on?*
DEMME: Well, a good example is a scene of the swing shifters watching a convoy passing by, filled with Japanese-Americans being transported to the nisei camps. For the moment, that scene is being taken out, as we're trying to find the strongest possible through line and approach a reasonable running time. But that scene serves two functions: It observes the dreadful thing that was done to Japanese-Americans, but there's also an emotional value in seeing Goldie and Christine share the upset and disturbance caused by this event— and *you* get to share that. I think that scene will wind up back in the movie.

QUESTION: *In a sense, the wartime period provides some very positive experiences for the women. How are we supposed to feel when the men come back?*

DEMME: There's no easy sociological resolution; it's all worked out in terms of the characters. It's easy for us to sympathize in a big way with the women who were yanked out of one life-style, into a deep involvement with the fate of the world, and then summarily pulled out of what the world considered "meaningfulness" and sent back to the home. But we complicate that by asking, "What about the guys coming back? Did they not deserve to get their jobs and families back?" It's an unanswerable dilemma.

QUESTION: *Now that you've put in a few years as a director, is your hero still Raoul Walsh?*

DEMME: I still like all the usual hardworking guys, like Budd Boetticher. You can tell the directors who are working hard to do their very best. Sydney Pollack is a great example of a guy who's achieved terrific commercial success and is also, right down the line, a terrific filmmaker, Martin Ritt is another one. I'm interested in the guys who try to take chances and shoot their wad every time out.

Start Making Sense: An Interview with Jonathan Demme

MICHAEL DARE/1984

JONATHAN DEMME is an American, with ancestors that trace back to Alsace Lorraine, and his films are pure Americana. Though he started out as a film critic for a Miami paper and the Canadian film magazine *Take One*, he eventually worked with Roger Corman directing such potboilers as *Caged Heat*, *Crazy Mama*, and *Fighting Mad*. He left Corman to direct a film for Paramount, and since then he's matured enormously. His grasp of the day-to-day realities of American life is simple, wise, and as whimsical as it is understanding. Only he and Hal Ashby seem capable of infusing comedies with an authentic sense of inner life. In a Demme film, humor comes from a deep recognition of the truth behind each character's idiosyncrasies.

Handle with Care/Citizens Band was a Capraesque parable of a working-class American community united by their CBs. It died at the box office. After directing an episode of *Columbo*, he made *Melvin and Howard*; in it, Melvin Dummar epitomized the American dream, where a simple act of kindness can bring fame if not fortune. It's a film of such understated beauty that it was totally ignored by the Motion Picture Academy for Oscar consideration, but it picked up three New York Film Critics awards plus the award for best film of the year by the National Society of Film Critics.* His next film, *Swing Shift*, is problematic to say the least. It was taken away from him, reshot, and reedited in a bitter dispute between him and the film's star (we talked about the film for an hour, and her name never came up). It was refashioned to

---

From *L.A. Weekly* (November 9, 1984): 20. Reprinted by permission of Michael Dare, http://www.dareland.com.
**Melvin and Howard* was actually nominated for three Oscars, winning two. See Filmography. — Editor's note

such a degree that he had "A Jonathan Demme Film" taken off all prints. Tell Demme you liked the film, and he'll thank you. Tell him you didn't like it, and he'll agree with you. It's a subject he prefers to avoid, and he vows never to become involved in another project with the slightest hint of a problem.

Compared to *Swing Shift*, *Stop Making Sense* was a free ride, and as much a joy to make as it is to watch. He brings to the Talking Heads' performance film the same sense of wonderment he's brought to his fictional films. We talked at his offices at Raleigh Studios with a cassette of Hawaiian guitars playing in the background.

WEEKLY: *Have you known David Byrne long?*
DEMME: No, I met David when I approached him last summer to see if he'd be interested in putting a film together of the concert.

WEEKLY: *You just saw the concert and decided to shoot it?*
DEMME: Yes. I go to a lot of concerts. This was the one time I came out thinking obsessively about getting this thing on film.

WEEKLY: *Was there something about the concert itself that seemed cinematic to you?*
DEMME: Yes, there were a number of things that attracted me to it. The visual design of the show itself is obviously highly cinematic. I think all the members of the band are unusually charismatic, hard-working, and exciting to watch. Beyond that, I thought the show had a funny kind of narrative feeling to me, one that I can't describe—one that I don't even care to *try* to describe—but I had a feeling I was seeing some kind of story, that I was meeting a group of characters as David attacked each new song. I came away feeling very moved, very exhilarated, very entertained. I thought it was a lot more than just another wonderful rock 'n' roll show. There was an underlying sensibility—all the humor that's in it, and all these little surprises. I hadn't seen the Talking Heads live since 1978 in Central Park. Those were the days when they stood there like four robots and just played. So part of the thrill of the show at the Greek was seeing the expansion of the band on every level.

WEEKLY: *And you shot that exact concert?*
DEMME: We made some changes. We dropped about four or five numbers because the show ran for two hours and fifteen minutes and we knew the picture couldn't, and shouldn't, play that long. We lost some great stuff like "Big Blue Plymouth" and "Houses in Motion." We talked a lot about how to build it just right, to give little dips in just the right places. In order to help the momentum, we also cut out two songs from the film, including some of

my favorites: the "Big Business/I Zimbra" medley and "Cities." We're going to put them back on the videocassette. I'd also like to clarify that this isn't a concert film; it's a *performance* film.

WEEKLY: *What's the difference?*
DEMME: A concert film may intend, like *The Last Waltz* did so effectively, to give you a sense of what it was like to be at an event the focal point of which was the music. In *Stop Making Sense*, I'd just as soon it didn't occur to people that they're watching a concert, but rather a band performing without the distancing factor of it being an event that happened once. That's why there's no audience in the film until the very end. I thought it was important if the film was to be as effective for filmgoers as it was for me watching the concert. I wanted to capture the energy and the flow and that unrelenting progression of music.

WEEKLY: *What was it like working with* [cinematographer Jordan] *Cronenweth?*
DEMME: We'd worked together once before, when we did *Handle with Care* together in '77. It's great working with him because he's an absolute tight-ass perfectionist. You can't get Jordan to back away from anything he's doing until he's got it perfect, and that can be exasperating because you've got one eye on the clock and you're desperate to get moving. But then when you see the dailies and you see the extra level Jordan was taking it to when he was driving you nuts, you go, "Thank God he did it." He's a painstaking artist.

WEEKLY: *Had he ever shot a concert before?*
DEMME: He had shot a Joni Mitchell concert. I wasn't sure how Jordan was going to respond to this. I had hoped that the lighting would have the obvious appeal that it did to him. David enjoyed working with him enormously because David conceived the lighting for the stage show.

WEEKLY: *Did it have to be redesigned for the film?*
DEMME: No, the big challenge for Jordy was the fact that certain songs had twenty to thirty lighting changes per number, so his film lighting had to keep up with that. There's no such thing as "take two" when you're shooting a concert, so it was really high-tension activity.

WEEKLY: *Does that mean there's an integrity to the songs as a sequence? Is it all one performance from beginning to end?*
DEMME: Almost entirely. We shot most of our extremely wide angles in one night, so those are interpolated throughout. We didn't mind having a little bit of camera presence. We thought it would be fun to see cameras occasionally. Since the show itself utilizes the actual stagehands coming on, in the

movie you get to see a little bit of the camera team. But for our wide shots, we wanted to play to the graphics and the lighting without intruding on it by showing cameras floating across in the foreground. So one particular night we pulled everything way back and shot the wide angles.

WEEKLY: *Did you watch the concert from a video booth in the back?*
DEMME: Yes, it was so exciting. I was standing in the back with Jordy and Sandy McLeod, the visual consultant. We stood there at this bank of monitors seeing what each of the eight cameras was getting at any given moment. I had an audio hookup to talk to camera operators during a shot and request adjustments.

WEEKLY: *Was this any different from the way concerts are normally shot for television?*
DEMME: I don't know. Perhaps this included another generation of design preparation. I went out on tour with the band a couple of times and I had a shooting script, shot by shot, that I was constantly revising and streamlining. I had a very strong sense of how I wanted to attack the different songs. I went over it all in great detail with the camera operators before the show, and during the show itself I'd be able to say, "Okay, here comes that movement we were talking about. Camera D, get ready to dolly left and tighten in on the conga player. . . ." That sort of thing. I'm not sure, but maybe we had more preparation than normal.

WEEKLY: *Have you ever worked in television?*
DEMME: I did a *Columbo*, but that was shot on film just like a movie. This was the first multiple-camera situation I'd ever been in. The first night was pretty disastrous. Suddenly it was all happening, and all the preparation and planning was put up against the reality of the show. Cameras ran out of film, the band was real nervous and uptight having cameras stuck in their faces. We kept getting each other in the background of the shots too much. It was a mess, but a superb camera rehearsal. The next three nights were spectacular.

WEEKLY: *All with an audience?*
DEMME: We talked about duplicating the Pantages stage on a film soundstage in order to do more complicated shots, but the band got nervous because the sense of feedback from the audience is so much a part of their work that they were doubtful about doing their best without one. We put ourselves on a very tight six-week picture cutting schedule with an equally tight two-week mix. We had a finished picture ninety days after we finished photography, which I'm very pleased with.

WEEKLY: *Inside the soundtrack album, there's a booklet, and on the last page there is a series of questions. I want to ask you a few of them.*
DEMME: Uh-oh.

WEEKLY: *Why no special effects in the movie?*
DEMME: I thought that any special cinematic effects would intrude on the richness of the pure performance. Therefore I didn't want to get into that, and didn't.

WEEKLY: *Why a big suit?*
DEMME: In order to make his head look smaller.

WEEKLY: *Where do the odd movements come from?*
DEMME: These are good questions. Where do the odd movements come from?

WEEKLY: *Why stop making sense?*
DEMME: That's a good question.

Could This Also Be the Start of Something Big?

HARRY HAUN / 1986

IT BEGINS INNOCUOUSLY ENOUGH—an accidental encounter at Sixth and Watts. He's the absentminded accountant who walks out of Felice's Hero Shop without paying; she's the mod young artist who runs after him and teases him with a citizen's arrest. The contrast is obvious—he buttoned-down conservatively, she in Early Funk—and the sparks are instant. There is something in the eyes. . . .

Orion's *Something Wild*, starring Melanie Griffith and Jeff Daniels, finishes filming here Friday, and, in true Hollywood tradition, they are only now getting around to shooting the beginning of the film—the "cute meeting," played out on the streets of SoHo. This could be—and, indeed, is—the start of Something.

Exactly what that Something is, however, is another matter. Security on the film—particularly in respect to the plot line pursued—is tight. If you read and/or believe in press releases, you'd find the picture characterized as "a modern American romantic thriller." This, presumably, is different from a modern Lithuanian romantic thriller, but the description isn't awfully enlightening.

"Good," says director Jonathan Demme, plainly pleased his secrets are safe. "It's a movie of surprises. That's what attracted me to the script in the first place—this succession of surprises that continually occurs throughout the story. So we're trying to be a little bit oblique about what it's about, beyond the fact that it's about two people who meet and fall in love and get engaged in a wild series of events."

From the *New York Daily News* (May 21, 1986). Reprinted by permission of the *New York Daily News*.

Because of the wildness that follows this brief encounter, Demme fusses excessively over the scene, shooting it from a variety of angles, fine-tuning the emotions as he goes slowly along.

He is also battling the elements: The firetrucks *and* the ambulances are out in full force today; there are backfires, street noises, clamoring crowds—a sound engineer's nightmare. "Happily, we have a good man on sound," says the director. "If he can't make sense of this, no one can."

The city's usual commotion contrasts starkly with the seven serene weeks of shooting the company has already put in down in Florida.

"The story of this movie travels out of New York through Pennsylvania into Virginia and then back to New York. We shot all those other states around Tallahassee because, appearance-wise, it's a perfect double. Also, everything gets green down there long before it does up here so we got off to an early start. We expect to have the film in theaters by October."

Plot particulars notwithstanding, Demme makes no secret of the fact he expects his leading players to emerge from *Something Wild* front-rank stars—a safe bet since both are already on upward curves.

Daniels, a Circle Rep reliable (*Fifth of July*, *Johnny Got His Gun*), has been making a steady ascent on screen—from *Ragtime* to *Terms of Endearment* to *The Purple Rose of Cairo* to the forthcoming *Heartburn*; just prior to beginning this film, he won raves for his work in the Off-Broadway revival of Lanford Wilson's *Lemon Sky*.

Griffith is also riding high via the terrific notices she garnered for *Body Double* and *Fear City*. Says Demme: "By page two of this script, I was thinking, 'Wow! This is a great, great opportunity to show what Melanie Griffith can do.'"

Daniels entered the picture not long afterward, when Demme sat down to discuss casting with the Orion executives. "They said, 'Well, here are the people we're really hot on nowadays,' and Jeff's name came up. I said, 'Whoa—that's a great idea!' It's funny—this has been a project where everyone involved had an immediate yes; nobody had to be talked into it."

Given the fact that Demme's films (most notably, *Handle with Care*, *Melvin and Howard*, *Swing Shift*) rarely move in a straight line, *Something Wild* should prove a pretty wild ride for both performers.

"I have a tendency toward the offbeat," the director readily confesses. "That's true of this picture, too—although it's more uncomplicatedly entertaining than anything I've ever been drawn to. It has suspense, it has humor, it has romance. It's kind of a moral tale, but, fundamentally, it's just an entertainment—full tilt."

Something Wilder

J. HOBERMAN / 1988

IF JONATHAN DEMME invented a new widescreen process, they'd have to call it Americarama. Demme is Hollywood's high priest of redneck chic and (more recently) tropical funk, which is why he's filming in a New York location so deep into Loisaida, as the locals call this section of the Lower East Side, that it's practically off the map. "The crummiest part of New York, they want to shoot a movie," a West Indian woman remarks to her friend as they step over the cables and cross Clinton Street. Clinton is Avenue B below Houston—a shabby, narrow stretch of bodegas, botanicas, wholesale zapaterias, and storefront shuls reborn as Pentecostal churches. The nabe is wildly ethnic, nobody's idea of Disneyland. But here's this Hollywood crew laying down tracks across from a Chinese restaurant called La Gran Muralla (The Great Wall) and acting less like a sightseeing safari or an occupying army than like lunch-hour entertainment for the polyglot locals, a diffident assortment of Hasidim, hipsters, and Hispanics.

We're all watching the exquisite Michelle Pfeiffer, wearing what looks like a Trump Tower doorman's uniform, being tailed by a gaggle of paranoid-looking Feds as she heads past Iris Maria Florist, Olga's Bridal Shop, and the Korean greengrocer, toward a moldering tenement on the corner of Rivington Street. Pfeiffer, who is familiar to onlookers mainly as the blondest witch in Jack Nicholson's *The Witches of Eastwick* harem, is playing the widow of a former Mafia hit man. She's left her Neapolitan Ponderosa-style ranch house in suburban Long Island for the liberating weirdness of the Lower East Side, but the boys, most particularly the cigar-chewing Dean Stockwell, still feel that they've got to keep an eye on her. So does the FBI, which has installed Matthew Modine in the apartment upstairs—after all, she's still married to the mob.

From *Premiere* (September 1988), pp. 80–84. Reprinted by permission of Wright's Reprints.

That's the premise of Jonathan Demme's new film, his second for Orion Pictures, following the critical (if not financial) success of *Something Wild*. Orion proposed the script to Demme, who supervised a couple of rewrites, shifted the Manhattan locations from Sutton Place to the Lower East Side, and put his mother in the movie. Like *Something Wild*, *Married to the Mob* is the saga of a character leaving the staid middle class for something a little wilder. It's related to those comedies of yuppie angst—Susan Seidelman's *Desperately Seeking Susan*, Albert Brooks's *Lost in America*, John Landis's *Into the Night*, Martin Scorsese's *After Hours*—that appeared in the mid-'80s and, in posing petit-bourgeois entitlement against existential risk, took the classic *film noir* situation and treated it as the occasion for screwball comedy.

Demme—a stocky forty-five-year-old wearing an MTV cap, an old high school baseball jacket, a pair of baggy khakis, an embroidered Indonesian scarf, and a FREE NELSON MANDELA button—dresses the way his movies feel. He broke into the industry as a publicist and can spot a journalist a mile away. At the next break, he comes over to say hello. Orion is describing *Married to the Mob* as "a gangster movie with laughs," but the director's enthusiasm has nothing to do with the script. Instead, he's raving about Pé de Boi, the eleven-piece "power samba" band he's hired for the big dance scene he'll be filming later in the week. He couldn't be more excited if he'd gotten Michael Jackson and the Rolling Stones.

As is evident from his work, Demme has a transcendentally amiable sensibility. His films are sweet but not cloying—they're too quirky to be Steven Spielberg goo. At once trendy and populist, Demme is both a professional cool guy and a total fan. His associates include such lower-Manhattan luminaries as David Byrne, Laurie Anderson, and monologuist Spalding Gray (whose one-man show *Swimming to Cambodia* Demme filmed in 1987), but his greatest character is the Las Vegas loser Melvin Dummar, the mysterious self-styled beneficiary of Howard Hughes's contested will, whose foredoomed struggle to cut himself a piece of the American pie provided the story of *Melvin and Howard*.

There is a bit of Melvin Dummar and a bit of David Byrne in Demme. His critical reputation far exceeds his commercial clout; his movies are difficult to characterize—and that's part of their cult status. Steeped in good-timey '60s values, his films glorify Third World energy while treating white-bread America with benign post-hippie oh-wowism. (Like, who needs Nepal? Check out K-Mart.)

Despite the critical accolades Demme's *Citizens Band* (a.k.a. *Handle with Care*) and *Melvin and Howard* received, audiences stayed away in droves. Nor were moviegoers certain how to respond to the offbeat rhythms and mood shifts of *Something Wild*—a romantic road film that brazenly telegraphed its hipness with lower-Manhattan locations, excerpts from underground super-8 movies, and cameos by John Waters and the Feelies.

Orion never really figured out how to package this New Wave *It Happened One Night*. Demme tactfully suggests that it fell "victim to the studio's over-enthusiasm"—a unique way to describe the paucity of press screenings and the uncertain promotional campaign with which *Something Wild* was rushed into distribution.

The world may be better prepared for *Married to the Mob*, which is at once more violent and more slapstick than *Something Wild*. Demme's touches are likely to be most evident in the cluttered, improvisational mise-en-scène. From the beginning, the hallmark of his career has been an appreciation for lower-class kitsch and the mass-produced fantasy it embodies. (How appropriate that his father was the press agent for Morris Lapidus's ineffable Fontainebleau, the most deliriously vulgar luxury hotel in Miami Beach.) From the Sleep-in-a-Wigwam Motel sequence in *Crazy Mama* through *Melvin and Howard*'s heady brew of casinos, trailer parks, and while-u-wait wedding chapels, from the impeccable period details of *Swing Shift* to the roadside attractions and schlock tourist emporiums of *Something Wild*, Demme has given the impression of rummaging around the American landscape like an antique hound in a thrift store. (That he actually is one can be verified by the most superficial investigation of his office, which contains a wall full of Haitian paintings and J.F.K. bath towels, a china Elvis clock set in the middle of a gold-rimmed guitar, and an assortment of voodoo altars.) *Married to the Mob* not only has major scenes set in a medieval-motif restaurant and a Borgia sleazoid "adults only" hotel, but Demme also gets to invent two fast-food franchises and stage a shoot-out in a honeymoon suite at Miami Beach's Eden Roc hotel.

In addition to showcasing the director's taste, *Married to the Mob* recapitulates the story of Demme's own journey from Long Island to Florida to lower Manhattan. Born in suburban Baldwin, New York, and raised in Rockville Center, he moved to Miami when he was a teenager and attended the University of Florida at Gainesville. Demme originally planned to become a veterinarian—until he encountered chemistry. His fate was sealed once he began reviewing movies for a campus newspaper. ("As you know," Demme told critic Michael Sragow, "when you start seeing movies for free, there's no going back.") His first break came about through an encounter with a minor show-biz legend. Demme's father showed his twenty-two-year-old son's clips to movie mogul Joseph E. Levine, whose boat was moored off the Fontainebleau's beach. Levine was pleased to see Demme's wildly enthusiastic review of his Third World spectacle *Zulu*, and he was further pleased to do the showmanlike thing by giving Demme a job in the publicity department at Avco-Embassy.

After working as a publicist for United Artists and the foreign-film distributor Pathé Contemporary, Demme moved to London in 1969. Two years later he found a job as the unit publicist on Roger Corman's *Von Richthofen and Brown*, which was filming on location in Ireland. When the shoot ended, Corman brought Demme back to the New World stable, where he joined such aspiring directors as Paul Bartel, Joe Dante, and Jonathan Kaplan. After writing and producing a motorcycle adaptation of *Rashomon* and a nurse-action film, Demme got his first shot at directing with *Caged Heat* (the campiest of women's prison flicks), followed by *Crazy Mama* (Cloris Leachman on wheels) and *Fighting Mad* (Peter Fonda walking tall).

Handle with Care, which Demme directed for Paramount Pictures, should have been his breakthrough film. Although audiences rejected this good-natured, goofy, *Nashville*-esque movie both times it was released, its redneck Renoirisms and delicate sense of CB radio as a form of corn-fed astral projection made it a critical favorite. *Handle with Care* was included in the 1977 New York Film Festival, and Ann Wedgeworth, who played one of bigamous truck driver Charles Napier's two wives, won the Best Supporting Actress Award from the National Society of Film Critics.

His career on hold, Demme moved back East and directed *Last Embrace*, a Hitchcock-type thriller, then inherited Bo Goldman's script for *Melvin and Howard* after Mike Nichols bowed out of the project. Something like a country-western remake of Preston Sturges's 1940 *Christmas in July*, *Melvin and Howard* treated the contemporary West—Vegas, SoCal, Utah—as a land of failed schemes and sweet disorder. The film is the real *Rocky*, celebrating Americans as feckless, media-blitzed dreamers and natural performers who think nothing of marrying the same person twice and spending their honeymoon playing the nickel slots. The film opened the 1980 New York Film Festival and died at the box office, although it won Oscars for Goldman and for Mary Steenburgen, as Best Supporting Actress, as well as the National Society of Film Critics' Best Director Award for Demme.

Demme says he tried to develop his own projects after *Melvin and Howard*, suffering "disappointment after disappointment" until he was hired by Warner Bros. to direct Goldie Hawn in the World War II comedy-drama *Swing Shift*. But Demme's first star vehicle turned out to be his greatest disappointment. He and Hawn, who was also one of the film's producers, disagreed on its final shape, and Hawn prevailed—ordering a number of new scenes added and substantially recutting the film. "I lost my footing there," Demme says. "I had to reassess my reasons for wanting to make movies."

Stop Making Sense, the no-frills Talking Heads concert film Demme made as a respite from *Swing Shift*, marked a turning point in his career—not just a "return to the joy of moviemaking" but also a return to his roots. "Music was my first love, movies came second," Demme told one interviewer. During the mid-'60s, Demme had written rock criticism for the Boston underground paper *Fusion*; his first movie credit was as "music coordinator" for the Irving Allen production *Sudden Terror*, and none other than the Velvet Underground's John Cale composed the score for his first feature, *Caged Heat*. (Cale also worked on the soundtrack for *Something Wild*.)

Just from the way he's prone to yell "Awright!" Demme seems like the kind of guy who whiled away a good part of his adolescence driving around blasting the radio in some six-pack-stocked deuce coupe. "I grew up with rock 'n' roll—literally," Demme says. "I was always following popular music. When I was nine years old I was religiously listening to Nat [King Cole]. The first rock song I really remember was 'Sh-Boom,' and since then I have never stopped obsessing on at least something."

Since *Stop Making Sense*, Demme has made a number of rock videos, working with UB40 and Chrissie Hynde ("I Got You Babe"), Suzanne Vega ("Solitude Standing"), Artists United Against Apartheid ("Sun City"), and Fine Young Cannibals ("Ever Fallen in Love"), as well as directing a nine-minute minifilm of New Order's "Perfect Kiss." All except "Ever Fallen in Love" (which was used to promote *Something Wild*) and "Sun City" are straightforward performance documentaries—along the clean, functional lines of *Stop Making Sense*. "It's a very limited time commitment, and it's a couple of thousand bucks," says Demme of making videos. "You get to design three minutes in a stylized way. You really get lost in a song you like, and you can shoot. You get a chance to shoot. That's what's great about it. Every time you shoot, you learn something. I want to expand my photographic language. I'm seeking a more dynamic approach. I want to figure out ways to cut quicker."

Demme has worked in virtually every format. It's hard to imagine another American director filling the time between Hollywood assignments by working as the director of photography on an underground super-8 production. Characteristically, Demme says he learned a lot from the experience. He maintains that as far as movies go, he has no game plan. He's open to all opportunities that present themselves. "I'll listen to any movie, any idea, any budget. If something good can come of it, I'll dive right in," he recently told *People*. (While we're talking, someone telephones to pitch a script about nuclear winter. Unlike Ron Silver's character in *Speed-the-Plow*, Demme is more than politely enthusiastic.) "It's tough enough to find an exciting script, something really worth making, and once you do find it, you need to find someone with millions of dollars who agrees with you," he says. Demme says he was involved with early versions of *About Last Night* . . . and *Peggy Sue Got Married* before discovering the script to *Something Wild*. Now he has a development arrangement with Orion. "I love making fiction movies, but I can't resist getting involved with other projects."

Among other things, Demme hopes to make a film of *Continental Drift*, Russell Banks's novel about anomie and Haitian refugees in Florida; in the meantime, there's *Haiti: Dreams of Democracy*, the hour-long documentary he made in collaboration with Jo Menell for Britain's Channel 4 Television. Shot entirely on video in the streets of Port-au-Prince and Jacmel one year after the overthrow of "Baby Doc" Duvalier, *Haiti: Dreams of Democracy* is a percolating mix of pulsating crowds and quick background sketches, toothless ranting and coolly delivered analysis, appalling statistics and voodoo ceremonies, visionary murals and sidewalk cynicism, made by an impassioned, wildly appreciative tourist with a taste for cha-cha fantasy and an eye for funky detail. With its engagingly empathetic populism, infectious herky-jerky flow, and deft, carnivalesque mise-en-scène, the documentary is not unlike a Demme feature.

If Demme has an overriding theme, it's America's optimism, the drive toward personal reinvention—Melvin Dummar's abiding faith in the American Dream, the way *Swing Shift*'s insecure heroines become confident factory workers, the transformation of the nerdy protagonists of *Something Wild* and *Married to the Mob* into relaxed urban hipsters.

The epitome of this transformational Americarama is the Demme production number: the Christmas luau at the dingy milk-bottling plant where Paul Le Mat belts out the Melvin Dummar version of "Six Days on the Road"; the high school reunion in *Something Wild* at which, resplendent in red-white-and-blue party hats, Melanie Griffith's erstwhile classmates cavort to "I'm a Believer" in front of a colossal American flag; the Saturday-night dance at a Loisaida social club where Matthew Modine takes Michelle Pfeiffer on their first date. She's "leaving everything familiar behind," says Demme. "She's discovering a new world out there."

Demme originally hoped to locate the dance at C.U.A.N.D.O., a hip community center that hosts everything from Brazilian percussion bands to Caribbean women's films. But there were problems, so instead he's using an old public school on Suffolk Street, near the corroding Williamsburg Bridge. The set is a small masterpiece of rampant tropicalismo—a storefront Copacabana as seen through the haze of too many cuba libres. The peeling ceiling of what was once a gymnasium is festooned with streamers and florid clusters of pink and yellow neon lights. There are red Japanese lanterns dangling from gold-and-green-foil palm trees and acres of artificial fruit, with strings of Christmas lights entwining the bunches of plastic grapes. The walls are covered with purple satin hangings, huge Coco Goya posters, and rainbow murals of toucans and parrots. Does Demme do his own art direction? "Uh-uh, I find a designer who is even more into this stuff than I am," he says.

Today's scene seems more like a party than a shoot. There's a conga line of extras and the samba-mad sound crew, their loud, orchid-emblazoned Hawaiian shirts a virtual uniform. Patterns that would sear your eyes on any other set are barely noticeable here. Demme is in the thick of this passion-flower rain forest, wearing a canary yellow shirt with a charcoal dinosaur pattern.

The stars are sitting at a grass-trimmed table under a flowered beach umbrella, toasting each other with concoctions served in plastic coconut shells and decorated with paper parasols. "Pretty wild, huh?" says Pfeiffer, in the nasal Long Island accent she developed for the film. She's resplendent in a red-polka-dot frock and prominent crucifix while Modine, his hair slicked back, is engagingly gawky in his skinny tie and ill-fitting blue FBI suit. Pé de Boi breaks into the eighty-seventh version of whatever it is it's been playing. "Let's dance," says Pfeiffer. Modine cautiously follows her onto the floor.

Demme's camera is circling the gyrating mob, a mass of plastic purple gardenias and glitter bolero tops, hoop earrings and flowing dreadlocks. He closes in on the stars and glides around them. Pfeiffer and Modine are the only touch dancers on the floor—her mildly inebriated shuffle matching his uptight boogie. Meanwhile, the Pé de Boi singers are ecstatically pirouetting; the sound crew is shuffling. Demme's party is totally infectious. The best dancing is going on outside the samba-crammed frame. You may not see it on the screen, but if *Married to the Mob* works the way it should, you'll feel it.

Kael and Demme: Meeting of Two American Film Heavies

ROB NELSON/1988

GETTING FILM CRITIC Pauline Kael and film director Jonathan Demme together to discuss the state of the art of filmmaking, and Demme's in particular, was something akin to "uniting the dog catcher and the dog." That's the way Bruce Jenkins, Director of Film and Video at the Walker Art Center in Minneapolis, phrased it before introducing his guests at a symposium held at the Walker late last month. "But if you're going to invite a dog catcher," Jenkins said, "you might as well get the best."

Indeed, Pauline Kael is widely respected within the field of film criticism. She has been writing for the *New Yorker* for twenty years, and has had ten successful and acclaimed books of her reviews published, including the classics *I Lost It at the Movies, Kiss Kiss Bang Bang, When the Lights Go Down,* and her most recent *State of the Art*. A collection of the last three years of her work at the *New Yorker*, tentatively titled *Hooked*, is scheduled to be out before year's end.

Cherished by countless movie buffs and despised by almost as many others, Kael is at very least an original, deeply opinionated and passionate about the movies. A year away from age seventy, she is still writing for the *New Yorker* and has lost very little, if any, of her vast knowledge of film, her acutely discerning eye, and her scathing wit. She adores adoring movies (the titles of her books illuminate her obsessive, incestuous relationship with film), but finds that amidst the Hollywood of the 1980s, a good film is almost as rare as true love.

From the University of Wisconsin-Madison *Badger Herald* (September 9, 1988). Reprinted by permission of the *Badger Herald*.

There are those few exceptions, though; the movies she appreciates she defends vehemently. Among these are the films of Jonathan Demme, including *Handle with Care, Melvin and Howard, Stop Making Sense, Something Wild*, and his latest, the recently released *Married to the Mob*. Her influential and zealous support of Demme has, from the beginning, been inextricably linked to his success. When Kael's exaltant review of his 1977 *Handle with Care* ("It could be that *Handle with Care* is almost too likable a movie . . . its comic style has the touch of thirties Renoir—who would have thought there could be such a thing as redneck grace?") included a formal damnation of Paramount for lopping off the film's original ending without Demme's consent, the studio quickly restored the film for a subsequent re-release.

Demme revealed that he has been equally interested in Kael's work. "If you're a filmmaker, you read what Pauline Kael says about you, and you read it in a certain way. I've had my mind changed on several occasions by her. She has a point of view, an artistry that's extraordinary for a film enthusiast [to read]. When the *New Yorker* comes out and you see that, by God, she likes your movie, it's a spectacular feeling, and you read it over and over. When she doesn't like your movie, you read that one only once."

Demme is still affected by Kael's opinion of his work. In one of the more inspired moments of the evening, when Kael casually mentioned that she thought *Married to the Mob* was "a wonderful movie," Demme promptly stood up, threw his hands in the air and shouted, "Yeah!"

Seated with Demme at a small table on stage just to the right of a movie screen (which would be used to show Kael's selected clips from Demme's films), Kael began the evening's conversation by summarizing her affection for the director's work. "What I love about Jonathan Demme is that he searches for the poetry in the tacky, the everyday. I value that much more highly than the so-called tasteful movies people make. It takes more courage to be as unhighfalutin and democratic as he. And movies are, or were intended to be ever since they were first shown, a democratic art form."

Demme, an energetically impulsive speaker by contrast to Kael's mannered reserve, responded with the first of his typically cryptic self-analyses: "I've been lucky enough to have been invited into a lot of different houses, and I guess I developed an eye for kitsch, to use your word, Pauline. The way I've applied that to movies is you try to get a good cast, a good script, and you don't screw it up."

After viewing the high school reunion scene from *Something Wild*, Kael described the Demme trademark of a mesmerizingly chaotic mise-en-scène. "I love the cluttered, messy screen in your movies. They're wonderfully busy." Demme: "I think that's one of things I learned from Roger Corman" (the infamous B-movie producer of the '60s and '70s who sponsored the first directing efforts of Coppola and Scorsese, among others). "When I first started working with him he took me out to lunch, sat me down, and said, 'Okay, Jonathan, we've got an hour. The most important thing to remember is that this is a visual medium, first and foremost. The eye is the primary organ, and if you can't keep the eye stimulated you're not going to keep the brain stimulated.'

"Working with Roger was just a great experience. It was like a big school. It was every bit as valuable as going to film school, only you were getting paid, not the other way around."

When the floor was opened for questions, an elderly man said he liked *Something Wild*'s first hour, but then felt violated by the violence in the film's second half. (The man was referring to the dark, Hitchcockian turn the formerly lighthearted comedy takes when Audrey's high school sweetheart Ray begins to terrorize Charlie). "In *Something Wild* I was trying to show that if you behave violently, you will taste violence," Demme responded. "That people were distressed by the film was distressing for me, you know? And I feel there are definite signals in the first half of the movie that the characters had better straighten up or else."

Kael elaborated: "Part of what is wonderful about Scorsese's earlier work [Demme had earlier mentioned Scorsese as his favorite director] like *Mean Streets* and *Taxi Driver* is that it does upset you, and it doesn't apologize. I don't think the violence in *Something Wild* is gratuitous, and I think it's absolutely crucial to the movie. Without that second half the movie would make no sense."

Kael and Demme are asked to name their favorite movies. After eluding the question a bit, Kael manages to name D. W. Griffith's *Intolerance* as a film she can always enjoy. Demme says that if pressed, he would choose Alain Resnais' 1967 documentary *Far from Vietnam*. "To me, that film is proof that movies can effect positive change, even if it's only in one person."

"Most of what's been playing in theaters lately is dead," Kael said. "Of recent films there's been *The Unbearable Lightness of Being*, a movie that speaks to you in a different way than anything else I've ever seen. And *The Dead*. It's amazing that Huston was able to conjure such a powerful film so near the end of life. And that's about it. And Jonathan's film. But most of it is just awful.

"As a critic, I hate it much more than anyone else can. The major studios' films are generally so much worse now. Most of what's out isn't worth seeing. And having to write about this stuff, you feel degraded. It's occupying your head and it has no right to be there."

Interview with Jonathan Demme

MICHAEL HENRY AND HUBERT NIOGRET / 1989

Q: *You were raised in Miami. How did you discover cinema? When did you discover it as art, as a means of expression? What films did you see?*
A: I moved to Miami at the age of fifteen. Before that, in Long Island, I went to the movies a lot, because as soon as I was old enough, my father would take me every Thursday evening to see movies like *Them!* My parents had very good taste. We saw lots of Fritz Lang films, for example. I had what it took to be more than a regular customer of popular American double features. My parents also went to see art films like *Black Orpheus*, the kind of film that could bring the whole family and its imagination together. It was wonderful.

When I was twenty-one, I went to college for a little while. There was a movie theater there that programmed a different film every night. In one week, I got to see *Wild Strawberries*, *Through a Glass Darkly*, and finally *Shoot the Piano Player*, which was an event for me. I love this movie and I love the fact that I love this movie. I still think it's an exceptional film. Seeing it and appreciating it allowed me to look at films differently, but also to look at myself differently, at a time when I was going through a very self-centered phase. Suddenly, I could appreciate a film like that, in black and white, coming from France, with subtitles. Just as Aznavour says: "May my mother drop dead if I'm not telling the truth" . . . there's a cut, and a woman drops dead. That was for me an essential moment. It was the first time I realized what

---

From *Positif*, no. 335 (January 1989), pp. 24–32. Interviewed at Deauville October 10, 1988; originally published as translated from the English by Hubert Niogret. Reprinted by permission of *Positif*. Translated from the French by Kathie Coblentz. Reprinted by permission of *Positif*.

montage was. This film really opened my eyes to the work of filmmakers. Afterwards, I could admire people who make films the way I admired people who write books. I had never been aware of that until then, when those images struck the screen. I had never considered getting involved with the movies in any way.

Q: *What was the following stage? Did you try consciously to work in the movies?*
A: There were two incredible combinations of circumstances. My father, who worked in the Fontainebleau Hotel in Miami, was in contact with Joseph E. Levine, who'd done *Hercules*. I was at college studying veterinary medicine at the time. Since I couldn't figure out chemistry, I gave it up, but in order not to waste the money I'd invested, I stayed in college. Since I didn't have any money to go to the movies, and I'd noticed that the campus newspaper didn't have a movie critic, I wrote a few samples and offered them my services. They agreed after reading a piece about a Peter Sellers film.

When I came back to Miami after the school year was over, I had gotten in the habit of going to the movies for free, and it was hard to give it up. I went to the local weekly newspaper and pointed out their need for a movie critic, and I got myself hired. When my father told Levine I was a movie critic, Levine asked him to introduce me to him and to let him read what I'd written. I'd written an enthusiastic review of *Zulu*—I'd probably have a different view of it today, but back then I thought it was a great movie. Levine declared that I had good taste and that I had to come to New York to work in his publicity department. So I went. And I was working in the movies! I had already done various jobs when I got a phone call from Roger Corman, who asked me to do the publicity for a picture he was shooting, one of the first films of New World Pictures, the company he'd just started. He was out in the boondocks of Ireland, looking for scripts . . . and here comes this American film enthusiast and publicist. He asks me if I like motorcycle movies. Yes, of course, especially *The Wild Angels*, but what did that have to do with my job as a publicist? "How'd you like to write a screenplay for me, for a motorcycle movie?"—"I've never written one."—"Try it and see."—"OK."

I hurried off to see my friend Joe Viola, an exceptional storyteller who at the time was a commercial director. We set to work, and we conceived a sort of version of *Rashomon*. There had been adaptations of *The Seven Samurai*, of *Yojimbo* . . . why not *Rashomon*? Roger Corman appreciated the idea of the fight scenes, the rape scene, but he wasn't convinced by the flashbacks. Nevertheless, we got the go-ahead to write the script.

When he read it, he told us: "Okay, kids. Come out to California to make the picture. Jonathan will produce it, and Joe will direct." All of a sudden we became filmmakers, in Los Angeles. I was twenty-six and I had a budget of $125,000 to produce a film. It was wonderful to make a movie that way, and terrifying.

Somehow, when you decide you like a film and you don't want to see it destroyed, if before going to bed you make a list of the things you're anxious about, and the next morning you solve them, then you are a good producer.

After this movie, *Angels Hard As They Come*, Roger Corman sent us to the Philippines to film the story of a nurse who was imprisoned during the revolution: *The Hot Box*. I shot a lot of second unit material, like shots of convoys and shootouts in the jungle, with a small camera team. A "spaghetti Western" remake of *O Cangaceiro*, directed by Giovanni Fago and starring Tomas Milian, was at the local cinema during the week when I had to shoot battle scenes, and every evening I went to see this film, which was remarkably well made and photographed. People sometimes ask you what films influenced you. In this case, I stole every shot of the movie to use in my second unit work. It's terrifically exciting to take a camera, along with some technicians, and make action shots.

When I came back to the United States I told Roger Corman how much I'd enjoyed doing that. He replied that if I wanted to write a script for a women-in-prison film, he would let me direct it. I wrote several versions of *Caged Heat*, and finally he greenlighted me.

Roger Corman has two major strong points. He really likes to make sure the screenplay has all the elements he thinks the picture needs. So long as you remain more or less within the limits of his specifications, he lets you shoot. Then, in the editing room, he again becomes very present, very demanding. He's very skillful in these two areas.

He liked *Caged Heat*. It was the era of *Walking Tall* and *Billy Jack*, which were hits in the drive-ins, and he wanted pictures like that. I began working on what was going to become *Fighting Mad*. When I was already pretty far along with this project, he was getting ready to produce a movie directed by Shirley Clarke, *Crazy Mama*, but ten days before the start they had an awful fight.

Q: *Roger Corman and Shirley Clarke seem like a very strange "connection" [laughter] . . .*

A: Julie Corman was the link between the two. There was a rather heavy feminism in the air, and Julie thought that Shirley Clarke, who had some talent, could direct a picture for Roger Corman, but Shirley Clarke wasn't prepared for the New World spirit, nor was New World prepared for Shirley Clarke's New York spirit, and the result was foreseeable. Roger Corman called me up: "Forget *Fighting Mad*. You're going to start shooting *Crazy Mama* in ten days. Come have breakfast before a casting session at ten o'clock."—"I can't direct a film when I haven't even read the script."—"Okay. Forget the breakfast. Come read the script before the casting session."—"And if I don't like it!"—"Jonathan, you're going to like it.... Believe me." I went over there and read the script, which was by Robert Thom. Some parts were fantastic, others were the sort of useless stuff you find in the first version of a script. Cloris Leachman and Ann Sothern had already been cast, and they'd said that the script was hopeless. In ten days, I was supposed to rewrite the script, complete the casting, find locations, etc. Roger Corman told me I could make *Fighting Mad* afterwards. And I answered that I didn't know how, but that I was going to have big problems with him on this picture.

At that time you could really test a title on a chain of movie theaters. For example, in February you would call some guys and ask them if they had some theaters free in the summer for *Crazy Mama*, the sequel to *Big Bad Mama*... and they'd agree, they'd rush in with $50,000: then $300,000 would arrive and Roger Corman would ask you to write a script for *Crazy Mama*, since the money was there. The script would get written, actors would be cast, the film would be shot in three weeks, the way we did it, and it would be edited in two weeks. On this picture, the two editors, who worked literally against the clock, were Lewis Teague and Allan Holzman (the latter also directed some interesting things for Roger Corman). It was a crazy experience. I had problems changing the awful things in the script that didn't work. It was supposed to be a comedy, but there was also a bloodbath with all the ladies killed at the end, and that seemed impossible to me. I eliminated the bloodbath, but I left in a police fusillade against the cars, with the ladies getting away. Roger Corman was disappointed, worried, and unhappy, and he told me to forget *Fighting Mad*. I had said I was going to have problems. People hated the script, it was shot too fast, the producer was pregnant (along the way, Julie Corman had to leave the set in an ambulance to give birth). How could I forget *Fighting Mad*, when we were doing bad work here? I wrote a letter to Roger Corman, telling him that what he had done wasn't good, going over everything I've described to you, and why all that made the director's work difficult. And Roger Corman called me to tell me that he was furious with me... but that we'd eventually be making the picture. I was very impressed, this doesn't happen often. The movie was shot, and Roger Corman was pretty happy with it. Shortly after, I received my first outside script, *Citizens Band*.

Q: *Crazy Mama was photographed very well. What was the role of Tak Fujimoto in the cinematography?*

A: *Caged Heat* was my first complete collaboration with him. In *Crazy Mama*, he only did second unit work, which was almost as important as the first unit, because the first unit cinematographer had been chosen before my arrival. He was part of the "package." Tak Fujimoto also did two weeks of second unit work for *Fighting Mad* in Arkansas (we had to use union technicians, because the film was distributed by Fox). On *Citizens Band*, which was distributed by Paramount, he wasn't allowed to work. Finally, Tak Fujimoto, Caleb Deschanel, Steve Katz, and others sued the union in order to be able to join. I love working with Tak Fujimoto.

Q: *The cinematography of* Crazy Mama, *in a style reminiscent of Russell Metty's work for Douglas Sirk, is very elaborate for a B movie shot in three weeks.*
A: The art director Peter Jamison is really excellent. I worked again with him on *Swing Shift*. The cinematographer Bruce Logan was very good, and with Tak Fujimoto for the second unit, it was a joy.

People talk about director debuts, but think about cinematographers of all categories also: Bruce Logan, Tak Fujimoto, Jamie Anderson, who's now coming up, John Alonzo, who shot *Bloody Mama*. Tak Fujimoto had studied technique in film school, and he'd worked in a laboratory, a brilliant thing that cinematographers ought to do. Then he found a job with Haskell Wexler, who was his mentor for a number of years. Because one cameraman had been fired, then another one fell sick, he became the cinematographer of Terrence Malick's *Badlands* by default, because he was the only one available. He was lucky enough to show what he was capable of on that occasion.

Q: *Do you develop projects? Do people send you scripts? Do you accept commissions?*
A: *Citizens Band, Melvin and Howard, Last Embrace,* and my last two movies are scripts that landed with me after they'd been refused by a lot of people. *Citizens Band* had ended up becoming a gag, it was turned down so much. Twenty-two people had refused it before me, but I didn't care, I loved the script. One of the things that interested me was that it was an "anti-formula" film, whereas I had been brought up on "formula" films. Of course, in the United States, it was a colossal flop; the picture is even famous for its extremely poor showing at the box office. And it's exactly the absence of commercial elements that made it so special in my eyes. To make a film about CB, without car chases, without crashes . . . it was abnormal.

Q: *How could Paramount have been mistaken about* Citizens Band *to the point of imagining it would be its greatest hit of the year?*

A: Amateur radio was a social phenomenon then. Everybody was doing it, going as far as to speak the jargon that went along with it. There were at least a dozen specialized magazines and some thirty million operators, and the backers were convinced they'd have a hit on their hands.

Q: *It's a film without dramatic tension, with intermingled stories, something you've done several times.*

A: When it works, I love it. But things didn't work out between the screenwriter and me. Paul Brickman, who later directed *Risky Business*, was very possessive vis-à-vis his script, and he couldn't believe that his Bible had gotten turned over to this director from Roger Corman's stable. He viewed me with horror. On the second day of shooting, the actors were coming to me to find out whether what they had done was OK. Paul Brickman was going to them to check on whether the way they read their lines corresponded to their idea or mine. I called the production manager, Ben Chapman, who had worked for Republic Pictures, and we decided to forget about the screenwriter. That afternoon, he was literally put on a plane, even though he had come to implore me, assuring me that he wouldn't start in again. I couldn't take that risk. From that point on, instead of watching me, he would be watching the rushes with the producer in California. It was quite a difficult shoot, I had to go through all that, but I survived.

I learned one thing: whether you're right or wrong as a director, you have to make your own choices, and protect them. If you don't, the film will turn out different from what you wanted, for better or for worse, and no one, not even you, will know what your work is worth. It's better to risk making a mistake. It's one of the reasons that makes me choose collaborators like the ones I work with today. Deep down, in the fourteen years I've been making movies, I don't think I have better ideas than anyone else: an actor, a cinematographer . . . I pay attention to the suggestions people make. It was the same with regard to our relations with actors in Roger Corman's time. He had a plan made up of what we were going to shoot every day, to make sure we remained within his specifications. On *Citizens Band*, there was more money, so we had better actors. Whereas with Corman, you hired what the budget permitted. One day Bruce McGill, who played the brother of Paul Le Mat, wanted to try something. I told him no, I showed him the plan outlining all the work we had to do. I saw in his eyes how disappointed he was at not being able to try out an idea. When we did the scene, I told him to forget the plan and try it out. You can't tell everyone what they have to do, how they have to move. It's necessary to let actors feel the scene, to let them construct something themselves, working together. If they need help, give them help. But they are probably going to arrive at a logical mise-en-scène that will benefit from their ideas. As a rule, from then on I've let the actors have as much responsibility as possible. I leave them to discover their character and shape their interpretation. I'm content to observe, only intervening for dramaturgical reasons, suggesting pauses here and there, modifying the rhythm, adjusting the timing.

Q: *One of your characters said: "This country promises everything. What does it give? Nothing." A lot of your characters are duped by the American Dream. At the end they are lonely and frustrated.* Citizens Band *is the first of your films to reveal a great sympathy for failures.*
A: It was one of the great attractions of the script for me. It's a theme that reappears in *Melvin and Howard*, when Melvin Dummar says that inheriting $156 million is something that couldn't happen to him. He's actually prouder of the fact that Howard Hughes sang his song. That was a marvelous thing: maybe this guy will never be rich, but it's the quality of his experiences that is going to determine whether or not he's had a good life, and not the mass of money available in his bank account.

Q: *In general, there are no "bad guys" in your films.*
A: No, not many. If you really study someone, he'll turn out not to be so "bad" after all. Can you make a movie with Hitler where in the end there isn't anything that makes you sympathize with this miserable loser? I doubt it. I don't believe it's important for the viewer, but I need to know the psychology of my characters. Characters who are just "bad"—it's never that simple. In *Married to the Mob*, Connie functions something like a "bad guy." She brings a negative power to situations. On the other hand, I also see her as an "operatic" woman. Whereas the character portrayed by Dean Stockwell is a vicious bastard. He's terrifying because he slaughters people, but Dean Stockwell gives him a certain charm. When he gets trapped in a shootout, I find myself once again on his character's side. But generally, I like scripts without "bad guys" and serious problems, but showing people with real conflicts.

Q: *Humor is an important element in gangster films, but rarely comedy, as in* Married to the Mob, *which is not bound to the genre. Were you looking for that for a long time?*
A: I've always wanted to do a gangster movie. It's one of my favorite genres, in both American and French cinema, and they're the two best in this genre. I've always been passionate about the genre, up to and including *Prizzi's Honor*. Onscreen, there's always something fascinating about gangsters' behavior. I've often wondered why. Is it the cut of their suits? Their skill with

guns? In real life, gangsters, actual ones, are revolting. I enjoyed making fun of them, making them look ridiculous. But it's hard to make innovations in a script for a gangster movie, as always with genre films. *Married to the Mob* is a gangster movie, but from a woman's point of view, with a lot of laugh lines. Like an Ida Lupino film, but funny. Maybe it's a little naïve to say that if she had directed comedies, they would have been like that, but I love Ida Lupino's movies.

I like to work with strong themes. *Married to the Mob* is a script in the style of Preston Sturges, one of my favorite filmmakers. He's a complete auteur, a wonderful storyteller, a superb stylist, even though that's not what strikes you about him right off. *Married to the Mob* is a movie that should make people laugh like *Sullivan's Travels*. It's got a great theme—a woman wants to get back on the straight and narrow, she has to take on the Mafia, in the end she triumphs—and it's a movie that ought to make you laugh. But it bothers me that organized crime is a real problem and the picture doesn't take that into account at all. I hope someday I'll have a chance to do a realistic film on organized crime: it would have to be a terrifying one.

Q: *What primed you to be so interested in Middle America, American kitsch, Americana, themes that are so frequent in your films?*
A: Middle America is where I grew up; I was raised on Long Island, then in Florida. And I was treated well there as a person. To me it seems a warm place to grow up. The word kitsch is fairly new in my life. I'm not quite sure there's even a consensus on what it means, but I think it involves images that recall home to us, things we use to decorate our homes, which partake of kitsch. It's also related to how you dress, the way you "decorate" yourself, things that express a certain image of yourself, of what you are or aren't. The word seems a bit condescending, maybe not malicious, but not very sympathetic.

Q: *The culture of kitsch goes from American blue collar to the culture of suburban gangsters. It's a mixture of tastes, colors, visual things without judgment. Everything's possible. You can mix everything up. It's evident in* Something Wild *and* Married to the Mob. *Howard Hughes is the high priest of kitsch. [Laughter.]*
A: It's a very flexible term. There are two levels in what we're talking about. On the first level, there's good old Roger Corman's Rule Number One: always, always keep the eye engaged. If your eye isn't engaged, your brain won't follow. It's something I always have in mind before shooting, and it really means something. When you look at a very full frame in one of my films, or in a certain way one of Roger Corman's, the things it's filled with come back at us with the notion of kitsch. That's part of the production designer's job. I've worked with a whole series of exceptionally gifted production designers: Toby

Rafelson, who is retired, was brilliant, very gifted. He worked on *Melvin and Howard*, but also *Alice Doesn't Live Here Anymore*, *Five Easy Pieces*, *Stay Hungry*. When you look at all those films, a common visual aspect becomes apparent. The production designer of *Something Wild* was an Australian, Norma Moriceau. It was her first job as production designer, but she had been costume designer for *Mad Max*; remember how much imagination there was in that movie. Kristi Zea was the production designer of *Married to the Mob*. She was a costume designer for pictures like *Terms of Endearment*, *Birdy*, a whole lot of outstanding films where the costumes were exceptionally well chosen. They're the kind of people to whom I say, "Make it fabulous. Go to it!" I hope I'll get to work with one of them again.

I always look for a production designer who has a great imagination, a great sense of observation. Someone who will take a set and enrich it. You can't underestimate the contribution of production designers. In the end, the director signs the work, but he's not necessarily the person who had the idea to do something or other. I've always been very well supported in this part of the filmmaking process. I've made it a habit to be surrounded by a bit of kitsch, that is by material you find interesting to look at and which is going to help the story along. There's also a pleasure that emerges from it, but the satirical aspect mustn't be too pronounced.

Q: *Is that your bond with David Byrne?*
A: He and I have talked about the look of the land, the people, their houses, their businesses, and I know that in *True Stories*, which is of course the perfect reference, everything you see, including the buildings that can be put up in twenty minutes, is true. In the beginning, I wondered how anyone could come up with some of it. David discovered an incredible beauty there. You could hear his commentary on everything you saw: "Ah! Look at those houses! Who lives there?" David has a great warmth, an artist's point of view about things. He has a very open mind, and he sees a wonderful world and falls in love with it. And why not? It's a response to all the people who want to decorate their houses. It's a refusal of all aesthetic judgment, and a welcome to everything that other people present you with. I'm devoted to this vision.

Q: *Did you help him on* True Stories?
A: I read all his various scripts, I talked with him about what we ought to do. We were finishing the editing of *Stop Making Sense* when he started his preparatory work. He started out with pictures, drawings on a storyboard that he pinned up in his house, which stretched out into a streamer. When he was finished filling in all those situations, all those pictures, the script was written. We made some trips to Texas to see marketplaces, festivals, brass

bands. I adored the movie and I would like to be able to say that my contribution was considerable, but that wouldn't be true.

Q: *Don't you sort of belong to the same spiritual family?*
A: Without a doubt. We've become friends, we live in the same city, we often hang out together, we go to movies, we laugh in the same places. While editing *Married to the Mob* I thought seriously about Ennio Morricone for the music because he's a remarkable composer who is constantly renewing himself. Besides, I wanted the picture to have a hint of spaghetti western. I also considered asking Carmine Coppola for a score for electric guitars. But when David offered to write the music for me, of course that became the obvious choice.

Q: *Was Martin Scorsese's* The Last Waltz *a source of inspiration for* Stop Making Sense?
A: It was one of our favorite references. I adore *The Last Waltz*, and so does David Byrne. I especially remember the magic moment where the dolly turns around the Staples Singers when the camera discovers them in the studio. It was an inspired marriage of the movies and music.

Q: *How did the filming of* Stop Making Sense *go?*
A: Seven cameras were filming at the same time. You looked at all the monitors at the same time. The picture was shot in three nights. But before that, we had a camera rehearsal in front of an audience. We were minutely prepared. David had storyboarded the concert in a series of close shots. Not for the film, but for a tour. From this storyboard, I started to develop a model of the film, which by the way never stopped being modified. I worked closely with my visual advisor Sandy McLeod, who made sure I was in constant contact with the Talking Heads while they were on tour. I traveled with them myself for one week in Texas, then, before our concert, I followed all their performances on the West Coast. So on D-Day, I had a precise idea about the best camera placements. Having said that, 50 percent of the shots were conceived on the spot. I was organized as if to shoot a televised debate: I had a video monitor and headphones, and I was able to communicate with the camera team at any moment, to make suggestions, to make it react instantly to what was happening on stage.

Q: *Wasn't* Swimming to Cambodia *a challenge?*
A: It sure was. You've got a guy sitting at a table talking. A priori, it's a gamble, it's anti-cinema. But it so happens that we're talking about Spalding Gray, who is surely one of the greatest storytellers of our time. After I'd spent two hours listening to him on stage, I knew it would be possible to make

a ninety-minute film out of it. Even though it was even more austere than *My Dinner with André*, since in our case the monologue was addressed to the camera, in other words, to a virtual spectator.

Q: *The lighting of the film is magnificent. Were you inspired by Gray's show or did you reinvent it visually with cinematic means?*
A: I couldn't find a better example to illustrate how exemplary the process of collaboration can be. Spalding called me and asked me if I was interested in filming his monologue. He'd been invited to a screening of *Stop Making Sense* and he had loved it. My answer was yes. My first idea was that it would be fun to create a real musical score for the film; instead of illustrating what you see, the music would illustrate what the monologue suggests. I was just about to begin the picture when John Bailey called me. He had just seen Spalding's show and he wanted to create a particular lighting scheme for the film. I'd planned to film in natural light, and here I inherited a complex visual strategy concocted by the artist of *Mishima*! Then, in the editing stage, an assistant asked me if I wanted sound effects. I hadn't thought of it, but I encouraged him to make all kinds of suggestions. Similarly, Carol Littleton, the editor, started using excerpts from *The Killing Fields* to illustrate various passages in the monologue. In the beginning, I didn't believe that would work, but she convinced me and the result is great.

Q: *What is* Haiti: Dreams of Democracy? *A documentary combining music and politics?*
A: It grew out of a trip to Haiti, at Christmas 1986, with a group of friends. After meeting emigrants in New York, I wanted to go to see the place, to meet music people, art people, cultural people. I fell under the spell of this people's charm, and I was moved by their struggle. Something extraordinary was happening there, one year after the departure of Duvalier, one year after the promises of elections. There was a growing awareness through music, street art, street theater, radio, all of which became important because it's a country where most of the population is illiterate. There was all this flux of information throughout the country, in the city, and in rural areas. There was a great hope of democracy, and there were promises. But there was also a lot of cynicism vis-à-vis the possibility that the old leaders would not abandon power so easily when the moment came. I came back to New York after ten days that weren't a vacation, but the kind of experience that is life-altering. I called Jo Menell, who's made a lot of documentaries for the BBC. He contacted Channel Four TV, which gave him $100,000 to capture with me what was happening in Haiti. We went back over there, at times with three teams, and we walked around in the streets. We found the musicians, the singers,

we sought out the painters. We told them all: "We want to be 'the voice of Haiti,' we don't want to impose a point of view, but to give a shape to all this energy." I am proud of this film. PBS refused it in the United States, because it's a discontinuous compilation of conscience, and not at all the documentary linear approach they're used to. They were furious.

Q: *You appear fascinated by street people, particularly by musicians. They always play a positive role, with a touch of magic, in your films. That's true of* Last Embrace, *where you linger on a ukulele player in Central Park, as well as of* Haiti: Dreams of Democracy *where you give the musicians the floor for a long time.*
A: Whenever I encounter musicians in the street, whether they're good or bad, I get on well with them right away. I like to make room for them in my movies because I like the source of the music to appear on screen. One of things I like, for example, in *Last Embrace*, a film that doesn't entirely satisfy me otherwise, is the opening sequence, the murder in the canteen, because the violinist's music dictates the choreography of the whole scene.

Q: *You are, with Scorsese and Rudolph, one of the rare American filmmakers to work both inside and outside of the system, to succeed in alternating experimental projects and big studio productions.*
A: But I'm an armchair experimenter! I have the privilege of being tied to one of the best studios, Orion Pictures. I made my last two pictures with them; they look for subjects for me. And they let me play around with marginal projects when that suits me. It's a very comfortable situation.

Q: *But you've managed to resist the megalomania, the budget inflation.*
A: I learned my lesson a few years ago, when they gave me $18 million to make a movie with Goldie Hawn. It was the worst nightmare I ever lived through. When you choose a project, you've got to only listen to your heart.

Q: *So what happened on* Swing Shift?
A: After the picture was shot and edited, Goldie decided that she didn't like our story and made another one out of it. For me, it was the story of a friendship between two women, of the solidarity that's established among all these women working in a factory to contribute to the war effort. Goldie decreed: "I've got a better idea. It's going to be a love story between Kurt Russell and me." Then she had another script written and some new scenes filmed. The result was a hybrid compromise, completely schizophrenic, between the two approaches.

Q: *You alternate between fiction films and documentaries. Are they two complementary experiences in your eyes?*

A: Fiction films demand so much work, you have to master so many different elements, that a documentary seems like a wonderful liberation. You don't have to worry any more about the script, the actors, the orchestration of themes. There is only you, your camera, and the reality you're confronted with. It's like a return to pure cinema: pictures and sound. I also believe that the documentary permits you to bear witness, to shed light on an intolerable social and political situation, like in Haiti. And maybe even to help the people you're filming. That doesn't have anything to do with the other function of the movies, a perfectly honorable function by the way, which is to entertain the audience, to make it laugh or be moved for the space of two hours. As you know it this isn't so simple, and I'm proud when I happen to succeed.

Q: Last Embrace *is a stylistic exercise, sometimes brilliant, but this homage to Hitchcock is quite unexpected on your part. It was more of a film for De Palma, wasn't it?*
A: I've always loved Hitchcock's films, and when they offered me the script I let myself be tempted. I was also very eager to direct Roy Scheider, I believed he was destined to become the Humphrey Bogart of the 1980s. In the background of the script, there was a true story: the Jewish organization that arranged for the trafficking of white slaves to New York really did exist. It seemed to me to provide a good framework for the movie. Undoubtedly we should have worked further on the script before we began to shoot. I would have so much wanted the picture to be up to the height of the magnificent score by Miklos Rozsa! It's hard that nowadays you acquire your education as a filmmaker . . . under the eyes of the public! You're not allowed any mistakes. And yet, you have to learn. Every time I see the movie again, these youthful mistakes jump out at me.

Q: *It seems you're more and more tempted by parabolas, as if reality were becoming more and more absurd and could only be captured by bewildering detours.*
A: Look at the world around us. Don't you think it's getting crazier and crazier? It seems to me I've hung around too long to be considered "new wave" as some people claim. I don't put the problem to myself in those terms. I see myself rather as a filmmaker who is passionately fond of a great variety of topics, one who tries hard every time to do his best. And the best way to do a good job is to be enthusiastic about your subject, whether it's fiction or a documentary subject.

Q: *You like to divert established genres and foil the expectations of the audience. Sometimes, as in* Something Wild, *you can change genres in the course of a film,*

and even do it repeatedly. Again in Married to the Mob, *you choreograph the rituals of the gangster film to the point of the absurd. Does metaphor fascinate you?*
A: Let's say that I see an evolution from *Melvin and Howard*, which was supposed to be anchored in reality, to *Something Wild*, which, within a quite realistic frame, describes some extraordinary events, to *Married to the Mob*, where I try to make a funny, screwball movie of pure entertainment. But perhaps this is only a coincidence. It happens that there were those three scripts that I liked for different reasons. Now I would like to make a very, very serious film, based on a book called *Continental Drift*. It would be the reverse of *Melvin and Howard*. Not a bit wacky. I hope you'll see a return to reality there. Reality also fascinates me. It's a very strong book by Russell Banks. There are two parallel stories: one is about a working family in New England who go to Florida to try their luck and the other is about a family of "boat people" who escape from Haiti and end up in Florida also. At the end, their paths cross. With tragic consequences. Once again, it's a quest for the American dream.

Q: *Why, in* Married to the Mob, *did you choose young Matthew Modine to play opposite Michelle Pfeiffer?*
A: He has an innate dignity, a little like James Stewart in his day, and I wanted the public to see him as a good guy, even though he works for a corrupt organization like the FBI. Besides, he has an incredible charm. This is not an aggressively erotic seductiveness, like that of Angela's husband. It's important, when she falls for him, that it's because of his warmth, his kindness. You understand that she's matured. Finally, Matthew, who in real life is a funny, multi-talented guy, was being cast mostly in serious roles. I thought the picture would benefit from his humor and his energy.

Q: *How did you get along with Michelle Pfeiffer?*
A: Michelle has qualities that too often go unrecognized: she plumbs the depths of her character, and she has a natural gift for comedy. To work with her is an extraordinary experience. Our experience was all the more exciting because she knew it was an ideal role for her. She had confidence in herself and came "fired up" to the set every day.

Q: *You roll the final credits over shots, or even scenes, that weren't retained in the final cut. Why?*
A: Above all, I wanted to apologize to some actors whose parts had been cut. For example, Joe Spinell's part. He's one of my old collaborators and his talent remains too unappreciated. He played a gangster in Dean Stockwell's restaurant and got himself killed. Unfortunately, this episode, a kind of gang

war, was too long and I had to cut it. It was a light story that required a lively rhythm. I had another reason: in offering a glimpse of something I'd cut, I thought it would be fun to make the audience think about the editing, to show it the process of making a film.

Q: *What is your favorite phase in the creation of a film?*
A: I take an immense pleasure in viewing the rushes. There is something raw, something clean, a fabulous purity, in this immaculate footage that hasn't yet been manipulated, where no one has repaired the shortcomings.

Q: *Did you have a share in the writing of* Melvin and Howard?
A: No. Bo Goldman had already written several versions of the script before I was contacted. He had even worked, I believe, with Mike Nichols, who had been approached to direct it. When it was proposed to me, it was a jewel. I only went over the last draft with him. At my request he wrote one supplementary scene, that's all. Originally, the TV game show in which Mary Steenburgen is a contestant was supposed to be *Let's Make a Deal*, but when the moderator Monty Hall, who was going to play himself, got cold feet and withdrew, we had to improvise, and Toby Rafelson and I invented a new game, which became *Easy Street*.

Q: *It's a very powerful fable about the American society of consumption. You explore it while espousing the blue collar point of view, but you have too much sympathy on their account for it to be a pure satire.*
A: That's the magic of Bo Goldman. What a magnificent script! But it's true that I'm interested in the way Americans live, and you can't avoid addressing the society of consumption when you situate a story in America.

Q: *After* Melvin and Howard, *your career diverges again and you shoot* Who Am I This Time?, *based on a short story by Kurt Vonnegut, for the cultural network PBS.*
A: The script was sent to me by the producers of the series *American Playhouse*, probably because Susan Sarandon, with whom I was in talks for another project, was supposed to play the main role. I liked the script a lot and I was very much attracted to the idea of working in 16mm with a minuscule budget and a non-union crew. At the time, nothing else was materializing. It was an opportunity to escape the routine of studio productions. No matter what the budget is or who the collaborators are, the process remains the same. And once I've been motivated by the story, or a character, or a song, or a topic if it's a documentary, that fascinates me. I'm surprised, by the way, that my colleagues don't make more videos or documentaries, because the brevity of these productions is so stimulating! A feature film takes you an

average of a year and a half, while with a video, you begin on a Monday and you can contemplate the result a week from Wednesday.

Q: *What is your role currently on* Miami Blues*?*
A: I'm co-producing the picture with Gary Goetzman, who produced *Stop Making Sense*. It was Fred Ward, the executive producer, who discovered the book by Charles Wilford, the author of *The Cockfighter*, which was filmed by Monte Hellman. Fred had submitted the project to me for me to direct. But I didn't want to do another criminal comedy and I suggested George Armitage as screenwriter and director. I had collaborated with him in the New World Pictures era.

Identity Check

GAVIN SMITH / 1991

WHEN PEOPLE TALK about A Jonathan Demme Film, it can mean several things. Which Demme Am I This Time? Born on Long Island and growing up in Florida, Demme, like local asthmatic Scorsese, was a sixties kid: movies vied with rock 'n' roll for their souls. Like a protagonist in one of his own movies, the quirks of character and chance, not destiny or Scorsesean grand obsession, brought Demme to film. Try this: his ambition was to be a veterinarian, but he lost the bug for it at college and wound up in the movie foodchain—moving up from campus film critic to publicist in the late sixties (that twilight of the student gods) to foot soldier in Roger Corman's army in the early seventies (mandatory service for a, well, *certain kind* of filmmaker. Was it a way of beating the draft?)

Now living in London, Demme commuted to the U.S. where he co-wrote and produced *Angels Hard As They Come* (1972), and to the Philippines for *The Hot Box* (1972), then moved back to L.A. in 1974 and switched to directing. He had assumed the first of his identities: Demme the Exploitation Filmmaker (from *Caged Heat* in 1974 to *Fighting Mad* in 1976). Jonathan Demme Mark II followed soon after and goes like this, according to conventional wisdom: warm-hearted documenter of small-town Americana, filled with affection for eccentric humanity and the quirky richness of life. This roughly covers the period from *Citizens Band* in 1977 to a little-seen one-hour TV drama, *Who Am I This Time?*, with Christopher Walken and Susan Sarandon, in 1982. It includes, of course, his much-loved *Melvin and Howard* (1980).

The next incarnation of Jonathan Demme was short-lived and doesn't count: Jonathan Goes to Hollywood and gets burned. He directs Goldie

---

From *Film Comment* (January/February 1991), pp. 28–30, 33–37. Copyright © 1991 by the Film Society of Lincoln Center. All rights reserved.

Hawn's project, *Swing Shift* (1983), and the film is rewritten, reshot, and recut at her behest. Full of Demme moments and people, *Swing Shift* is the Demme movie that never was, his dark night of the soul. He returns to New York, his base since 1978, and before long Demme Mark III emerges: still quirky, still doing his own thing, but now the words most frequently attached to him by critics are "hip," "urban," "multi-ethnic," "wacky," "kitschy," "*subversive.*" Somebody somewhere must have called him a Downtown, as in hip, filmmaker—after all, his office is in NoHo, no-man's-land between the Village, SoHo, and Little Italy. Yup, that's Demme, always on the edges.

This period began in 1984 with *Stop Making Sense*, the start of an occasional professional association with Talking Heads' David Byrne, whose first film, *True Stories*, is reminiscent of the earlier, Middle-America Demme. (Byrne acted in Demme's *Trying Times* episode *The Family* for PBS.) He became visibly involved in political issues, notably the anti-apartheid movement (he directed the *Sun City* video, a breathless piece of rap-graffiti agit prop), and in efforts to publicize the political situation in Haiti and promote Haitian music and culture. He made music videos for the likes of New Order and Fine Young Cannibals, and a performance film with Spalding Gray, *Swimming to Cambodia* (1987). Recently he contributed a music video of New Orleans's The Neville Brothers to the international AIDS benefit event, *Red, Hot + Blue*, in which a dozen world-class directors directed videos of bands interpreting Cole Porter numbers.

Somehow he also found time to direct two features, *Something Wild* (1986) and *Married to the Mob* (1988), which reflect Demme's expanded sensibility in their offcenter subjects and styles, their almost in-jokey cameo appearances by the likes of John Waters, David Johansen, and Al Lewis, and above all in their music soundtracks which burst at the seams with rock, rap, reggae, and Latin music. It sounds like a case of Anything Goes, but when you look at those films again, actually they're pretty well-controlled. Still, Demme's level of productivity has become quite alarmingly high. He is currently completing *Cousin Bobby or: The Isaiah Rowley Story*, a documentary commissioned by Spanish TV about Demme's cousin and, in Demme's words, his "lifelong push for social change via his church work."

If all this dissecting and cataloguing of Jonathan Demme the filmmaker seems like glib overkill, go see his new movie, *The Silence of the Lambs*, adapted by Ted Tally from Thomas Harris's bestseller. It may be the distillation of everything Demme's done up until now (though he'd insist that's making too much of it). Some reviewers will surely announce that Demme Gets Serious (i.e., it isn't a comedy); others will say Demme Sells Out. But that would be to misunderstand his whole career: *Silence* is charged, compulsive filmmaking, full of darkness, urgency, and uncanny movement. It is every inch a Demme film.

In cinematic terms it precisely inverts the psycho-chases-girl format, in accordance with Harris's novel. But the film version's reinvention is in some way more potent because the genre is *essentially cinematic*, its central device the voyeuristic-subjective camera. Demme grasps this need for inversion and applies it elsewhere—in the casting and in the look of the film.

There's nothing hip about *Silence*, and you'll search in vain for Demme trademarks and tics. But the director has almost always been concerned with one notion, and Jodie Foster's Clarice Starling, FBI agent-in-training, is its latest instance: The film's opening image is of an ordinary-looking young woman in sweats, dragging herself up a steep slope and running through a wooded training course. Not fleeing from the killer, but maybe fleeing from her past, or her average self. It's Aspiration that drives her obsessively—to change herself, to become something better, to achieve the "Brand New You" that Angela, like a score of other Demme characters, discovers in *Married to the Mob*. There's really only one Jonathan Demme, and he understands what it is to want another life. The filmmaker has already had a few.

Q: *Aside from the fact that it's a good story with good characters, what was it in* The Silence of the Lambs *that really resonated in you?*
A: Ever since my days of working with Roger Corman, and perhaps before that, I've been a sucker for a woman's picture. A film with a woman protagonist at the forefront. A woman in jeopardy. A woman on a mission. These are themes that have tremendous appeal to me as a moviegoer and also as a director.

Q: *You weren't drawn to the serial-killer aspect?*
A: No, I was repelled by the idea of doing a film about a serial killer. Quite apart from do you want to make a film of it, do you want to see a film of it? [Then] I started reading the book, when Orion sent it to me, and I leapt at the chance to get involved with characters of such dimension, and a story with so many complicated and interesting themes.

Q: *Why is it that you are drawn to women's stories?*
A: It has to do with the fact that just in everyday life, in this male-dominated society, women are operating under some handicaps. For women to achieve what they want is harder than for men to achieve what they want. That brings a touch of the underdog to them, and I respond to that. So I'm partial to women in that sense. I think they're better people, by and large.

Q: *Also, the male characters in* Melvin and Howard, Something Wild, *and* Married to the Mob *are not men's men in their masculinity—there's a sensitivity to them, a more feminine side in some way.*
A: Well now, Gavin, I don't want to come across as some kind of sissy in this interview! But I'm pleased you feel that way. Because from what I understand on the subject, we've got our female hormones and our male hormones regardless of which sex we happen to be. If I have a female side to me, I value it for the reasons I said before. And I like it when men feel free to not show that they're the toughest guy around. I find a lot of fault with aggressively tough guys. On every level, globally, personally, this is the sort of attitude that gets us into trouble. I don't think I've particularly done anything with the characters as written, to sort of take them away from a 100-percent maleness. But I may be more drawn to men who are willing to show their vulnerability.

Q: *Did you see* Silence *as having a kind of subversive potential?*
A: No. I need to find good scripts that I have regard for in order to do what I do. And apart from constantly searching for a script that would work in the race-relations arena, I don't really seek out particular kinds of scripts. *Something Wild* I thought was a wonderful screenplay. I liked its originality. I liked very much that E. Max Frye was able to start us out thinking that we're seeing one kind of story, and then gradually take us into a much darker kind of story. If there were certain themes about the dark side of America lurking beneath the surface, terrific. But it's not like a deep-seated vision that exists already within me, and now *Something Wild* comes along and gives me an opportunity to express that. I just respond to writers' work.

My whole process is really, come to think of it, a series of responses. First, I respond to a writer's work, and then the next big thing is responding to the work of the actors. And finally, in the cutting room, I'm responding to the footage we've wound up with.

I did like that *The Silence of the Lambs* was a woman's picture. Is that vaguely subversive?—I don't know. I haven't talked to Tom Harris about this, and ultimately I don't think this is of special interest to moviegoers, but I love that he's taking some really good pokes at patriarchy while spinning this tale. And I think the movie sort of manages to do that, too.

Q: *Some people say directing doesn't require the creativity or imagination of acting or writing. You talk about responding to things instead of, say, "the director's vision."*
A: The director doesn't have to take the creative responsibility of dreaming up what all the actors and crew should be doing. When you start out you

think you have to. If you're working on tight budgets and fast schedules, you think you have to know everything, because if you don't then how's it all going to get done in time? But the better the people you work with, the more you realize you can relax and perceive and enjoy and respond.

Q: *How did you arrive at your portrayal of Dr. Lecter? There's almost an abstract quality to him, and you place him in very stylized, gothic settings—not quite real.*
A: More than anything, I was trying to be utterly loyal to the spirit of Lecter as I understood it from the books [*Red Dragon*—filmed as *Manhunter* in 1986—and *The Silence of the Lambs*] and the script. You read them and you just get a certain kind of feeling about Lecter which stands apart, I think, from all other characters in all other works of fiction. And now he's got to be on screen. And luckily, it's going to be Anthony Hopkins bringing him to life. Anthony really knew exactly what to do there. He got this joke.

Kristi Zea—the production designer—and I spent a tremendous amount of time trying to deal with the bars on Lecter's cage. We were never happy with the different looks we were experimenting with. And finally we went to glass. The looks of Lecter's environments are sort of one step beyond, one step into active imagination in the presence of a lot of ultrarealism elsewhere in the picture.

Were we on some level trying to make it easier for the audience to deal with Lecter? One of the big challenges for this movie was, how do you depict some of the shocking scenes described in the screenplay? Like when the police officers burst into the room in Memphis to discover their fallen partners. Ted wrote, "What greets them is a snapshot of hell." [*Laughs.*] Thanks, Ted. But it's okay, we got that.

It was very hard, because you want to own up to the content of the book and script. But you don't want to cross the line with people, make people physically ill. You don't want to compromise them to that extent. You want to give them the good old-fashioned kind of shock they paid their money for without mortifying them. I'm not against mortification in films, by the way, as a moviegoer; but in my own films I think I will always stop well short of it.

Q: *But, again, the look of Lecter's cell block was gothic, even medieval—anything but modern and institutional.*
A: I didn't want people to feel, for a second, they were seeing anything remotely like a prison movie. When Clarice and Lecter square off against each other, one on the inside of the cage, one on the outside, I didn't want to settle into a someone-visiting-a-prisoner scene. We aspired to creating a setting for these encounters that would not evoke any other films, that would have a freshness and a scariness all their own.

Q: *To me, those encounters are staged somewhere between psychoanalysis sessions—given that Lecter is a psychiatrist—and Catholic confessionals.*
A: I thought it was essential that the movie really put the viewer in Clarice's shoes. That meant shooting a lot of subjective camera in every sequence she was in; you always had to see what Clarice was seeing. So as the scenes between her and Lecter intensify, inevitably we work our way into the subjective positions. And maybe that brings that heightened sense of intimacy we associate with confessionals or with the psychiatrist's couch.

Q: *You had the actors looking as close to the lens—without looking into the lens—as possible. Standard over-the-shoulder shots or matching singles are done with plenty of distance between the eyeline and the lens—but you cut them as close as possible during those scenes.*
A: Well, in most of them, one is looking slightly off—just slightly—and the other one is smack into the lens. We really pushed for that.

Q: *Then in the final sequence in Gumb's basement she can't see and the subjective shooting shifts to the killer's POV through his infrared nightvision goggles.*
A: Exactly. I relished that on a technique-of-making-a-movie level: the idea that we'll be predominantly in the shoes of the protagonist throughout, and then when she's deprived of her sight, we'll be in the shoes of the killer. And perhaps that abandonment of Clarice's point of view will make the situation even more distressing on a certain dialectic level.

Q: *In that scene I felt he was way too close to her. In the book I visualized him stalking her across the basement, instead of on top of her. You made it more claustrophobic.*
A: The idea that Gumb would try to get as close as he possibly could, and touch her hair and—given that he holds the power, he has the gun—he would play with this proximity: that appealed to me as a way to stage the scene.

Q: *Overall, how did you approach the material stylistically? What were you aiming for in terms of the look of the film?*
A: It started off with wanting to have a film that was rich in closeups and subjective camera. One of the reasons I work so consistently with Tak Fujimoto is that Tak comes up with a brand new look for every movie. Which is what gifted DPs are supposed to do. I've almost stopped talking to him about lighting going into films, because his conception of a look for the film is inevitably going to be a lot more interesting and appropriate than what I might have dreamed up. Because that's not really one of my strong points—conceiving the kind of lights and shades of a look for a movie.

My only thing was, I didn't want the film to look like another modish, stylish, moody broody long-shadow catch-the-killer movie. And because of the incredible heaviness of the subject matter, it was important to aspire to a certain brightness whenever possible. To that end, Tak and I looked at *Rosemary's Baby* together a couple of times. A very bright picture most of the time. Tak then spun off from there.

Q: *But as a director, how do you make sure you're all making the same movie? Do you sit down with your key people and give them a concrete image to work from?*

A: Noooo . . . no . . . no . . . [*Laughs.*] I wish I had, but no. We sit down, Tak, Kristi, and Chris Newman—our soundman—and we swap views and impressions. The thing is, we were all responding to the book and the screenplay. You read that book and you're going to come away with an impression of what that stuff looks like. None of us were thrilled about having to depict some of the more shocking aspects of the story. It took months during the pre-production process to get over being appalled at the subject matter. By the time it came to film it, I was happily desensitized, to the degree that I could go out and just do it with great gusto and abandon.

Q: *Did the demands of making a real down-the-line, narrative-driven film result in a suppression of your tendency to direct the viewer's attention towards what's going on at the edges of the story—the incidental details you have a fondness for?*

A: No, all that energy gets channeled into what the new demands are. I was thrilled to have such a strong story, told at such a relentless pace, to focus all that energy on. What was at the forefront was too important to be distracted by the details on the fringes.

It's the same thing with any kind of comedic aspect, because most of the pictures I do try to have a very active sense of humor about them, whether or not they're comedy. And I was just delighted to be freed from the discipline of comedy—not to have to think in terms of where are the laughs going to be, and is this funny enough?

Q: *What are you aiming for when you go off at a tangent in a film, as you often do?* Something Wild *comes to a dead halt during the high-school reunion sequence—and then coming out of that, becomes a different movie.*

A: That was an important part of what *Something Wild* was about. I wasn't just having fun off to the sides—it was a film about this guy's awakening. Jeff Daniels was a total shades-down bonehead at the beginning of the story. And when he goes with Lulu [Melanie Griffith], she takes him on an exhilarating journey that opens his eyes to the life out there. Therefore it was important to populate the environments their journey took them [through] with a tremendous amount of human activity—lifeforce kind of stuff. So I was actively seeking kind of fun things—most of which were drawn from things I was seeing around Tallahassee while we were shooting. Just the kind of things that a lot of us ignore if our minds are turned inward and we're walking around, you know, thinking about our problems and our day's work . . .

Q: *Same thing with* Married to the Mob. *From the closed world of the Long Island Italians, she goes into the Lower East Side.*
A: Yes, exactly. I like that theme a lot.

Q: *It's also part of the Jonathan Demme stereotype—Demme, he loves all that quirky kitschy stuff; he's wacky, he's zany. Does that bother you?*
A: No, I don't mind. I don't pay much attention to that. In terms of my stereotyping as a director, that's one of the least offensive stereotypes that we see around us all the time. If you get to pick what you're going to be perceived as, I would pick being perceived as unpredictable. 'Cause for *me* I'm unpredictable: I haven't got the foggiest idea what's going to turn me on next, and what's going to speak to me as something that I want to make. I haven't got a clue what the subject matter is going to be, as proved by *The Silence of the Lambs.*

Q: *You do a lot of other projects, apart from features—music videos, documentaries. Do you ever worry that this diverts your energies and undermines your ability to make the breakthrough personal project that really counts?*
A: [Firmly, laughing.] No. I think I bring an uncommon amount of enthusiasm to the feature films I direct. And I think one of the reasons I'm able to do that is that I don't feel chained to it. I get away from it, I explore other mediums, and get to work away from the discipline of the big box-office success, which allows me to come back with great enthusiasm to go for it again.

Q: *But there must be that one special project that still eludes you.*
A: More than anything I hope one day to do a movie that has a lot of meaning for people in the area of race relations. Also, as the father of two kids I suddenly have this deep desire to make a wonderful film for children.

Q: *Ten years ago you said in* Film Comment *that you weren't interested in violence anymore. Why has your interest revived since* Something Wild?
A: I'm sure that has something to do with becoming more distressed again, in my life, about the violence in our society and around the world. I'm not sure if that's me reading the newspapers more than I once did. I'm not sure if it's me having discovered children. Not my own children, just children. I'm

probably a little more concerned on a specific level with humanity. I'm just appalled with what's going on.

Q: *But I bet you enjoy violence in movies when it's well done.*
A: Well, what do you mean by "enjoy"? I'm not sure I get the same kick out of violence I once did. I'd have to go back and see *The Getaway* again to tell you; I might not respond the same way I once did. It doesn't mean I hold it in any less esteem, but I may not get off on that quite as much as I did.

The most violent thing I've ever seen in a movie was when Jack Palance got his arm run over by a tank in *Attack*—which right on the spot made me, without realizing it, absolutely antiwar. I was the typical American boy who played with his tin soldiers all the time, loved the idea of GI Joe and so on, and then I saw *Attack* one day and that was it. Just to see that kind of destruction being done to a person, and to contextualize it in war.

So, ever since then I've had sort of standards about violence. I loathe and despise fun violence. I feel it's important to have violence in movies so that people can see how awful it is. *The Getaway*—that kind of violence is in its own little corner. I wish I could explain my complex feelings about screen violence to myself, much less you.

Q: *Isn't the violence in* Married to the Mob *fun violence?*
A: Well, it definitely treads in there much more than I'm pleased with. Yeah. That one particular Burger World shootout . . .

Q: *I bet the audience cheers when Chris Isaak gets shot through the car windshield glass—'cause it's so cool.*
A: Yes. Well, see, that's a little bit of prostitution going on there, probably. But that scene contains what I, quote, "like" about violence, and what I don't like anymore about violence. I like when Paul Lazar, who plays Tommy, says "Don't," because I think there's a moment of truth there. When Dean Stockwell pulls out his .45s and does his Gatling-gun, two-handed thing, the adolescent moviegoer in me thrills to it. And the anxious-to-have-a-movie-that-pleases-people director in me goes, That's a great shot. And then another part of me goes, Be careful there, 'cause you just crossed the line. You just turned violence into fun, you really must strive to not do that anymore.

One of the themes that I was working really hard to put across in *Something Wild* was how awful violence must be. And I know that the first time we previewed the movie, and there was a moment when Charlie turned the tables on Ray early on in the fight and got his handcuffs around Ray's neck, some people in the audience cheered at the reversal. And I just thought, Oh—they totally got the wrong idea what this scene's about. I have an aversion to the idea of cheering death. I don't think it's fair to the character who lives, as much as anything else.

In *The Silence of the Lambs*, when Jodie finally shoots down Jame Gumb, I wanted to avoid the obligatory triumphant shot of Clarice's face. I wanted to respect her privacy at the moment of having just taken a life. And the camera doesn't travel to her. It goes in on Gumb.

Q: *What did you think of Michael Mann's* Manhunter? *Did it affect your choices?*

A: I saw *Manhunter* when it came out. I found it very effective, very disturbing. [*Pause.*] Then, when I knew I was going to make *The Silence of the Lambs* and it was pointed out to me that this was Tom Harris, and Dr. Lecter and Crawford had appeared in *Manhunter*, I felt immediately that it would be smart to look at it again. And I started watching it, but I didn't get very far. I felt my feelings for what *Silence of the Lambs* should be like were so strong that it was impossible for me to learn anything from *Red Dragon/Manhunter*. And I stopped watching it. I saw one Lecter scene, and I thought, "Oh, my God. That's not *my* Dr. Lecter." [*Laughs.*]

In no way is *The Silence of the Lambs* reactive to *Manhunter*, because the gap in seeing it was too long. Now I should see it again.

Q: *You cast Anthony Hopkins and Scott Glenn both against type. You would've expected Scott Glenn to be the serial killer and Anthony Hopkins to be the father figure.*

A: [*Laughs.*] Right. With Tony I just got a bee in my bonnet early on about him in this part. I think he has the ability to project an extremely heightened intelligence, which was key to Lecter as a lover of words—words just roll off Tony's tongue.

Jack Crawford should've been a couple of years older than Scott. And I was thinking of actors older. Scott came into the equation late in the game, and it was funny because I've worked with him in the past; he was in *Fighting Mad* and, indeed, the first movie I produced, *Angels Hard As They Come*. Scott is a very cerebral guy; I felt it would be fun to give him an opportunity to really work with his mind in a part, to put on a great-looking three-piece suit—'cause Scott's in exceptionally good shape—put some glasses on him, and completely leave everything he had ever done before at the door.

Q: *What about Ted Levine's portrayal of Gumb? What lines did you draw in terms of visualizing that character?*

A: The one thing that was more important than anything else, in terms of the character, was that the pathology be as accurate as we were capable of understanding. We received a lot of guidance from the FBI Behavioral Sciences Unit on that. Before Ted was even cast, I was working on profiling Gumb. I wanted my understanding of this deranged person to be as accurate as possible. So I would write my own profile of Gumb and send it to the guys at Behavioral Science and have them critique it for me. In a way, understanding Jame Gumb is comprehending the incomprehensible.

Q: *But the guy has his own logic.*
A: Yes. And his own motivation, and his own methods. Ted Levine had a lot of good ideas for that; there were certain guidelines drawn. Also, obviously, we knew that it was tremendously important to not have Gumb misinterpreted by the audience as being homosexual. That would be a complete betrayal of the themes of the movie. And a disservice to gay people.

The scene where he dresses up and talks to Kathryn in the pit, when he appears to be a transvestite—we didn't want people to think he's a transvestite. It was critical to understand that he *shouldn't* be doing this. He's *dead wrong*. (Lecter explains it; hope the audience is paying attention.) This is someone who is so completely, completely horrified by who he is that his desperation to become someone completely other is manifested in his ill-guided attempts at transvestitism, and behavior and mannerisms that can be interpreted as gay.

Q: *Is Charles Napier going to be in every movie you do?*
A: I certainly hope so. I'd love to see his parts get larger again. Some people say, "Oh, is Chuck your good-luck charm?" It doesn't have anything to do with that. Chuck is a wonderful actor; I think any film with him in it benefits enormously. Same thing with Tracey Walter. When I know I'm doing the script, I send it to Tracey and say, Tracey, please pick something out. We have a lot of fun working together.

Q: *Is that George A. Romero we glimpse in the courthouse where Lecter is being held?*
A: When I first called him up it was like, Hi, I've come to Pittsburgh to make a scary movie. And you've got to call the king when you come to town. So, we're here. And he said, Good, welcome, thank you very much. Then later, I thought, gosh, I wonder if we could get George to do a secret cameo. So I called him up and he came in.

Q: *How come Roger Corman gets to be the director of the FBI?*
A: Well, he was so good as the senator in *Godfather II*; I always thought that was brilliant casting on Coppola's part. I'm so fond of Corman. The only way

to get to see him, he's always so busy working on his empire, is to offer him a part in a movie. He's in *Swing Shift*; he played the owner of the factory, Mr. McBride.

Q: *Why did you choose to have the last scene with Lecter in Haiti? I know you've got a thing for it—the music, the culture . . .*
A: It's not necessarily Haiti.

Q: *Yeah, but it is.*
A: [*Laughs.*] I thought you really had to get a sense in a very brief time that Lecter had tracked Chilton to the ends of the earth, to a place that redefined "off the beaten track." So, because I'm very familiar with Haiti and the Creole language and the atmosphere, it seemed like a good choice.

Q: *What creative involvement did you have in George Armitage's* Miami Blues, *which you exec-produced?*
A: I participated a little bit at script level and later a little bit at the editing level. And I scrupulously avoided anything to do with the shooting of it.

Q: *How do you work with screenwriters?*
A: You've got to have a gifted writer in order to get a good script, 'cause no director, no matter how many ideas he has in his head, is going to help make a good script out of the work of a bad writer. It's important to sit down, and you tell the writer what you like and what you don't like. And you tell him if you feel there's something missing, and you discuss it a little bit, and then you let him go write it. And then come back and read it again. I'm not too into sitting and working out scenes in great detail. Every once in a while that happens.

Q: *You seem interested in people who want to change, who transform or experiment with their identities, who want to become something better.*
A: Isn't that one of the great old chestnuts, though?

Q: *No, I think the old chestnut is, "I like a movie where there's a strong conflict."*
A: [*Laughs.*] Of course, it's not a story—it's the theme of change. I don't know the answer to that. But I do know, as you know, that one of the ways actors decide if they want to play a part or not is, is there a good *arc* there? That wonderful, wonderful word, right? It's always, Well, she's not that different at the end of the film than she was at the beginning, so what happened to her in the course of the story maybe isn't interesting enough to make a movie about her. So the whole idea that you must witness change in a character to have a meaningful story is now taken to extreme.

Q: *But the main character in* Melvin and Howard *doesn't really change, and that's a more truthful portrayal of life. He has a few new insights, but his life hasn't altered radically.*

A: I'll tell you what appealed to me so much about *Melvin and Howard*. Once again, it must be said, a brilliant screenplay. What appealed to me tremendously was the portrait of a hardworking man, an American guy working his ass off in a million different kinds of jobs and never getting ahead—always pursuing the dream. It's a quintessentially American story. In the typical Hollywood version of that story, he would achieve his dream. But Bo Goldman's screenplay remains true to the truth of the actual American Dream—that far more don't achieve it than do. The poetry of Melvin's story is that at the end, in fact, he *had* changed because he has come to realize that maybe it's more important to treasure your experiences and your interactions throughout the course of your life, rather than the amount of material goods you're able to amass.

Q: *That beautiful line that sums it up—"Howard Hughes sang Melvin Dummar's song."*

A: It sums up this idea of, it's the experiences that count, not the size of your bank account. That was the measure of Melvin's growth. You think about how obsessively he was chasing the golden ring. The end of the trial was, I guess, his great moment of truth—he's put to the test, where his values were. He went into the trial wanting to get that money. And then suddenly all his integrity was on the line, and the truth of his life became more important than what he was going to walk away with financially.

Demme's Monde

AMY TAUBIN / 1991

"THE SILENCE OF THE LAMBS employs an archaic plot device—that the saving of one life is profoundly important. Not catch the motherfucker, the crazy killer, but get to the girl while she's still alive. Such an old-fashioned idea." Jonathan Demme shakes his head and emits a wary middle-aged laugh that does nothing to alter the dorky high school set of his permanently pleated features.

Deliberately, unabashedly, and uncompromisingly a feminist movie, *The Silence of the Lambs* also has the makings of a breakaway popular and critical success. It's to the psychological thriller and slasher genres what Angela Carter's *The Bloody Chamber* is to classical fairy tales like *Little Red Riding Hood* and *Bluebeard*. Both take familiar stories—so familiar that they've become part of our cultural unconscious—and turn them upside down.

"One of the great things about the script," says Demme, "is its genre base. It's a suspense movie with a female protagonist who's never in sexual peril. It's a slasher movie that's devoid not only of slasher scenes, but of the anticipation of seeing them."

Demme is a director who knows his genres but has never been able to resist messing with them. Starting out in the film business as a publicist, he was soon hired by Roger Corman as a script writer and then as a director. His first feature, *Caged Heat* (1974), about women in prison, became a cult classic. It shows up regularly in alternative and academic film venues, satisfying the guidelines of neither fetish object nor feminist critique.

Corman's rules for filmmaking, which mandate either the revelation of some bit of bare torso or some show of physical violence for every three

---

From the *Village Voice* (February 19, 1991), p. 64, 76–77. © 1991 Amy Taubin. Reprinted with permission.

pages of dialogue, are as good a lesson in the meaning of the misogynist aspect of voyeurism as Laura Mulvey's pioneer essay "Visual Pleasure and Narrative Cinema" and the flood of feminist film theory that followed. It's paradoxical, if not downright perverse, that Jonathan Kaplan, who directed *The Accused*, which, in its mix of feminism with genre violence, is comparable to *The Silence of the Lambs*, also toiled for Corman. And it's probably not altogether coincidental that Jodie Foster is the star of both movies.

While *The Accused* had only one complicated character, *Silence of the Lambs* has two, the fledgling FBI agent, Clarice Starling, and Dr. Hannibal Lecter (performed with cobralike relish by Anthony Hopkins), whom Clarice so impresses with the purity of her pursuit that he yields her his secrets. *The Accused* is played totally for social realism; *The Silence of the Lambs*, however, evokes the fantasy life of the unconscious, where sexuality and sexual roles are determined. Demme's film suggests that these fantasies can be exhumed and examined, and that their meanings can be shifted. In that sense it's a deeply positive movie.

In his earlier films, Demme intermittently evidenced an interest in assertive women characters, but they were inevitably subsumed in romance and marriage. His all-time low was the conclusion of *Something Wild* (1986), which backed away from the male homoerotic can of worms it had, I suspect inadvertently, opened, taking refuge in a quick trip to the altar with the heroine properly, though unconvincingly, relinquishing the driver's seat to her man.

In any event, however charming, intelligent, and increasingly socially conscious were his previous nine features, his made-for-TV comedies, his one documentary, his handful of music videos—all sparked by an appreciation of pop culture (and more recently, world-beat music), an intuitively postmodern sensibility, and a passion for quirky underdog characters—none of them suggested that he was capable of the cathartic mixing of fantasy and realism, the sustained structural clarity, and the understanding of female experience that distinguish *The Silence of the Lambs*.

AMY TAUBIN: *How did you get involved with* The Silence of the Lambs?
JONATHAN DEMME: I may have read the coverage of the novel when it first came out, you know, "young female FBI agent hunts down serial killer with help of demented psychiatrist." It wasn't the kind of thing that I find interesting. The idea of a film about a serial killer repels me. Then Gene Hackman read the novel and got Orion to option it for him. He wanted to make it his directing debut. Ted Tally was hired to write the screenplay. I have a special relationship with Orion, and when Gene Hackman withdrew his in-

terest, they came to me and said, these are exceptional characters. I read the novel—the script wasn't finished at that point—and I said sign me on. It was Clarice that got me.

TAUBIN: *As it turns out, your Clarice is a more radical character than the Clarice of Thomas Harris's novel. In the novel, you have the sense that Clarice's heroism is a way of proving herself to the good fathers—her real father who died when she was a child and Jack Crawford, her FBI mentor, with whom she has an intensely Oedipal relationship. In the film, the father is barely present, and Crawford seems almost as much of a problem to her as Lecter.*

DEMME: After Crawford says that line to Clarice, "Your father would have been proud of you," it cuts to a close-up of Jodie, who gives him what I think is the most complicated smile in the history of cinema. I don't want his statement to be taken literally. I see Clarice as a woman who has to unencumber herself from those velvet shackles. I also found it impossible to believe that people like Clarice and Crawford, faced with a terrible dilemma and with the clock ticking, would have the time to notice whether the person they're working with is sexually attractive. Besides, it would have been a movie cliché. The unrequited spark—boring and cliché.

You know, there are movies about women from an external point of view and then there are movies that get the joke—that understand about the endless abrasive difficulties of wading through the patriarchy in the course of a day. When you watch debates on abortion on TV—you hear a lot of discussion about fetuses that are the result of rape and is it okay to abort them. Holy shit, we live in a society where rape, at that level, isn't even questioned. It's taken for granted, accepted, tolerated. I wish the president would get on TV and condemn rape and lynching. Instead the attitude is men do this kind of thing. Where can young people get exposed to the idea that rape is a cowardly act, that what happened in Bensonhurst was a cowardly act.

TAUBIN: *But there's no rape in* The Silence of the Lambs.

DEMME: No, I wanted to make a gripping entertainment in which the heroine was never sexually threatened, and I wanted to take a subtle poke at the patriarchy. And in case that wasn't enough reason to make the movie, I wanted to get in the meaning of child abuse. Behind every serial killer is a profoundly abused and neglected child. When you're making a movie like this, you think about why this whole country is fucked up, why child abuse and family violence, and violence toward women and rape is tolerated. We need a legal mechanism to respond to that aspect of male dominance.

I wanted to get this meaning of child abuse in there so bad. We tried a scene with someone from the Behavioral Science unit [of the FBI] lecturing about how serial killers were always abused as children. We tried to get in dialogue about it. It just stuck out—like standing on a soapbox: In the end we cut everything except one line: "You are looking for someone who was abused as a child."

What I'm trying to say is there is an awesome movie to be made about child abuse and the way we practice it on a societal level, on whole sections of cities, on the vast majority of kids in Harlem and in Brooklyn.

TAUBIN: *Given what you've implied about the government, how do you feel about making a film in which the hero is an FBI trainee?*
DEMME: I continue to read in the paper about damage done to people and organizations that I respect by the FBI, and I continue to be alarmed by the way the organization functions. Who will police the police, investigate the FBI? On the other hand, I feel great about the Behavioral Science unit and what the movie says about it. The way our society operates, we breed serial killers. Behavioral Science are the pioneers, not only in looking for ways to catch them, but to prevent them from being produced.

TAUBIN: *So what about the character of serial killer Jame Gumb? Are you aware of the reaction of some gay critics to the film that this is just one more gay psycho?*
DEMME: I don't think it's there. I don't feel defensive about this. We went into the movie knowing we had to protect the movie and we had to protect gay people from negative interpretations. Clearly there is a problem in society; homophobia is one of the cowardly manifestations of the sickness of American males. But we wanted to trust the intelligence of the script. If you don't understand that this guy isn't gay, you don't understand the story. It's about a man who doesn't want to be a man, he wants to become as different from himself as he can. He wants to become a woman. When he gets into his special room, he's transformed. He's not the person he loathes and despises. But at a gigantically key moment you are meant to understand that these efforts are pathological, that he's doomed to endless failure. That has nothing to do with being gay.

TAUBIN: *But the criticism is that a mass audience already steeped in negative gay stereotypes won't understand the subtle distinctions between a psychopath who's totally confused about sexual identity and a gay man.*
DEMME: Then perhaps the movie will provide a forum for this, hopefully there will be a dialogue.

TAUBIN: *To switch to more formal issues, you showed considerable restraint in your trademark use of tchotchkes in this film. On the other hand, for me, one of the most powerful moments is that series of close-ups near the end in Jame Gumb's* lair. First the newspaper clipping "Bill Skins Fifth," then the old velvet cloche hat with the American flag propped against it, and then the blue paper mobile with the giant painted butterflies, like some imperialist trophy from Vietnam. Those images said more about who that guy was, about the fantasy he lived in, than thirty pages of Thomas Harris's prose, notwithstanding my admiration for the novel.

DEMME: I'm glad you liked it. Maybe the way this film looks is a response to reading criticism about kitsch and tchotchkes in my films. Not that I have any regrets about the tchotchkes in my past, but maybe I don't want to be identified that way. I do feel the things we put up in homes and workplaces tell what we care about. You want to engender certain things in the viewer through what you show them. [For the record, the walls of the reception area in Demme's Noho office are covered with Haitian paintings.]

TAUBIN: *You've been talking about very serious issues—child abuse, murder, rape—and yet you characterize the film as entertainment.*

DEMME: It's a subtle and recorded truth that people love to be terrified in the safety of a work of fiction. Little kids love Halloween. No one's figured that out yet. People have potential for good and bad. What we read about in newspapers are acts that define how bad we can get. I believe in the positive aspects of experiencing certain kinds of catharses. When I saw *Rosemary's Baby* or *Texas Chainsaw Massacre*, I left the theater feeling purged and cleansed. The filmmaker and the moviegoer in me loved making *The Silence of the Lambs*. It had integrity and it's frightening.

Still Burning

AMY TAUBIN / 1992

AWKWARD AND ENTHUSIASTIC, Jonathan Demme's *Cousin Bobby*, a film portrait of the Reverend Robert Castle of St. Mary's Episcopal Church on 126th Street, mixes memory and desire, history and prophecy, the personal and the political. Reverend Castle takes Demme on a guided tour through his Harlem parish where, he explains, people feel as if they have to organize an entire civil rights movement in order to get the city to fill in a pothole or hang a streetlight at a school intersection. A liberation theologist, he believes that "this country should not be allowed to have peace until there is justice, and right now there is no justice for black people or poor people."

Asked to contribute to a series of personal documentaries produced by Spanish TV, Demme decided to make a home movie about his cousin, whom he had lost track of nearly thirty years ago. "At first, I thought he was strange and quixotic in this rage-filled battle that he was waging against the establishment," Demme says. "But I came to admire him—his magic is infectious, and hopefully people who see the film will feel as I do about him and about people who work for social change."

In charge of a Jersey City congregation throughout the sixties, Castle became involved with the civil rights struggle via the Black Panther Party. He was particularly close to Panther leader Isaiah Rowley, whom he describes as "a person of great compassion who was also capable of being very violent." Rowley, who was gunned down nearly twenty years ago, remains a touchstone of Castle's politics and his emotional life. "I was very glad that this film gave me the opportunity to tell Isaiah's story," says Castle in his hectic rectory office. "He was a real threat to the forces of oppression—the police as well

---

From the *Village Voice* (June 9, 1992), p. 66. © 1992 Amy Taubin. Reprinted with permission.

as drug dealers. I believe he was killed by drug people, but the police never bothered to investigate his death."

Completed nearly a year before the recent events in L.A., which Castle terms "a rebellion, not a riot," *Cousin Bobby* concludes with a montage of what Demme describes as "American race war footage from the sixties." As KRS-One raps a "Wake Up" to history African American style, we see cities burning: Detroit, Boston, Watts . . .

"I had intended to end the film with this overhead shot of Bob walking down 126th Street," Demme explains, his voice blaring over Castle's speaker phone. "It had this feeling of sweet heavenly resolution, as if there were serenity on 126th Street. What was left out was the profoundly justified rage of this advocate for social change. And then I came across this archival footage, and I was shocked by it—seeing white American soldiers shooting at and humiliating the black citizenry of these cities. I wanted to send a warning—to show it would happen again because of the horrendous downward spiral, because people are living in despair.

"I share Bob's feelings and I marvel at his devotion, but I'm not an activist and I hate sounding as if I thought I was. I'm a taxpayer who hates the way my government is behaving. My response to the riots is as a filmmaker; and luckily, I have a chance to channel my rage."

Castle adds that the epilogue to *Cousin Bobby* allows the black community to express its outrage. "It's not for Caucasian people to determine how African Americans take control of their liberation," he explains carefully. When pressed, however, he adds that "we applauded the community for not burning down 125th Street. We're not going to play into the hands of a system which wants to see oppressed people destroying themselves."

As for himself, he refuses to be "one of Bush's points of light" or to be part of "the white church's patronizing of black people as opposed to making it possible for black people to have jobs and housing and self-determination. The problem is not that there aren't enough good people but that the good people don't give a damn."

Demme's Philadelphia Story

ANN KOLSON / 1993

HERE ON the East Mount Airy set of his movie *Philadelphia*, director Jonathan Demme's voice booms out: "He's young, gifted and scared. We got *action!*"

The camera rolls as Denzel Washington, playing Joe Miller, a swaggering, low-rent lawyer, visits his family doctor after meeting with a prospective client who has AIDS. He can't recall if he even shook the man's hand: "We were sitting in the same room. We were three, four, maybe five feet apart," he says.

Still in character between takes, Washington introduces himself to a visitor: "I'm a member of the NRA and a damned good shot. A personal-injury lawyer. I do commercials—in fact, I'll give you a card. I can get cash justice for you," he riffs, pulling out one of Miller's business cards.

It's the final day of a three-and-a-half-month shoot, and spirits are high on the set. (The production has taken over an actual doctor's office, in an old stone house on Sedgwick Street.) Demme, who's wearing rumpled khakis, a baggy maroon sweater, and hiking boots, stands in front of a monitor, watching the scene, shifting his weight from foot to foot and swigging from a big bottle of Evian, as crew members step over cables, whisper into walkie-talkies, consult clipboards.

Dr. Armbruster, played by Philadelphia actor Bill Rowe, speaks to his patient in his deep, comforting voice. ("I wanted to find my fantasy of a great doctor who you always believe," Demme says.) The physician solemnly educates on the ways AIDS can and cannot be transmitted. Sensing his patient's unease, he begins gently to prod: "Have you had unprotected sex with someone you didn't know very well any time over the last twelve years?"

From the *Philadelphia Inquirer* (February 28, 1993), N1, N5. Reprinted by permission of Reprint Management Services.

After endless takes, Washington finally loses it. "Only once—with a midget in Albuquerque," he answers. As everyone on the set breaks up, Demme, laughing too, shouts, "Cut!"

Philadelphia is a drama about a big-league lawyer with AIDS (played by Tom Hanks) who sues his powerful law firm when he is fired. After a long search, he finds personal-injury lawyer Miller to represent him.

Directed by Demme, who last year won an Academy Award for *The Silence of the Lambs*, the $20 million-plus TriStar production filmed in and around town from October 21 until February 4. Written by Ron Nyswaner (*Mrs. Soffel*), the project also stars Jason Robards as the head of Hanks's law firm, Mary Steenburgen as the lawyer hired to defend the firm, Joanne Woodward as Hanks's mother, and Antonio Banderas as Hanks's artist lover.

Accessibility is key to the success of *Philadelphia*, which is, after all, a major Hollywood film, the first about AIDS. "If it's not a mainstream movie then we've wasted our time and failed in our mission," says Demme, who turned forty-nine on Monday.

"This isn't just for people with AIDS and their families—they know about it. This is a movie for those of us who read in the paper about AIDS but whose lives haven't been touched yet," he says. "We've wound up with a script that, yes, is very much about AIDS, but it's about so much more than that. It's about human nature, it's about life in America today, it's about finding the humor in the saddest of situations."

The campaign to lure Demme's production to Philadelphia was launched last April when the filmmakers approached Sharon Pinkenson, executive director of the Greater Philadelphia film office.

"She wooed the living daylights out of me," recalls Robin Fajardo, assistant to co-executive producer Kenneth Utt, at *Philadelphia*'s twelfth-floor production office in the Suburban Station building.

New York also was under consideration, but Utt, whose career goes back to the age of live TV dramas, says that "Jonathan just fell in love with Philadelphia immediately."

Concedes Demme, a Long Island native who lived for years in Manhattan, "I had no idea about it—the typical arrogance of the New Yorker." (The director may get to know the town even better: He's considering a request by Mayor Rendell to do a promotional film for Philadelphia.)

The moviemakers knew they wanted to shoot in a metropolis that hadn't been seen too much on screen. They wanted a "real American city." And, says producer Edward Saxon, choosing his words carefully, it did seem appropriate to shoot in a town where the lawyers "are known as a kind of plentiful and, ummm, famous species."

Rendell contacted the filmmakers at once to see what it would take to bring this movie—and its $20 million or so—to town. The main requirement was the use of an empty courtroom for about twenty working days. ("I said, 'If we don't get this courtroom, we don't get this movie,'" Pinkenson recounts.)

The request "was granted to us instantly," says Utt, referring to use of the City Hall's grand Courtroom No. 243, where they eventually shot the movie's trial scenes.

Over the months, filming took place all over the area. Washington's storefront law firm was at 19th and Chestnut Streets. Scenes were done at Famous Delicatessen (a Demme hangout), Fourth and Bainbridge. Julius Erving appears in a scene at the Spectrum. Hanks and his lover live in a loft at 10th and Bainbridge. Hanks's parents (Woodward and the Rev. Robert Castle, Demme's cousin) reside on Merion Road in Merion.

Washington's nineteenth-century home was on Tulpehocken Street in West Mount Airy. Hospital scenes were shot at Mount Sinai, Fourth and Reed. A law library scene was filmed at the University of Pennsylvania's Fine Arts Library, which was designed by Frank Furness. And Hanks's powerhouse law firm occupied the spectacular quarters of Mesirov, Gelman, Jaffe, Cramer & Jamieson (Rendell's former firm), high above the city in the Mellon Bank Center at 1735 Market Street.

Often the way had to be smoothed. The film office sent out three-page letters that addressed the concerns of families and businesses that would be affected when tractor trailers, motor homes, cast, and crew took over their streets. *What does it mean when a movie comes into my neighborhood? Why do they need all those trucks? Who do I go to if I have a problem?* Location manager Neri Tannenbaum also distributed letters door-to-door. Town meetings were held at the South Philadelphia hospital and near 10th and Bainbridge.

Out-of-town members of the cast and crew needed assistance finding lodging. (More than half of the two-hundred-member crew was hired locally.) Hanks, Washington, and Saxon, among others, moved into the Rittenhouse Hotel on Rittenhouse Square. Much of the crew stayed within walking distance of the production offices, at Oakwood Apartments at the Windsor, 17th and the Parkway. Other accommodations included the Omni Hotel at Independence Park, Carlton House Apartments, 18th and JFK, and the Wyndham Franklin Plaza Hotel, at 17th and Race.

Demme rented a house in Society Hill (as did co-executive producer Ron Bozman) and immersed himself in the city. His children, Ramona and Brooklyn, attended nearby schools; his wife, Joanne Howard, an artist, rented a studio. Demme was frequently spotted at neighborhood places such as TLA Video, near Fourth and South, where he rented children's movies.

"It feels like Philadelphia is a city that hasn't given up," says Demme, who has moved his family from Manhattan to a small town along the Hudson River.

The director also involved himself with Philadelphia's AIDS community, publicly taking part—with some of his stars—in World AIDS Day on December 1 and an AIDS Walk-a-thon on October 25.

When he heard about the production coming to town, Bruce Flannery, media coordinator for Philadelphia's ActionAIDS, wrote to the filmmakers and offered assistance. But "I never expected the phone to ring," he says.

Not only did Demme's people call, they sought the group's help in scouting locations and acquainting them with the local AIDS community. ActionAIDS provided answers to all manner of questions, such as the one from a wardrobe assistant who wondered what a Philadelphia AIDS activist would wear. ("Anything but acid-washed jeans," Flannery responded.)

In November, *Philadelphia* spent a day filming at the ActionAIDS office, a fourth-floor loft in a former garment factory at 12th and Arch Streets, and hired twenty of the agency's clients for walk-on parts. "I think Jonathan is one of the coolest human beings I ever met," says Flannery, who worked as an extra.

"On the day they shot here at ActionAIDS, there was a very strange kind of chemistry that just kind of developed spontaneously," he recalls. "The crew [was] confronted with people, many of whom were visibly suffering from HIV. I think in many ways it was jarring and galvanizing."

"Hanks was very real," says ActionAIDS executive director Ennes Littrell of the star's interaction with the true AIDS patients. "Here's this famous guy who was really very moved by what he saw," she says of the actor, who gets sicker during the course of the film, loses weight, and wears a bandanna to camouflage his hair loss.

Says producer Saxon of the day at ActionAIDS, "That was an important moment in the life of this movie. I think it gave everybody a deeper sense of what the work was about."

Demme says that he initiated what was to become *Philadelphia* about four years ago, before filming *The Silence of the Lambs*.

"One of my dearest friends was diagnosed as having AIDS about five years ago. And that's probably—I didn't realize it at the time—but I think that's probably what actively kicked me into seeking a script about AIDS," he says.

His friend died a few months before *Philadelphia* got under way, but, says the director, "he helped me with the script a lot. He was the script's toughest critic and he was the one who kept saying, 'Make it funnier, make it funnier.'"

"From the beginning, in developing the script, we found the reality was more interesting than anything we could make up—and more dramatic, too," says Saxon, thirty-six, a St. Louis native who lives in New York.

Cathy Wickline of Walton Wickline Casting in Northern Liberties says that 2,400 local extras were cast during the shoot. Union extras earned $99 a day; nonunion $75.

On the technical crew, there was "an immediate melding" of local and out-of-town people, says Utt, a New Yorker. And Philadelphia's reputedly uncompromising unions earned praise from the filmmakers—although "the Teamsters cut a tough deal and an expensive deal," one insider says.

"We want the production companies to return," says Harry Koplin of Manayunk, a prop man and the film's union shop steward. And Demme hopes to oblige: "Philadelphia is going to be our city of choice for urban subjects," he vows.

As for local talent, Saxon, Demme's longtime partner, says, "It's an ongoing fantasy that you go to a new city to shoot and you discover this vast assortment of wonderful people. Sometimes you do and sometimes you don't—and this time we really did."

To win their roles, Rowe, who plays Washington's physician; Lisa Summerour, who plays Washington's wife; and Joey Perillo, who plays his law partner, "all blew off really heavy-duty New York people," Saxon says.

At the outset, *Philadelphia* was only a working title.

"Philadelphia was the city of choice to set the story in and to shoot in, but we were just having terrible trouble with the title," Demme recounts, between takes.

"Finally, as shooting approached, we promised a dinner at Le Bec-Fin to whoever could come up with a title we liked. On Ron Bozman's list—we owe him a dinner!—was *Philadelphia*. And it kind of just popped for me. . . .

"I like the ironic undercurrents to it. As we say in the script, 'Here we are in the birthplace of the Declaration of Independence, but look at the discrimination present here, as in all American cities and towns. Here we are in the City of Brotherly Love, and yet there's tremendous prejudice here, as in all other American cities.'"

The title imposed "a certain discipline" on him, says Demme, "to really involve the city of Philadelphia more, and to live up to the title, and to justify the title.

"So we started going bonkers on a really interesting, idiosyncratic title sequence that would capture the unique feeling of Philadelphia. [We were] just working Philadelphia—getting more and more skyline shots . . . always with a slight eye toward Woody Allen's *Manhattan*, which showed how wonderfully the name of a city can suit a story.

"I don't think [the title's] going to change," says Demme, though TriStar's marketers may have other ideas between now and the time the film is released, next fall or winter.

These New York filmmakers could not be kinder to the city in which they spent so much time, working long, gray winter days and sometimes frigid nights. Utt, for one, is positively rhapsodic.

Making the movie here was "absolute heaven," he says.

"We're going to run ads in the trades: 'Philadelphia, thank you.'"

The *Rolling Stone* Interview: Jonathan Demme

ANTHONY DECURTIS/1994

IT REALLY SHOULDN'T surprise anyone that Jonathan Demme would defy Hollywood taboos to direct a movie about AIDS, homophobia, and social justice or that the movie *Philadelphia* would ever earn over $40 million dollars in its first two months and nab five Academy Award nominations. *Philadelphia* was fueled by three of the director's staunchest convictions: that helping out people who are having a hard time is less a duty than a pleasure; that bigotry is more the result of ignorance than evil; and that for all the country's political outrages, goodness is deep in the American grain. Despite his impeccable downtown New York credentials, Demme, who just turned fifty, is less a card-carrying member of the cultural elite than a suburban product who, however astonishingly, believes what he was taught in civics—and is determined to act on it.

Certainly little about Demme's early history, first on Long Island, where he was born, and later in Florida, would indicate either his idealism or his eventual success. His ambition to be a veterinarian evaporated when chemistry class at the University of Florida proved insurmountable. He was writing about movies for local papers when his father, then head of publicity at the Fontainebleau Hotel, in Miami Beach, introduced him to studio mogul—for once, the term can be used unironically—Joseph E. Levine. Levine glanced at some of Demme's reviews—a rave over *Zulu*, one of Levine's movies, natch—proved especially persuasive, and Demme was offered a job as a press agent in New York.

From *Rolling Stone* (March 24, 1994), pp. 60–65, 90. © Rolling Stone LLC 1994. All rights reserved. Reprinted by permission of *Rolling Stone*.

A few years later, while working in Ireland as a publicist on the set of a film by B-movie titan Roger Corman, Demme was invited to write a screenplay for Corman's new company, New World Pictures. The result, *Angels Hard As They Come* (1971), a motorcycle movie based (*very* loosely) on *Rashomon*, began Demme's film career in not exactly earnest. He continued working for Corman, making his debut as a director in 1974 with *Caged Heat*, a quite literally revealing look at women behind bars, and following it up with *Crazy Mama* (1975) and *Fighting Mad* (1976).

Demme's uniquely sweet American vision began to manifest itself after he split from Corman. He directed *Citizens Band* (1977, retitled *Handle with Care*), an eccentric, bighearted exploration of CB-radio culture, and later, *Melvin and Howard* (1980), about Melvin Dummar, the working-class Nevadan who claimed that Howard Hughes had named him the heir to his fortune.

Demme's baptism by fire came with *Swing Shift* (1984), which he conceived of as an exploration of the lives of working women in factories during World War II but which Goldie Hawn, the film's executive producer and female lead, saw as a star vehicle for herself. Hawn played the heavy, and faced with adding thirty minutes of scenes he couldn't stand, Demme walked.

Following that debacle, Demme delivered a run of films that established him as a significant new directorial voice. *Stop Making Sense* (1984), a splendid rendering of Talking Heads' exultant 1983 tour, won a National Society of Film Critics Award for Best Documentary. Then *Something Wild* (1986), a comedy of urban manners that veers into a violent suspense plot, managed to capture every nuance of life in New York in the mid-eighties, from bohemianism to stockbroker paranoia—all set to a fun and friendly, if dauntingly in the know, soundtrack.

Swimming to Cambodia (1987), a documentary of performing artist Spalding Gray's riveting monologue about his experiences in Southeast Asia on the set of *The Killing Fields*, seems indistinguishable from Gray onstage. All of Gray's intelligence, neurosis, humor, and sheer humanity are palpably, and somewhat eerily, present. *Married to the Mob* (1988) features Michelle Pfeiffer as a mob wife looking to go straight: In its affectionate send-up of gangster movies, the film, like *Something Wild*, demonstrated Demme's ability to be simultaneously parodic and unapologetically emotional. Even when his characters are cartoons, he seems to love them.

Demme became an industry powerhouse himself—Goldie Hawn, beware!—with *The Silence of the Lambs* (1991), based on the terrifying serial-killer saga by Thomas Harris. The film racked up five Academy Awards (including Best Director for Demme, Best Actress for Jodie Foster and Best Actor for Anthony Hopkins); particularly estimable was Hopkins's gripping portrayal of

Dr. Hannibal "the Cannibal" Lecter, which lifted the grisly character into the pantheon of American film roles. Despite criticism from gay activists over the depiction of gender-bending murderer Jame Gumb, *Silence* earned more than $130 million.

With *Philadelphia*, Demme took on the story of a gay lawyer with AIDS (Tom Hanks has been nominated for an Academy Award for the role) who is fired by his firm and wins a wrongful-termination suit with the help of an initially homophobic lawyer (Denzel Washington). The film has realized Demme's hope of bringing a gay-oriented AIDS drama into the heartland, though again, not without generating fierce controversy.

Some gay activists—most notably Larry Kramer, author of *The Normal Heart*—have attacked what they consider to be *Philadelphia*'s avoidance of gay sexuality (between Hanks and his lover, played by Antonio Banderas) and its too rose-colored view of Hanks's extended and supportive family. Few people with AIDS are quite so fortunate, they say. In addition, the family of a lawyer who died from AIDS in 1987 has brought a $10 million lawsuit against the creators of *Philadelphia*, including Demme, for allegedly basing the movie on the lawyer's life without acknowledgment. TriStar Pictures, the studio that produced *Philadelphia*, has denied the claim. Demme has refused to comment.

Both as a director and a producer (through his company Clinica Estetico, which roughly translates into Portuguese as "beauty parlor"), Demme has had a hand in a number of small-budget documentaries focused on social issues, including the ongoing series *Haiti: Dreams of Democracy*; *Cousin Bobby* (about the director's cousin Robert Castle, a radical clergyman in Harlem); and *One Foot on a Banana Peel, the Other Foot in the Grave*, an AIDS film directed by Demme's late friend the artist Juan Botas.

Demme has been busy for a man who now says that he hopes to cut back his activities in order to better enjoy life with his wife, Joanne Howard, an artist, and their two children in Nyack, New York, where the two interviews for this story took place. His unstoppable enthusiasm, torrent of words, quick, explosive laughter, and energetic engagement of any idea put in front of him suggest that any slowing down of his pace might prove undetectable to the rest of us.

Q: *Why did you want to make an AIDS movie?*

A: My friend Juan Botas became sick. Juan was my wife Joanne's soul mate. They had the kind of friendship that was completely without restraint. Juan and I also became good friends—you can see him in his documentary, *One Foot on a Banana Peel*. So when Juan said that he was HIV-positive, I reacted in the only positive way I could, which was to try to work somehow.

I talked to my partner Ed Saxon, who was very keen on the idea, and also to Ron Nyswaner, who had done the shooting script for *Swing Shift*—a wonderful writer. That Ron was gay didn't hurt. Anyway, the desire to do a film on AIDS was born of Juan's sickness.

We looked for a story for a long time, and we decided it would be pointless to make a film for people with AIDS. Or for their loved ones. They don't need no movie about AIDS. They live the truth. We wanted to reach people who *don't* know people with AIDS, who look down on people with AIDS.

Q: *You made a conscious decision about that?*
A: When I read in the papers that *Philadelphia* was "targeted for the malls," part of me goes, "Oh, my God, that sounds so calculated." But we *were* calculated about it. We calculated what audience we aspired to.

Q: *How exactly did you do that?*
A: We started off with angrier scripts, very politicized. Scripts that were informed with the rage I felt when confronted with society's not only indifference but hostility to my sick, courageous friend. Ron and I were pissed, and we were not only aggressive, we were *assaultive*. There was a desire to just, like, stick AIDS in your face and say, "Look at it, you scumbags."

Q: *Tom Hanks's character displays conviction and intelligence but very little anger. Where did that aspect of the story go?*
A: If your immune system is imperiled, the best way to stay alive is to strive for as much serenity as possible—stress is debilitating and will hasten the onslaught of the illness. We made a choice to get spiritual. We had scenes of Tom meditating to tapes, things like that. We felt this guy is so committed to staying alive, at least long enough to see his name vindicated, he is going to identify rage as a wasted emotion. Maybe we went a little too far on that side.

I find it admirable that he isn't more actively angry. The whole time we're talking, though, I keep picturing ACT-UP demonstrations—and I admire that, too. People who are afflicted with this disease are entitled to all the anger they feel like venting. Our choice for this particular guy was he was going to avoid rage.

Q: *What about the charge that the gay couple in the movie doesn't get a bed scene?*
A: We had one scene showing the guys preparing to go to sleep. It was like "We've *done* it! They're in *bed* together! And, sure enough, one of them wears pj's, the other one doesn't. And, gosh, they're a lot like you and me." But then you're back in court, and all this other shit's happening. So we made a

choice: The film was edited, finally, to tell its strongest story in the best possible way. And that was the story about the fight for vindication.

I feel the film is richly permeated by feelings of love and attachment between Tom and many people in his life, including Antonio. Their scene together toward the end of the picture in the hospital is one of the most intimate, beautiful scenes between two people I've seen in a long, long time. I think it's stunning.

Q: *But didn't Denzel Washington reportedly tell Will Smith that whether you play a gay character or not, you never kiss another man onscreen?*
A: I wouldn't fault Denzel for telling Will Smith that. That's Denzel responding to the same concern that Ron, Tom, Antonio, and I had. It's a real concern. When we see two men kissing, we're the products of our brainwashing—it knocks us back twenty feet. And with *Philadelphia*—I'm sorry, Larry Kramer—I didn't want to risk knocking our audience back twenty feet with images they're not prepared to see. It's just shocking imagery, and I didn't want to shoehorn it in.

Denzel ain't a homophobic guy—he had difficulty understanding some parts of his character's extremes. I think he was saying: "You'd better watch out, with the kind of climate that exists, you don't want to be identified as the guy who makes out with other guys. It could work to your detriment in seeking other roles."

Q: *It also becomes the only issue that gets discussed. The movie is two hours, but it becomes the movie in which two guys kiss.*
A: Well, in *Prelude to a Kiss*, which I didn't see, Alec Baldwin kissed an old man—wasn't that considered the *coup de grâce* of that movie? I think we found that there was no way people were going to pay to see that.

Q: *There was also a lot of speculation that you made* Philadelphia *to atone for offending the gay community, which perceived* The Silence of the Lambs *as homophobic. Did that whole flap have much of an impact on you?*
A: I hadn't been paying attention to the absence of positive gay characters all that much, so I came away from the protests enlightened—and it made me happy that I was already working on *Philadelphia* before *Lambs* came out.

By the way, maybe you can explain something. Who on earth would get the shit kicked out of them and then turn around and do something nice for the people who kicked the shit out of them? I don't get that.

Q: *Well, the reasoning runs, "Jonathan so much wants to do the right thing, to advance the cause of people he sees as oppressed, that it would sting him to get criticism from them."*
A: Right.

Q: *"So whether he believed it was justified or not, he would in some way try to make up for it."*

A: Well, I try to be nice—but not *that* nice [*laughs*].

The thing about *Philadelphia*, targeting the malls and everything: I didn't have some *better* version—some deeper, more complicated version—of this movie that we turned away from. We set out to make a movie dealing with AIDS discrimination, and there it is. And I've got to tell you: When I sit in a theater, and Denzel says, "Let's talk about it, our fear, our hatred, our *loathing* of homosexuals," I'm like "*What?* An American movie is saying *that?* Holy shit! I *love* that."

Q: *You started out making films with Roger Corman. What are some of the things you learned from him?*

A: As the years slip by, my mind goes to this luncheon I had with Roger, one week before starting my directorial debut. That was Roger's ritual—this unbelievable sixty minutes of *rules*. It remains quite vivid. My favorite—because it has the word *organ* in it—is this one: "Jonathan, never forget what the primary organ is for the moviegoer. It's the *eye*. You must keep the eye interested." He goes: "Have a lot of foreground action. Have interesting things going on in the background. Move the camera—always find some motivation, don't *just* move the camera but find motivation to move it. If you're in a room too small to move the camera, get a lot of different angles, so you can cut a lot. And don't forget, your actors are the greatest source of inspiration for the eye. Choose actors who look tremendously interesting."

Q: *You've earned a reputation as an actor's director. How much do looks affect your casting choices?*

A: It's imperative. I need to want to see their face a lot. If I can't be interested for fifteen minutes, how can an audience be expected to go with this person for two hours?

Another imperative is that the actors take full responsibility for the characters. I can't work with actors who look to the director each morning for guidance, actors who ask historical questions—you know, "Where did my guy go to college?" I'm like "*Uh*-oh."

Q: *Has anything else from the early years stayed with you?*

A: Roger used to refer to himself—and we heard this *endlessly*—as being 40 percent artist and 60 percent businessman. That was *soooo* Roger—to have a formula, even for that. But I'll be damned, twenty-some-odd years later, boy, he's right. You'd *better* be 60 percent businessmen, because if you don't have an eye, a *passionate* eye, on getting the picture done at the right cost, you just ain't going to get to make a whole lot more of them. So, the terror of going over budget remains happily with me to this day. It's a healthy aesthetic.

Q: *Corman also stressed that movies should contain an element of social critique, something that's obviously stayed with you. Even in a jail-girl titillation like* Caged Heat, *you had a plot about the medical exploitation of prisoners.*

A: This is before *Cuckoo's Nest* came out. I thought [*laughs*], "It may only be showing in drive-ins, but it shows what's going on in prisons: We are lobotomizing patients to make them nonviolent." It's true, that's Roger's formula: Your picture must have action, nudity, humor—and a *little bit* of social statement, preferably from a liberal perspective. I'd love to get in deeper with Roger, as to "Is the social statement there because audiences like it? Or, *finally*, is that a little bit of *you* getting in there?" [*Laughs*.]

Q: *Another way that has played out for you is that you've always created strong roles for women.*

A: I just admire that extra something that women bring to getting through the day, faced with all of the hassles that we males put in their face. I'm appreciative of that, and I'm glad my movies reflect that.

I root for the underdog. One of the things that made us think *Philadelphia* might have a chance of succeeding was that we came up with the David and Goliath one-liner: It's the little guy going up against the big guys. I'm much more interested in that than the eminently capable guys vanquishing their lessers. I mean, my Stallone movie would be *Rocky*, not *Rambo*. Rambo's better armed, he's smarter—superior firepower doesn't interest me.

Also, as someone who's been force-fed things European and male, I long for more variety—in my own life and in what I see onscreen. I'm not interested in boy movies, and I'm not interested in white-people movies. I want to see movies that reflect the country I live in.

People have found fault with *Philadelphia*: "Oh, look at this. You got the noble gay guy who goes to the black lawyer and who lives with a Latin. How PC." *Excuse* me—that's America. We got black attorneys now. We got tons of Latins. The ongoing melting pot has a lot of appeal to me.

Q: *It also makes for texture in your movies. Something like putting Michelle Pfeiffer at the center of a gangster comedy helped make* Married to the Mob *distinctive in an overwhelmingly male genre.*

A: What really made me excited about *Married to the Mob* was the same secret theme as *Silence of the Lambs*. A woman wants to go straight, and the men just won't let her. The bad guys won't let her. The good guys won't let her. And she is able to carve out a positive trajectory through other women.

I think every picture, however light, needs to be saying something. I need that for my work—just something, just some kind of theme. *Something Wild* also had that, showing how awful violence is when it occurs. It's not fun. It's not exciting. It's slow and awful and tragic.

Q: *Something Wild also had that "when worlds collide" element that you seem to be drawn to. Even in* Swing Shift, *you have a World War II movie and a factory setting, and suddenly women are introduced into this otherwise alien environment.*
A: My grandmother, by the way, worked on the assembly line, making fighter planes during World War II. So a story like that had great personal resonance for me. That's one of the reasons it was devastating to have the picture changed so much. I loved that theme of women going up against adversity and rising to the occasion. And this was *true*. You know, we looked at the documentary *Rosie the Riveter* a lot in preparing for the movie and always walked away blubbering. The goal of our fiction was to try to match the emotional impact of that documentary. And in the first version, we did a pretty good job.

That's the sort of thing that got cut out of the picture. I was sad when it got all chopped up.

Q: *There's been talk of your version of the movie being released. Any chance of that?*
A: The agents I work with talked to the folks at Warner Bros. to see if it would be possible. We were told that all the outtakes and supportive material of the other version had been destroyed. So the material doesn't exist to do that.

Q: *How did the* Swing Shift *experience affect you?*
A: I emerged from it exhausted and damaged, because it was a long, drawn-out fight. I wondered what it was about making films that made it worth trying again and risking a similar experience. It's the opposite experience of what I love about making films. I thrive on collaboration. I thrive on trust. When people are trying to hurt and damage you, that's a face of human beings you don't really wish to see.

Luckily, I committed to *Stop Making Sense* before the shit hit the fan on *Swing Shift*, and we were too deep into preparing for *Sense* to not do it. It boiled down to three days where I was sort of . . . not directing so much as *officiating* these new scenes that I hated for *Swing Shift*. And at night, I would go to the concert and direct the cameras for *Stop Making Sense*. It was literally going from hell to heaven.

Oh, what a thrill it was to be doing those concerts! Even as I was having the horror of the animosity with *Swing Shift*, I was enjoying the intense collaboration and trust with the Talking Heads and my crew. That really helped me get through the whole thing. Then I moved back to New York—I'd been living in California—and went out to make *Something Wild*. It really felt like a first film. I was clean as a whistle. It was like a student film.

Q: *In situations like* Stop Making Sense *or* Swimming to Cambodia, *how do you capture a performance?*
A: It's a simple discipline. I know how transcendental this performance is live. With Spalding Gray, there's no impediment to your enjoyment of what he does, that he's just sitting in a chair, talking. In fact, it's part of the magic. So the discipline is simple: Help the moviegoer get that whack. And you have some added tools. You have the camera, which can provide emphasis. You can bring in sound effects. You can bring in music. The way you make it work onscreen is honoring the material and the artist, not trying to make it cinematic. Trust the source.

Q: *You've been inventive in your use of music. What do you see as the role of music in films?*
A: I love manipulating the viewers' emotions through music—and I think it's fair. Music is such an inescapable part of reality—our lives are infused with it. We go to the cleaners, and there's a certain aural mood there as a result of whatever's on the radio. You go home, there'll be a different mood. You've got to honor that dynamic. It's just another tool to try to suck people into the experience.

Like you're watching the scene between Denzel and Tom in the library. One guy is poised to extend himself, overcoming certain hurdles to do so. The other guy is daring to think that maybe someone who had rejected him is reaching out to him. I think it's okay for a movie to now send you some musical signals to reaffirm that this is a significant moment.

Q: *Of course, there's also the now-famous opera scene in* Philadelphia, *where Tom Hanks uses an aria that's playing as a way of confronting his impending death. It's very long, and it's one of the most controversial scenes in the movie. Did you foresee that response?*
A: No. It wasn't until I watched the first cut of it after the picture was finished that I . . . You know, there's two schools of thought on this. There are those who can't believe this overly theatrical, ludicrous sequence and are

completely untouched by it. There are also those, myself included, who have a big emotional epiphany through that scene. I mean, I was *devastated* the first time I saw it cut together—tears coming down my face. I was so moved, I couldn't believe it.

But back in the script, I never knew. I knew nothing about opera. I wasn't sure how it should be played. But I always trust great actors. Truthful actors will discover the truth of the scene. Tom and I never discussed how it should be played. Denzel—we didn't talk, either. That's Take 1 in the movie.

Q: *Was the scene in which Hanks and Banderas wear sailors' uniforms a joke about gays in the military?*
A: No. That was just for elegance. Having a party hosted by gays, now you're in a minefield. Are you going to have drag or not? Then I realized, they're an elegant couple, they would throw a swellegant, Cole Porter-type party. So the idea of the guys in dress naval—they'll look so handsome, they'll look so elegant. The gays-in-the-military thing came after that, and we were chortling.

Q: *It had a timely resonance.*
A: When we showed the picture at the White House, shortly after the shot of the guys, dancing in uniform, President Clinton left the room—he had to relieve himself. But I thought that was kind of . . . interesting timing.

Q: *What was it like to screen the movie at the White House?*
A: I'm greedy. It wasn't enough that the movie was seen at the White House—I hoped that with the fifty or so guests, there would have been ten minutes devoted to a discussion about AIDS in our country. But instead, President Clinton took the guests on a guided tour of the White House. I was disappointed by that.

Q: *The enormous success of* Silence of the Lambs *really put you on the map as a major director. You probably couldn't have made* Philadelphia *without it. Has that success affected you in more personal ways?*
A: At certain points, I was afraid there was something—a missing chink of skill—that was going to prevent me from having a movie that was financially successful. That frightened me. So when *Silence of the Lambs* became an unqualified success, I took a huge sigh of relief. I mean, I can't tell you how wonderful that felt.

Q: *How do you account for the fear?*
A: I didn't go to film school; I didn't work toward being a filmmaker. I stumbled into writing movie reviews so I could get into the movies for free.

Then my father introduces me to Joseph E. Levine, and Levine offers me a job in the movie business. "A huge stroke of luck" doesn't catch it.

Then I wind up crossing paths with Roger Corman, and Corman has just started New World Pictures and needs scripts. My best friend is Joe Viola, one of the most gifted storytellers I've ever known. So Joe and I write a script for Corman, and then, because Joe directs commercials, suddenly Roger wants us to make this motorcycle movie. Again, "an enormous stroke of good fortune" doesn't fully characterize it. I mean, people bust their butts for decades to get to make a picture, and I fell backward into it.

Maybe that's one of the reasons I work so hard, I'm still trying to justify that luck. It's also why I'm amazed when I get to actually finish a picture, because I'm still afraid of being found out: "*He* can't direct! *Look!* What? Look! He's . . . he's a *phony!*" So there's that still, but I try to use it healthfully—"But, wait, I've made several pictures, now surely I'm entitled to . . ."

Q: *Well, before* Silence of the Lambs, *people were always predicting breakthroughs for you that never seemed to happen.*
A: Yeah. Sometimes my pictures would get good notices and, with *Melvin and Howard*, even a lot of notoriety. That's one picture I can go, "That is truly a good movie." Again, luck goes into all this: Thom Mount, who was the head of production at Universal in those days, would open his door to people who weren't happening, such as I. Thom had seen *Citizens Band* and liked it. Mike Nichols was supposed to direct *Melvin and Howard*, but he couldn't cast it to his satisfaction. Thom thought of me as someone who might do a good job on *Melvin and Howard*. Thom went from *Mike Nichols* to a *zero* and trusted me with that picture.

On such things do careers hinge. I will never forget, I was calling Mike Medavoy, trying to persuade him to give a "go" to a little script I had found after we'd done *Married to the Mob*. And Medavoy goes: "Oh, gee, you in your office? I'll call you back in five minutes." Hang up, five minutes later, the phone rings, and Mike goes: "I'm going to send you a book. See what you think of it. It's called *Silence of the Lambs*."

Actually, as we sit here discussing these things, I get very terrified of the whole bizarre process [*laughs*].

Q: *Speaking of good fortune, how did you get Bruce Springsteen and Neil Young to write original songs for* Philadelphia? *[Each song has been nominated for an Academy Award.] Did you expect them both to write such introspective ballads?*
A: I thought: "Let's reassure people. Let's get these guys who, if anything, are identified with a testosterone, machismo kind of thing." Like "Hey, if Bruce and Neil are part of this party, it's going to be something for the unconverted."

I thought: "What we need is the most up-to-the-minute, guitar-dominated American-rock anthem about injustice to start the movie off. Who can do that? Neil Young can do that." So we edited a title sequence to "Southern Man" to help him see how his music could power the images we were working with. He said, "I'll try." Six weeks later, "Hi, it's Neil, I'm sending a tape." So in comes this song. We were crying the first time we heard it. I went: "Oh, my God, Neil Young trusts this movie more than I do. Isn't that pathetic?"

But now we're back to Square One. Even as I'm going, "He trusts the movie more than I," I *still* don't trust it, because now I'm going to call Bruce Springsteen! The same exact dialogue goes on—"So we still need to kick ass at the beginning." Then, one day, this tape shows up. Again, it was not the guitar anthem I had appealed for. Springsteen, like Neil Young, trusted the idea of the movie much more than I was trusting it.

Q: *So, after* Philadelphia, *what's ahead?*
A: Well, the great thing about documentaries is that if you're interested in social issues, you don't need a $20-million-dollar budget to put them onscreen. We made *One Foot on a Banana Peel* for less than $30,000. It's wonderful. It sheds light on the experience of having AIDS in a very different way than *Philadelphia* does. We're also working on *Haiti: Dreams of Democracy, Part IV* now.

That's taken away my fervor to do big-budget versions of social issues—unless they offer the possibility of making some wild *magilla* of an entertainment, like the project we're working on based on Taylor Branch's biography of Dr. Martin Luther King, *Parting the Waters*.

Q: *What do you have in mind for that?*
A: I'm picturing a cross between *Nashville* and *Battle of Algiers*! But I couldn't be more excited by anything than making the next Tom Harris book.

I'm probably not as open to full-tilt entertainments, "Never mind the message, let's just have a ball" kind of films, as I might have been five, certainly ten years ago. I'd rather read books and be a lazy person than just make a movie anymore. That's probably a function of age and the fact that I've got a family life. I don't need to make movies.

The *Guardian*/NFT Interview: Jonathan Demme

ADRIAN WOOTTON/1998

JONATHAN DEMME has managed to successfully divide his career between Hollywood blockbusters, low-budget independent movies and documentaries. On the release of his latest film, *Beloved*, the Oscar-winning director of *The Silence of the Lambs* talked to Adrian Wootton.

ADRIAN WOOTTON: *In a few minutes I'll ask you about* Beloved, *and about* Storefront Hitchcock, *but before I do I'd just like to do a little canter over some other parts of your career. I know you've talked a lot about your time in the Corman stable in the 1970s and your development through the work you did there and the movies you made with Roger Corman. I wanted to ask you about what the single most important thing was that you learnt from Roger Corman in terms of that background that really gave you the opportunity to become a director?*

JONATHAN DEMME: I think it was probably that it was completely understood that if you didn't complete the day's work on any given day that you would be replaced. That instilled in me a very strong discipline and a sense that first and foremost your priority was to keep the movie on schedule and on budget, and that's one way you get to stay on the job. That was very valuable. Roger also said something I'll never forget. He said that as far as he was concerned the formula for a director was 40 percent artist, 60 percent businessman. He also had a little pat speech that he'd give you before you did your first directing job, a lot of really good rules—stuff that most movie goers know anyway—just ways to keep the eye entertained, the value of well-motivated camera movement... that kind of thing. He was great. We called it the Roger Corman school of film technique. You really did learn on the job.

AW: *That was really quite an interesting period for U.S. independent cinema in the 1970s. Were you aware at the time that it was an exciting period, with all these directors coming out of that Corman stable, the people who went on to become really major film-makers?*
JD: I was really excited during that period of time making my Hell's Angel movies and my women in prison movies . . .

AW: *You cashed in . . .*
JD: Of course now there's the book *Easy Riders, Raging Bulls* that documents that period. I think sometimes in a very unflattering way. I don't know if many people have read the book, but it seems sometimes like the writer is trying to see the downside of the film-makers he was covering. I think that a lot of the people, like Hal Ashby, were a lot more complicated and there was a lot more magic going on in their lives and their work than the book indicated.

But yeah, it's funny, now that you mention it, I can remember going to a theatre out there and seeing an almost finished version of *Apocalypse Now* and being overwhelmed with excitement. But that's just what was going on because I was a young guy in town on a fluke making a movie for Roger Corman and then a couple more, and this was all going on. It was very heady.

AW: *And then in the seventies you left the Corman stable, and made a series of critically acclaimed—though not necessarily massive box office—movies, things like* Melvin and Howard. *They established you as a renowned filmmaker—I know* Melvin *won a lot of awards at that time. But then you went on from there and had your first big studio experience with* Swing Shift, *which didn't work out terribly well I think. Is that right?*
JD: It turned out very poorly, yeah. We did a film and I hope that very few people here have seen it!

AW: *It's played a lot on British television I think.*
JD: Oh great! Well, an extraordinary thing happened. We made this film and it told the story a certain kind of way and it was a very different kind of movie for Goldie Hawn to make. When the picture was finished and the studio looked at it, they perceived this great chemistry that existed between Goldie Hawn and Kurt Russell—who had fallen in love while making the movie. So a very high profile Hollywood writer was brought in to rewrite the movie as more of a kind of Tracy and Hepburn film, a light romance. We had this hard-nosed feminist, all women together thing, and Kurt Russell was supposed to be a bastard, and suddenly all these scenes were being rewritten, and I found myself in a very awkward position because I had to co-operate

with these new scenes. I actually had to shoot them, otherwise I would have been in violation of my contract, and so in order to protect the movie that I thought we were making I had to shoot these very bad scenes.

Finally we shot the scenes and had a screening for the Warner Brothers executives. Everybody trooped in, really proud of themselves because they had sort of made me do this, and we screened the movie for them. They saw the new scenes and they came out slightly pleased but also, probably, scratching their heads because it didn't quite work.

There was a preview that night and the editors and I had gone back to the cutting room and restored our version, so they all sat down in the theatre again and saw what they hated. I lost my control after that. I was called into the office the next day for a list of changes, and I told them then that I was finished with my work.

AW: *After* Swing Shift *you, well I won't say retreated, but you diversified in terms of not jumping into doing another feature film. Particularly in the 1980s, but I know you've continued to do this, you started making documentaries. What led you to start making documentaries? Because I think I'm right in saying that you hadn't done that many in the 1970s.*

JD: I don't think of *Storefront Hitchcock* or *Stop Making Sense* as documentaries, I think of them more as performance films. I went to see a Talking Heads concert with Gary Goetzman, who was the producer of *Stop Making Sense* and the executive producer of *Storefront Hitchcock*. What went through my head was that there was a movie waiting to be made here, which is also what I thought when I saw Robyn perform for the first time a couple of years ago. I'm a real music enthusiast and I think it's exciting beyond description to work with a musical artist that you admire, and be filming and trying to capture his magic.

AW: *When you started making performance films did you develop any general principles for how to deal with them? It's very easy to make clichéd rock movies and clichéd concert documentaries that are incredibly flat and non-atmospheric. It happens a lot on TV and video, but you manage to avoid those dangers. When you started making things like* Stop Making Sense, *how did you approach it?*

JD: One of the things that was great for David Byrne when we did *Stop Making Sense* was that David really got to design the lighting for the show—and by extension for the movie. He hadn't got to do everything he wanted to do lighting wise with the stage show because of the limitations of technology at that point. But David got a chance to work with Jordan Cronenweth who shot *Blade Runner* and was a great master of American cinematography, and he could do all the little tweakings and brushstrokes that he had dreamed of doing with the stage show. Nobody goes to concerts or performances and spends the time looking at members of the audience or going backstage, so the trick is to try as you can on film to create as close a thing to a live experience as possible.

AW: *That has been a theme throughout your movies. What seems to be the aesthetic principle is that you're always looking for a straightforward shooting style, but actually in quite an original setting. Obviously in* Stop Making Sense *you had that, but it's the same with the Neil Young thing,* The Complex Sessions, *in terms of setting it in a studio and now you've got a storefront with Robyn Hitchcock. Is that what you're looking for? Instead of actually doing tricks with different shooting angles, to try and find an interesting setting? It seems to be very common in your work. It's also true of New Order, the wonderful "Perfect Kiss" video . . .*
JD: One of my favourite things in watching any performance on film is when there isn't a lot of cutting going on and when you get a chance to become really absorbed in the artist in hand. The same way we do, hopefully, at a concert, when we get a chance to really trip in to something that's happening on stage. Whether the singer's singing, or one of the other musicians is playing, we sort of stay there instead of cutting round with our eyes a lot.

Making a film with Robyn I went back to the Roger Corman idea of trying to keep the camera moving and the interest sustained. If you're in a cramped space and you can't move the camera around a lot to keep the eyeball interested, then you should be able to cut and you should try to get a lot of angles to cut. With David Byrne and Talking Heads you had a whole stage full of musicians to cut to, so you were obliged to cut to a certain extent. With Robyn it was basically "there he is"—except for when Tim and Deni joined him—and it's just one guy and one guitar. That was challenging. We didn't want to do it just in one room, in an enclosed space, because the eye might get too familiar with the surroundings.

I recalled this wonderful Dutch [Hungarian] theatre group, called the Squat Theatre, that had been in New York in the seventies and eighties, and they did their performances in a storefront space. Often you came in and just like in our film there would be a drape, and then they would find some excuse to open this drape and reveal the street. On one amazing night they did this piece called *Mr. Dead and Mrs. Free.* In New York City traffic they had this military jeep, with four soldiers in it, do a screaming U-turn in the middle of Twenty-Third Street. The jeep goes up on the sidewalk while people are walking by, the soldiers jump out of the jeep, run into the theatre, grab one of the characters in the play, put them in the jeep and then they're gone.

You never see them again, and that was the most amazing moment in live theatre I've ever seen!

So when we were trying to think of how we'd make the Robyn show have more going for it visually, we thought, "Ah! Homage to the Squat Theatre."

AW: *How did you come to work with Robyn? Had you known him for a long time?*

JD: I knew his work on disc for a long time, and I had been quite an admirer but I'd never seen him live. Then my wife noticed that he was playing at a club near where we live in upstate New York one night a couple of years ago, and we went to see him. I was completely blown away by every aspect of his show, and I approached him afterwards to see if he ever needed a director for a video or something like that, and told him that I would love to do it. We started talking and both agreed that it was absurd to do videos lip-synch, and that if we were going to do a video together then it should be a live performance video. Then we realised that if we were going to have all the equipment there we might as well go to the trouble of doing the whole set, since it was such a terrific piece and Robyn changes his character so many times. So we were up and running.

The people at Orion pictures—who are dearly missed—were very happy because there were a lot of Robyn Hitchcock fans up there and they leapt on the idea.

Can I go back to one thing and really reveal my inner guts for one second? I'm sitting here very calmly and telling you the *Swing Shift* story, and about how they took it away from me. For a film-maker, in your professional life, it's hard to imagine anything more devastating, because you haven't just had your work taken away from you. You've worked on it for more than two years, first with writers, then through pre-production, then with the editors and the composers, etc. etc., so everybody else's work is being taken away. And the director is the kind of custodian of all the collaborative artists' good work, and it is his job to maximise everybody's work and present it in the best way possible. So when they took this movie away and started chopping it up, I knew that this would happen, so it wasn't the usual ego thing—like my God, they're going to take my movie away—it was also this investment of everybody else's hard work.

This high-priced Hollywood writer—who I've never mentioned—came in and saw this as an opportunity to really endear himself to Warner Brothers, who were mad at him for a movie he did where he went grossly over budget. So this guy came in and started writing scenes but had some difficulty writing them and was taking time, and meanwhile there was this one thing that we had been planning to do, *Stop Making Sense*. It was scheduled for three nights in the beginning of December and September rolls by and October was rolling by, and Bob (oops, sorry!) isn't providing the scenes . . .

He was the second person they went to actually. Originally they went to Elaine May. This is on the up side actually. This was a great moment. Elaine May came to see the movie in its original form and then came to lunch with Goldie and Goldie's partner and me to—as far as Goldie and Warner Brothers were concerned—launch into things. Elaine May who I'd never met before, God bless her, came walking into the room and said, "Are you Jonathan? What a wonderful movie, it's fabulous! Are you guys out of your mind?" And they explained to her the vision of what the film could be, you know more of this Tracy and Hepburn kind of thing. And she said, "Well all these ideas sound great for some movie, but they go completely against the ecology of this movie as it now exists, and you'll never pull it off." (I love that, the ecology of a movie!) But anyway, we did it and then this extraordinary thing happened. Finally these pages come in and they weren't very good, and the Warner Brothers executives, God bless 'em, are going "Ah, um, well jeez." We knew there was going to be a scene in the living room and a scene in the kitchen and a scene in the backyard, and they all involve Goldie and Ed Harris (who played her husband) and Kurt, for some other scenes, but there are no details.

The scenes come in and we're two days away from when we're meant to be shooting and now the Warner Brothers guys say, "Jonathan, what are we going to do?" And I'm like, "Are you kidding? We'll throw them out, we'll forget the re-shoot, we've got a nice movie, let's get it out there." And they say, "Oh, God, that's just typical of you." So they push it back another week, right into the three nights when we're shooting *Stop Making Sense*. So now suddenly—as if it wasn't hideous enough before—I'm not going to be able to be there during the daytime preparing the night's shoots. There was this one day where we got the day's work done. But on the second day—there's this practice when if you're a director and you object to how things are going, you put your name upside down on the slate—I put my name upside down on the slate. Directors always hear about this upside down on the slate thing and you never know if it actually happens, and then one day your name is upside down on the slate! So we did that and we finished the shooting at six o'clock and then I jumped in the car. Ed Harris came with me, and we raced to the theatre and shot it. And the next morning I got up and started getting ready to do these re-shoots, and, all I can tell you, I don't know how I got there, but I just remember finding myself sitting in the bathtub at six thirty in the morning, just crying. I was just so low. But we continue shooting that day.

By this stage, all the Warner Brothers guys hate me so much now, and they come in and they're like, "Hum, it's going rather slow today, and you're meant to shoot about six pages of work. You may have to miss your shooting tonight if things don't speed up a little round here." I'm doing a take and the whole directing thing was horrible. I'd turn to the actors and say, "Okay, actors, what are you going to do?" And then I'd turn to the cameraman. They'd fired my cameraman, Tak Fujimoto, because he didn't make the actors look young enough or something and the whole point of the re-shoot was to make everyone look younger. So I turn to Bill Fraker, another wonderful cameraman, and say, "Well Bill, any ideas on how to shoot this?" And he'd say, "Well we could . . ." And I'd say, "Actors, how does that sound to you? Good, okay, great, let's set it up . . ." And that's my job.

So finally, it's about six o'clock. We're not finished and there's a certain amount of relishing going on on the sidelines because now I'm really going to pay, I'm not going to show up on my shooting on the other thing. Ed Harris, God bless him, sees what's going on and he says, "Oh Jesus, I've got a terrible headache, I've got to wrap. I've got to get out of here." So Ed walks out the door and I'm like, "It's a wrap!" And I go running out and go rushing to my car, and there's Ed Harris in the car seat and says, "Let's go!" So the movie gets made and they took *Swing Shift* away. They trashed the score, put the new scenes in, etc., and I was really depressed about all that. As joyful as I was about how *Stop Making Sense* had turned out, I remember more the horror of what can happen to you in this line of work. Not so much that stuff I was talking about but just seeing how tough people can be and how mean they can be to you. I didn't want to see that again. I went on a really lonely trip to the Caribbean and walked around on my own for a couple of weeks and decided that I would hope to continue making movies, but only with people I really liked. So that's my new rule, since 1984.

AW: *And has it worked out?*
JD: It's worked pretty good so far. I moved back to New York and made *Stop Making Sense* and so on. Anyway, that was a very long story and I apologize for going on. I had to get it off my chest.

AW: *I apologize for bringing back such painful memories!*
Just going back to documentaries for a second, you did start making documentaries around that time and you've made a lot of them, and executive produced a lot. You've talked about the aesthetics of making performance movies. How different for you are the aesthetics of making documentaries compared to fiction films? Do you use a completely different mind set? Is it freer? What rationale do you employ?

JD: Well, you're out there with the crew, and you're all out there for a particular reason which is hopefully to capture something really fascinating about the subject that you're pursuing. But what's interesting is that when you're doing a fictional film the whole aspiration most of the time is to try and make it as real as possible, but when you're making a documentary—I've discovered—you try and make reality as entertaining as possible. I like the difference.

I also love the absence of pressure, any kind of pressure, with documentaries. I know what Roger Corman's talking about when he says that a director has to be part businessman. Obviously if your film is overtimed then you're not going to get the investment back, and you'll probably stop getting opportunities to do that business. With documentaries it's usually very minimal pressure. Everybody knows it's a documentary. It will probably be on television. Nobody expects it to set the box office on fire. Although we made a documentary a couple of years ago, an amazing documentary directed by Jo Menell, *Mandela*, that we were convinced we had made a documentary that would finally blow the roof off theatres. It wound up not making any money in the theatres, even though we thought it was such a great story and Jo, and Angus Gibson who collaborated on it, had done such a magnificent job. Anyway, at least it made it into some theatres.

AW: *You say you changed where you lived, you adopted a new principle of working, and it obviously did pay off, because apart from making some of the best concert documentaries and other kinds of documentaries, your fictional film career appears to have gone from strength to strength. You have had massive blockbuster success with* Silence of the Lambs *and* Philadelphia. *Has that success changed your approach to movie-making in the way you select your projects or the kinds of pressures that are now upon you? Has the box office success and critical acclaim for those movies changed things for you? How come there was such a big gap between* Philadelphia *coming out and your next big movie?*

JD: I think the biggest change in my film-making life was when I got married and started raising a family, probably quite late in my life as a guy in my forties. I suddenly didn't want to make a movie every year. I wanted to enjoy my life more. Movies were essentially my life, in a way, the great source of joy, but now I had another thing that was making me a little lazier. When *Silence of the Lambs* did well commercially it was more than anything. My partner Ed Saxon and I were just so relieved that finally we had made a movie that had made some money! At a certain point you've just made a lot of movies that have come in on budget and are pretty good or whatever, so you're given another shot, but they aren't making money. You get nervous.

And certainly as a filmmaker I started thinking, "What is it I'm not understanding here? Why can't any of these things achieve?" 'Cause I love them and believe in them etc. So it was just a relief when *Silence of the Lambs* did well, and when *Philadelphia* did well also it was an even greater relief.

In a funny way, instead of increasing any pressure I think that it kind of alleviated it. I think that the conventional wisdom is that if you make a movie that does quite well from time to time then you're allowed some bombs. So it sort of helped. I've come to a point, or a realization—what with the family etc.—that it's such hard work for such a long time when you make a picture. It's about two years from when you get involved in it at script level to when you say goodbye to it in the theatres, and I've realized that you've got to be very enthusiastic about it. As a director, you have to be really, really glad that you're there. It's just finding something that gives me the confidence just to satisfy myself and amuse myself is the trickiest thing. I don't think it's possible for me to pick a movie just because it's going to do well at the box office. I just don't have that knack.

AW: *Were you, along with your producer and your agent, deluged with scripts after the success of* Silence of the Lambs *and* Philadelphia*? Was everybody trying to get you to make the next $60 or $70 million motion picture?*

JD: I wasn't deluged necessarily, but there were certainly a lot of opportunities, especially to do movies about serial killers!

AW: *You have now made, aside from* Storefront Hitchcock, *a big movie which has come out in the States but which we're going to see a little later on, perhaps at the beginning of next year, and that's* Beloved. *Could you tell us a little bit about that? What attracted you to Toni Morrison's novel and how you got involved in it. It's an incredibly famous novel, and I know that it's been very much a personal project of Oprah Winfrey's.*

JD: Oprah bought the book shortly after it came out, which was about ten or eleven years ago. I got involved two years ago. I know that she had talked to other directors and that there had been other drafts of the script. When it came to me, two years ago at Christmas, I find it hard to believe that such an aggressively different kind of movie was actually going to be financed. That was one reaction I had. The movie deals with a very difficult subject, and it's not a subject that America is dying for opportunities to confront and that is the unresolved, tragic subject of slavery in our country. It's arguably a subject that the entire world has to come to terms with appropriately. It's not just that we were a colonial territory where slavery, this horrendous thing between the races, was acted out. It started in other hemispheres. It's a deep, challenging piece that just, to me, had incredibly emotional rewards.

And also it's a ghost story and it has a deeply suspenseful, deeply disturbing, supernatural dimension to it.

The American history books—taught in our public school system—and most of the popular literature and movies rarely look at this amazing part of American history. An entire people were set free, in the sense that slavery was abolished, and then turned out in an extraordinarily hostile environment to create lives for themselves and future generations. So this great heroic initiative began on the part of the black race in America and there's just so little about that in this period that we call Reconstruction. I just think that the light Toni Morrison shed on it, and the way she dived into this fresh terrain with such imagination was just an amazing opportunity for me as a film-maker.

AW: *What was it like working with Oprah Winfrey when it was her project and she was going to be one of the main characters in it? She was effectively going to be the producer on the project. Did that lead to tensions or was it always a plain sailing relationship?*

JD: There were never creative tensions. Oprah is certainly one of the credited producers, and later, especially in the editing phase, her opinions and points of view came positively into play—along with her partner Kate Forte, Ed Saxon, Gary Goetzman, and the rest. We had a five-person producing team working on the movie. Maybe that's why it's so long. It's two hours, forty minutes long and there's a lot to produce there for us! Oprah felt and rightly so, that with such an able team working on the producing that she could concentrate on the extraordinarily difficult task of bringing her character, Sethe, to life. As *Beloved* is unique to cinema there's never been a character like Sethe. Oprah doesn't act that much but she's incredibly gifted and as exciting an actor as anyone I've ever worked with, both with the ideas she brings to the table and her ability to change focus, she was a joy to work with. She was just so pleased to act her part that there was never a moment's aggravation whatsoever.

AW: *Well I think that's whetted everybody's appetites to see the film, but you're going to have to wait a little bit longer. I think at this moment, as time's running out, I think that it's time to throw the floor open to the audience.*

QUESTION ONE: *How do you work with actors to create such strong performances?*
JD: Thank you for that question. What I do is I only work with actors who take full responsibility for their characters. There's never a moment in my process where I sit down and explain the character to the actor, I figure that that's their responsibility and their job. If they have any questions about

their character from what they see in the script then that we should talk about beforehand, but other than that I like to go to the set and have the actors show up and start doing whatever it is they've prepared.

I like to start filming as quickly as possible. I like to get what the blocking is going to be like and then I like to start filming, rehearsing on film. It amazes me that so many directors rehearse so much—and with great effect I have to say—but I always have this terror that, "What if your actors do it perfect and you're not filming? What if they find exactly the best way to do it and you're sitting there waiting?" Where I do collaborate with the actor has more to do with ideas about a change this way or that way, an emphasis within the body of any particular scene, or maybe perceiving that doing it the crying way isn't working so suggesting doing it the laughing way. I also have a spoken agreement with the actors that this is okay with them. I very much want the actors to feel that they get to do the character the way they have prepared it, to their satisfaction on film. And they have to allow me to express a different way that I would like to see it done and they will do that wholeheartedly for me.

One of the reasons for that is that I feel that in terms of human relations this works better. Acting is by far and away the toughest job, in terms of film-making and maybe even the arts. How they do it I don't know, but they have to be allowed to get their satisfaction. Since bringing that rule in and realising that the best way to get my way is to let them get their way too, I've sometimes discovered in the cutting room that hey, they were right. So I get to get my ideas out of my system and they get to get their ideas out of their system and in the cutting room we find out what works.

QUESTION TWO: *How do you go about choosing composers for your films and how do you decide that you're just going to use source music?*
JD: I was a sort of rock journalist—whatever that is—in London in the late sixties. It was a very exciting time to be a rock journalist, and because I was writing these columns in the music magazines, I got the opportunity to be a musical co-ordinator for Irving Allen, who was an American producer based in London. He was just finishing a film called *Eyewitness*, with Mark Lester in it, and the producer decided that he wanted a contemporary, kind of rocky, soundtrack. So he hired this stoned-out rock journalist—me—to find some musicians or bands or what have you. So I went to two of my favourite bands: Kaleidoscope, which did a very lyrical, beautiful, lush, emotion-filled music, and Van der Graaf Generator. My idea was for Kaleidoscope to do the more romantic sequences in the movie, and Van der Graaf Genarator were real freak-outs so they could do the suspenseful, terrifying schemes. Ironi-

cally, the fact is that Kaleidoscope wound up doing stuff far freakier for the suspense scenes. So I don't know.

In terms of casting a composer, well, I wanted to work with David Byrne because we had such a good time doing *Stop Making Sense* together. I wanted to warm him up for Bertolucci so that he could get his Oscar nomination, so he did *Married to the Mob*.

With *Beloved*, I had been in touch with Rachel Portman because I admired her work so much, and it struck me as great that I'd have a woman to score *Beloved*. The irony there is that this movie is very much about motherhood, in addition to the other things, and Rachel ended up doing the score while pregnant and having the child and that whole process. It's wall to wall music, and so amazing what she did.

AW: *It's interesting though because a lot of noted directors, especially those who care so passionately about music as you do, can often work with the same composer over and over and over again, but you seem to have distinctly decided not to do that. Instead you've selected a composer per film and put source music and baroque music in it. That's quite uncommon for a director in some ways, because we know big directors—depending on scheduling—often work with the same people.*

JD: Well I love to work again with someone who I've had a great experience with. In fact, Tak Fujimoto who shot *Beloved* is one such person. I think this is our thirteenth movie together or something like that. And I do love that, but I also feel that the only thing more gratifying than working with someone who you've worked well with is working with someone new and coming up with something great. Music's tricky too. I think cameramen are always looking for something different to do, but composers seem to have some kind of musical demon to get out of their system and are looking for ways to do this. That probably doesn't make any sense at all. In fact I don't buy it. Next question . . .

QUESTION THREE: *When you're filming do you know you're onto a good thing?*
JD: You finish the day's work and then you go on to dailies and see what you shot yesterday. Usually you go into dailies really tired from the day's work. You got up far too early, you've been working hard and you've had a lot of strain and stress. And if the dailies perk you up again and get you all excited and looking forward to the next day's work then you know you're onto something good. So I think that that's the best gauge.

Also, while it's happening, the first three or four movies I made I was always so astonished that I had made it through the process and my name was on the movie. I never had any training as a director and had never aspired to be a director and kind of fell into it in strange kinds of ways, so I didn't really understand what directors were supposed to do. Over time I've come to understand that the trick of making really great movies is to try to find a script that has potential to be a splendid movie in one way or another and then working with fantastic people in all areas. The more you get into that trip, the more the director can relax and enjoy what is going on.

When we made *Beloved*, more than any other time previously, we got to a certain point in the day, and the cameras rolling, and you realise that there's theatre going on. I feel that I don't even have to wait for dailies now. If you find yourself transported by what's happening then it's got to be good. Well, you've got to believe that it's got to be good anyway.

QUESTION FOUR: *Would you call yourself an independent film-maker or would you sign the three-picture deal with Paramount if the money were right?*
JD: You mean if the money was really right? Well it's complicated. I think yes, yes, yes. I mean, *Storefront Hitchcock* was a Clinica Estetico production—that's a company I'm involved with and our office is paid for, is always being paid for, by one of the big movie studios. In return for that we have to go to them first with any idea that we find interesting—whether it's a script we come across or a story in a magazine, whatever. So long as it isn't tied up elsewhere, we're obliged to take it to Universal—currently that's whom we're working with. So I do have a deal like that, but there's no pressure to make a movie because of that. The pressure is to find something that can be a successful movie to justify the investment they make in keeping the office running all the time.

I think we're very independent though. We're developing a certain amount of exciting ideas for Universal—one with Paul Thomas Anderson (director of *Boogie Nights*) and various other people—and we're shooting a $3 million, extremely independent movie in New York called *The Opportunists*, which Christopher Walken is starring in. And hey, we did *Storefront Hitchcock* and we make documentaries on videotape, so we do all kinds of stuff. I think we are as independent as they get, but we're also deeply enmeshed in the bowels of the industry, as well, because they pay our bills.

QUESTION FIVE: *I love the book* Beloved, *but is the movie compromised at all because it has been made by such a big company like Buena Vista?*
JD: Not in the slightest. We were allowed to make exactly the movie—to the best of our ability—we wanted to make. There are two reasons for that. One of them is that this was a cherished project for Oprah Winfrey. Even Toni Morrison told her, you'll never make a movie out of this book, and I don't know why you want to buy it. Oprah was just utterly committed both to making the movie and playing the part. She has a tremendously success-

ful television show, of course, in America, and that's all very involved with ABC and Disney. So, on one level, Oprah and what she does is such a corporate asset—in the best sense—for Disney and ABC that I can imagine few people there wondering whether to back Oprah's vision here or not! That's one thing.

The other thing is that the guy who was most responsible for running Disney films is a guy called Joe Roth, and he was desperate to make this movie. The only pressure we got from him was to make sure we gave it our collective best shot. So there was no tampering. This is it.

QUESTION SIX: *Do you have final cut?*
JD: Yes. It's a beautiful thing to have. Let me elaborate slightly on that. Being the kind of collaborative film-maker that I am I really do believe that it's not just one person making a movie it's a whole bunch of people. My realisation is that other people can have ideas as good as mine and sometimes even better. So it's easy to be a sponge-like open receiver of good ideas when you have final cut, because you can take and choose what you want. After having the experience that I had with *Swing Shift* this is very important. The next film I made after that was at Orion Pictures—who aren't around anymore—and they were noted for giving an implicit final cut to film-makers. Orion's thing was, we're financiers, you're the film-maker, we trust you, and we don't give notes. Starting with *Something Wild* I had a de facto final cut anyway. And with the success of *Silence of the Lambs*, that we did for Orion, my agents were able to build this final cut into the contracts.

QUESTION SEVEN: *Why do you make films?*
JD: Hey, it's what I do . . . Well, gosh, I don't know. I feel that I need a deep answer to that. I suppose it's because I love movies. I love humanity and I'm fascinated with the way humanity gets at each other, in good ways and bad, and as a film-maker it gives me the opportunity to trip out on that. I love visual things. It's a very exciting job to have.

I don't have an agenda, particularly, although from movie to movie there's a momentary agenda. I really wanted to make a movie that addressed the issue of AIDS. A friend of mine, who I love very much, got AIDS and it really got me in a very intense way how tough life was for people with AIDS. Again Ed Saxon and Ron Nyswaner who wrote it had similar motivations to say something like that, and to say something about the unspeakable discrimination that was being visited on people with AIDS who were up against a very heroic, tough struggle to begin with. With *Beloved*, I was given the opportunity to have very intense personal feelings about race relations and the state of racial affairs in my country and indeed the world. I had very strong feelings, so the chance to make a film that deals in an imaginative way with stuff you care tremendously about is a real high. It's a really amazing thing to be able to do.

AW: *And rock and roll is the lighter side in that sense . . .*

JD: One of the most significant scenes in any movie for me is in *Sullivan's Travels* when the director wants to make really meaningful movies. He winds up through a series of events taking a walk on the wild side and ends up imprisoned in this hideous work camp in the South and he's there and they show a movie that night. And he sees all these tragic, broken people laughing at the comedy on the screen, and he looks around and he realises that that's what he should have been doing all the time. There's no greater gift in this kind of field than to make people laugh their socks off.

QUESTION EIGHT: *How much artistic control do you give your editors and how do you choose your editors?*

JD: Well, until *Storefront Hitchcock* and *Beloved*, I'd only worked with one editor since *Melvin and Howard* days, which was about twenty years ago. This was an incredibly gifted editor named Craig McKay who is now directing—he's decided now, damn him, to direct!

I give the editor full creative control on the first cut and by the end of the editing process I know why, exactly why, every single cut is exactly on what frame it's on. The "why cut there?" is such a huge question in the making of a movie. Why not sooner or why not later. At first I tried to give the editors a lot of notes about how I wanted them to put the scene together. But once you start working with gifted editors you can always get to see it the way you want to see it—because you're the director—but you only arguably get to see a very gifted editor's first take on this material that's coming in. So I long ago stopped doing that. Now I'm dying to see what the editor is doing to it. We discuss it now, and stand side by side and get a feel for it. I feel it's a director's job to question every take, unless it's really working great.

QUESTION NINE: *Will we ever get to see the director's cut of* Swing Shift*?*

JD: You must have read that article in *Sight and Sound*. That was great! When *Swing Shift* came out, the critics universally trashed it, even some of those critics that I particularly admired and even some that I had previously considered almost friends. This motif was running through the reviews: this guy looked as though he had some kind of promise, but looking at this thing, forget about it. And I thought, my God, if my work is bad, then trash me, but this isn't even my work. There was nothing I could say about it. You can't go whining to the press. But then somehow a videotape of the original—the scripted movie—found its way over to *Sight and Sound* and an article was written saying it was very good the original way. And it went to great pains to enumerate why it was much better than what Warner Brothers had done. But it will never be seen anywhere, because now the videotape's all faded out and the Warner Brothers post-production people trashed all the outtakes and our version as soon as I lost control, so you'll just have to take my word for it that it was really something!

QUESTION TEN: *What advice would you give film students if they really want to become a director?*
JD: To get their hands on a video camera and photograph things that interest them—either make up stories or find a subject. Become a film-maker. The more radical people would say, if you can't buy one, steal one . . . whatever, but just start filming, because then you're a film-maker. And if you've got something going on then you can get these things seen by agencies and production companies and it happens every day, somebody with that particular kind of drive ends up getting a chance to do it that way.

QUESTION ELEVEN: *Did you look at Robyn's concert video from the 1980s before you made* Storefront Hitchcock?
JD: No, I didn't want to pollute my thing. For me it isn't good to do that kind of research. In fact, when I did *Silence of the Lambs* I started watching the previous Thomas Harris movie which had Hannibal Lecter in it and, not that it was good or bad, ten minutes into it I suddenly felt that I shouldn't be seeing it. It was the same with *Storefront Hitchcock*. We diligently tracked down all of Robyn's videos and I started looking at them and again I thought I don't want to see these. I wanted the memory of what he was like in performance and do it as seems best at the time.

QUESTION TWELVE: *Are you interested in the new multi-media technology?*
JD: No. I know I should be, but no!

QUESTION THIRTEEN: *What's happening with the* Silence of the Lambs *sequel?*
JD: Thomas Harris, author of *The Silence of the Lambs*, has been working on his new book for the last seven or eight years.

AW: *It's been announced that it's coming out several times, hasn't it?*
JD: Every couple of years, though it's not necessarily true. Thomas and I have become quite good friends and he's—amazingly—a very delightful man, and I don't think that he would mind me telling you this story. I went to visit him in person before shooting the last scene of the movie, because I thought it really important to be as faithful as possible to that book. I thought that the book was so powerful, and I didn't want to fall into the trap of trying to

improve it in the making of the movie. Now the book ends in a certain kind of way. If you've read it you'll know that it just sort of wafts away. It hits a certain kind of climax with the confrontation between Jame Gumb and Clarice Starling, and then there's a series of letters that are exchanged. It ends in a very fascinating way for a book but which wouldn't work, we didn't think, on film.

I had this idea of taking what the book did, which was that in the letters there was a very serious kind of threat to Doctor Chilton, the former keeper of Doctor Lecter, from Doctor Lecter, so we tried to play on that. Ted Tally, the author of the screenplay, and I came up with this idea. But I felt that I didn't want to make this major departure and shoot the ending without Tom Harris's blessing. I'd spoken with him on the phone a couple of times. During our first conversation, I'd told him that when we were having the first cut of the movie he was invited to come and look at it because I'd value the author's criticism—because he'd be likely to be the toughest critic. And he said, "Don't take this the wrong way, I'm glad you're making the movie, but I'll probably never see it." And I asked him why, and he said an interesting thing. He said that he read in an interview with John le Carré that after le Carré saw Alec Guinness play Smiley that he could never write Smiley again. This was a character that he thought he would write for the rest of his life, but Alec Guinness had stolen Smiley from him. And he told me this in a very salutary way, because Harris likes to revisit his characters and he didn't want something like that to happen, especially in the hands of someone like Anthony Hopkins. So he gave us his blessing and decided he probably wasn't going to see the movie.

He was very soft spoken on the telephone, a real Southern gentleman, and finally I phoned him up and said I need to come and see you, because I need to get permission to change the ending. So my wife and I went to visit him at his house in Miami Beach. We went outside and had a little food and were chatting, and he was very soft spoken and intense and interesting. And I finally said, "By the way Tom, I need to talk to you about a possible change to the ending to the film." And he says, "I tell you what John, why don't we go to the rose garden and talk about this." And he picks up these great big shears and says, "Well, John, you know, if you're going to make a departure from the book . . ."

And he told me an interesting thing. I told him that I pictured Hannibal Lecter going to a tropical country, not unlike Haiti, and he said the greatest thing. He said, "Well Jonathan, I'll tell you, I imagine Doctor Lecter going to somewhere in Europe. My image is of him strolling round the back streets of Florence or Munich, gazing in the windows of watchmakers. But I'll tell you, if he did go to the tropics he wouldn't sweat!" So if you ever see the movie, you'll notice that everybody's perspiring profusely in the last scene, except Doctor Lecter. Anyway, those of us who made the first movie hope that we'll get the chance to make a movie of his work in progress, which may be finished in a year or so and which we believe includes Doctor Lecter. But my hunch is that it won't be a straight sequel. I don't think that he's the kind of writer to do it that way.

AW: *What a tantalising prospect. I think we've got time for one last question.*

QUESTION FOURTEEN: *When you cast Tom Hanks in* Philadelphia *did you think that it was a gamble?*

JD: I guess you mean a creative gamble because he'd essentially done lighter parts thus far. We got the script to a place where we felt we could go forward. Sony Pictures were our parent company at the time and financed the development of it. They were adamant that a movie that was going to be about AIDS and homophobia in some way or other—subjects that they didn't think moviegoers were hungering to visualise—really needed some kind of terrific acting and star power. The part that Denzel Washington played was written very much in the hope of attracting someone like Robin Williams or Bill Murray, someone with a comedic profile. We understood what we were up against in getting an audience for a movie about AIDS so we thought that if we could get someone who could send a funny signal—and this character would certainly be amusing—that would be a step in the right direction.

We started seeing actors and a number of things happened. A lot of actors didn't really want to consider playing a gay man with AIDS at that stage. So two things happened. One was that our producing partner, Gary, was on a plane with Denzel. He read the script and called up and said he wanted to play the part of Joe Miller, which really thrilled me. Denzel is obviously one of the great American actors, and the idea of casting a black man in that part was fantastic. I got on the phone with Denzel and said that I was very excited by his interest but that we'd really envisaged a comedian playing the part, and he said, "Jonathan, I'm hilarious!" And I said, "This character was written picturing a white man, do you think we have to do any work on this script if we choose to cast you in this movie about prejudice and what have you?" And he said, "Do you?" And I heard myself say, "No," and he said, "Good, I don't either."

But Denzel at that point couldn't get a movie off the ground on his own—well not on that subject anyway. Then we got a phone call that Tom Hanks was going to be in New York, where we were based, and he would love to come by, just for a general meeting. So we thought, great. And we were actually in the editing room, editing our latest Haiti documentary, about the quest for democracy in Haiti, and Tom came in. And we chatted a little bit, and then I walked him to the elevator and he told me he'd read the script for *Philadelphia*. I wasn't looking for someone like Tom at that time, but he said he'd read it and he'd love to throw his hat in the ring for the part of Andrew. By the way, he said, in case I thought that he'd be appropriate, his agents had been told that the price was not the object. So he was essentially saying that he wanted to play the part and he knew that we had to keep the price down because of the subject matter. By the time I got back to the cutting room from the elevator, I was thinking, my God, we can actually get this movie made.

I trusted that Hanks would be really good, but I have to say he was even better. I thought he was magnificent in the movie, and I never imagined him being as good as he was.

AW: *I think at that point, with that very interesting answer, we're going to have to wrap. But I still haven't asked you what the significance of the traffic cones is in* Storefront Hitchcock.

JD: That'll be revealed in the sequel to *Storefront Hitchcock* . . .

AW: *Excellent.*

JD: I'd like to thank everyone for coming out on a school night. Thank you so much.

Breaking the Rules for *Beloved*

ERIC HARRISON / 1998

THE IRONY OF Jonathan Demme directing *Beloved*, the film adaptation of Toni Morrison's acclaimed novel, is that it came about by coincidence.

As far back as the mid-1980s, Demme was scouting around for a movie project that dealt with race. Demme chiefly was known back then as the director of quirky and well-made comedies that reveled in offbeat Americana. His reputation since has soared with works that were so expertly crafted (*The Silence of the Lambs*), and so poignant and brave (*Philadelphia*), that he rose to the first rank of American directors. All the while, he was quietly searching for his movie about race.

Oprah Winfrey was trying to get *Beloved* off the ground at the same time. But when she sent Demme the script, he says she had no idea it would dovetail with his longtime interests. "It was a dream come true," he says now of the opportunity.

The process of making the film, however, was far from easy.

Beloved, which won the Pulitzer Prize for fiction in 1988, is a densely written novel that deals with the aftermath and legacy of slavery. In poetic prose that fuses down-in-the-dirt reality with symbolism and the supernatural, the book centers on Sethe, a former slave, as she struggles with her daughter, her lover, and a mysterious young woman known as Beloved to overcome physical and psychic scars left by slavery.

Period films are always difficult. But adapting this one was made tougher by the way the novel combines elements of several genres into a work that refuses to be pinned down. The filmmakers had to extract a slice of *Beloved*'s epic story line from the tangle of flashbacks, interior monologues, and shifting points of view that obscures it.

"There are probably at least a dozen levels that the book operates on," says Demme, fifty-four. But he called the book's difficulty "part of the excitement. That was the challenge."

Beloved sprawls, pitches, and swerves as it transgresses genre boundaries on its way to achieving an aching kind of beauty. While watching it, a viewer may long for a little more of the discipline Demme imposed on *Philadelphia* and *Silence of the Lambs*, but if he had done that, *Beloved* would not be what it is—a brave if flawed tour de force, a bravura performance by a man who, based on his past movies, might have seemed an unlikely choice as director.

The sly humor and oddball style of Demme's earlier work in films such as *Melvin and Howard*, *Something Wild*, and *Married to the Mob* is hard to discern in his recent harder-edged films. In *Beloved*, all notions of what constitutes "a film by Jonathan Demme" are obliterated.

"Oprah said, 'There ain't never been a movie like this before,'" Demme recalls with a laugh. "I feel that's true. That doesn't mean it's what's good about the movie, but it is a fact about it."

Making the film would have been even tougher than it already was had he known more about the book's history. A large portion of the African American intelligentsia so treasures Morrison and *Beloved* that a literary controversy erupted in 1988 after she failed to win the National Book Award. Forty-eight writers and academics published a letter of protest in the *New York Times* that praised Morrison's work while deploring the "oversight and harmful whimsy" that had denied her the recognition they felt she was due. Morrison went on to win both the Pulitzer for *Beloved* and the Nobel Prize for her body of work.

Given that history of protectiveness, and given the mind-set that persists in some quarters that African American history should only be interpreted by African Americans, Demme's first and perhaps greatest act of bravery was merely signing on to direct the film.

"I'm really glad I had no idea of that," he says of the 1988 controversy. "Adapting the book was intimidating enough as it was."

As for a white man directing a work about African Americans, he says it was never a concern. "Probably eight or nine years ago it might have had the potential to be problematic," he says. "But that was before the wonderful proliferation of black filmmakers and more African American subject matter being dealt with in films.

"I do feel that as a human being we all have a lot more in common than the race and gender things we use to entrap each other," he says. "I have no difficulty relating to, feeling empathy with, and deeply sympathizing with people of different races and different genders."

In the 1980s, when films featuring African American themes were relatively rare, Demme tried in vain to launch several projects. "I sought those films out as a filmmaker," he says, because "as a moviegoer I wanted to see more African American subject matter. But I couldn't get anything off the ground."

Beloved is a ghost story. It is a family drama. It's a romance. But it also at times is an excruciatingly visceral depiction of the lives of black folk in the years during and after slavery. The film is inspiring in that it shows the triumph of the human spirit, but it also can be painful to watch. By necessity, it depicts the degradations that its characters had to face, and it shows the tragic, unthinkable lengths to which a woman who "loves too much" might go to shield her young.

To prepare audiences, Touchstone Pictures, the film's distributor, last week unveiled stage two of its advertising campaign. Without discontinuing earlier television ads and trailers that emphasized the inspiring side of the film, new trailers were put in play that suggest the challenging and deeply disturbing nature of the subject matter.

Reviewers praised *Philadelphia*, Demme's film about AIDS, as daring when it was released in 1993. It was daring in subject matter. But in truth, everything else about that movie—from the decision to show just a tad of gay affection to the casting of all-American Tom Hanks to the inclusion of a comically bigoted character who could become enlightened by movie's end—was designed to make a difficult subject palatable to mainstream viewers. *Beloved* makes few such concessions.

With the earlier movie, "as we worked on the screenplay and started thinking it through, trying to characterize that struggle, we gradually came to realize that homophobia was our biggest hurdle," Demme says. "We wanted to make a movie that was as friendly as possible to the group we were trying to reach, hoping to move."

But with *Beloved* the filmmakers took chances. "We felt that to back off in any manner from what the book was trying to achieve thematically and narratively would blow it. We felt that the book, being the exquisitely made piece of literature that it is, we really had to honor it."

In adapting the book, Richard LaGravenese, one of three credited screenwriters, said he threw out the rule book. He did not try to force the material into standard three-act structure. "The thing with *Beloved* was that I found it very musical," he says. It felt to him that the book was written in movements, like a symphonic piece, and that is how he tried to write it.

He turned in a script that was much less linear than the finished film; it contained more flashbacks to the main characters' lives on the Sweet Home plantation.

"If the film works, it's because of Jonathan knowing what to cut away," he says. "Jonathan's a great filmmaker and he knows much more than I about what you can condense and still have an audience be able to follow the story."

After LaGravenese left the movie to work on *Living Out Loud*, his own first film as director, Demme brought in Adam Brooks to polish the script. Akosua Busia had written an earlier version of the screenplay.

"The challenge to the adapter is figuring out what story are you going to tell—there're at least three fantastic motion pictures that could be made from this book," Demme says.

The movie easily could have focused on life at Sweet Home, the plantation where Sethe was a slave along with Paul D, an old friend who eventually would become her lover. The slaves enjoyed many freedoms under the benevolent hand of Mr. Garner. But when he died, the cruel man known as Schoolteacher took over, and life became a living hell. This hypothetical movie could have shown the pregnant Sethe's escape and the birth of her youngest daughter along the banks of the Ohio River with the help of a wandering white girl. This is included in the finished film, but Demme says this could easily have worked as a climax, with the film ending with Sethe crossing the river to reunite with what's left of her family. "Wow, what a movie!" he enthuses. "God!"

A second movie lay in the hardships Paul D faced during his eighteen-year sojourn as he crossed several states trying to locate Sethe. The unsettled years after the end of slavery form a period that has been ignored not only by filmmakers but also by society at large, says Demme, who has continued to study the era. One powerful and unexpected element of the book, hinted at in the film, is the way people wandered the land trying to reunite with family members, looking for a place to call home.

The filmmakers eliminated most of this, however, as they chose to focus on what seemed to them to be the heart of the story: what happens in the house at 124 Bluestone Road after first Paul D and then Beloved arrives, and everyone's lives start to change.

"Richard had wanted to try to fuse all three of these movies," Demme says. In paring it down, the director eliminated all flashbacks to Sethe's and Paul D's previous life except those that seemed absolutely necessary. When he did this, he found embedded in the story a multilayered domestic drama that he says could've been written by Ibsen, Chekhov, or O'Neill, only set in a haunted house.

Even with all the paring away, *Beloved* still does not resemble a typical Hollywood movie. In a film that takes numerous chances—in its subject matter, its ambiguity, and its searing images—Demme made two daring and unorthodox choices in the way the narrative is put together that he realizes could do even more to put off viewers.

Winfrey and Danny Glover drop almost completely out of the last third of the movie. The story is turned over to Kimberly Elise, who plays Denver, Sethe's youngest daughter, as she grows into her own, breaking away from the house and the past.

"On paper it breaks rules to lose touch with your main character for so long," Demme acknowledges, but he said he had "tremendous faith" in the power of Denver's story. "For me this is what brings the element of triumphant hope and uplift to the story.

"The other thing that breaks the rules is the eight-minute-long mini-movie in the middle of the film in which Denver tells Beloved the story of her birth." The flashback comes at a point of tension in the main story. "The scary part was when we return to the present how difficult would it be to pick up the pieces of the characters," he says.

"The book could just take off into another direction whenever it damn well pleases," he says.

A Conversation with Director Jonathan Demme

CHARLIE ROSE/1998

CHARLIE ROSE: *Jonathan Demme is widely regarded as one of the leading directors in American film. He learned his craft making B-movies with Roger Corman in the early 1970s. He made his feature directorial debut with* Caged Heat *in 1974. In 1991, he broke into the mainstream with his first blockbuster—*Silence of the Lambs. *The film took home five Oscars, including one for Best Director. His current film,* Beloved, *is an adaptation of Toni Morrison's Pulitzer Prize–winning novel. It stars Oprah Winfrey. It marks his first return to the director's chair since* Philadelphia *in 1993. I am pleased to have him at this table at long last. Welcome, sir.*
JONATHAN DEMME: Thank you very much.

CHARLIE ROSE: *It's great to have you here. And congratulations on* Beloved.
JONATHAN DEMME: Thank you.

CHARLIE ROSE: *We talked to Oprah, which will be on later this week. And we talked a lot about—in a sense, the making of a film. When you saw the script, what was it that so emotionally grabbed you to say, "This is for me."*
JONATHAN DEMME: You know, what I remember so clearly is I picked up the script, I started reading it, and at about page 30, 32, something like that, was the scene that takes place in the clearing, when Baby Suggs calls the men and the women and the children to come out of the woods. And I found myself with tears running down my face at this imagery, at the thoughts and feelings that the descriptions evoked. And I thought, "I don't know where this script is headed," 'cause I hadn't read the book, "but I love it." I was

---

From *The Charlie Rose Show* (October 26, 1998). Published by permission of Rose Communications.

already—I've never been so completely hooked and seduced so early in a script in my life.

CHARLIE ROSE: *And so what happened then?*
JONATHAN DEMME: Well, I finished the script and saw that it was arguably the opportunity of a—of a—I feel it's the dream I never dared have come true. It's a movie that combines a lot of my favorite genres while addressing—thematically—stuff that's just been, you know, tremendously important to me for a long time.

CHARLIE ROSE: *What are those things that appeal to you? I mean, in terms of the genres that it touched, that it gave you an opportunity to deal with.*
JONATHAN DEMME: I guess a ghost story, first and foremost. And then a movie that dealt in dreamtime. Which I loved—dreams and nightmares. I've always wanted to do—I think most filmmakers want to do their Western. I haven't done mine yet. And, when I started picturing this farmland and the people on horseback—It's a Midwest Western, but it's also a chance to get into a period that I've always adored in motion pictures and never had a chance to work with.

CHARLIE ROSE: *Directors want to do Westerns because it's so uniquely American, I guess.*
JONATHAN DEMME: Well, you know, for me that was the first genre that I ever fell in love with. I guess Westerns and horror movies. And just the whole idea of guys galloping up on horses and leaping down and pulling their six-guns out is kind of a very stirring thing for a kid, and that which makes you fall in love in the first place is something that stays with you.

CHARLIE ROSE: *When you read the script, did you think that Oprah wanted to be Sethe?*
JONATHAN DEMME: I figured she must. I mean, she'd be nuts if she didn't want to play Sethe.

CHARLIE ROSE: *Whatever else she might be—smart she is.*
JONATHAN DEMME: It didn't come with any kind of articulated attachment like that. But I made that assumption.

CHARLIE ROSE: *And you were prepared for that. Or did you have to see her, meet her, talk to her, decide if she was up to it?*
JONATHAN DEMME: You know, it had been so long since Oprah had done a movie. And she has done so few movies. And, since her last movie, she's become such a gigantic American figure—

CHARLIE ROSE: *Icon almost.*

JONATHAN DEMME: Definitely a living icon. For all the best reasons, by the way. I've been an admirer. I wasn't a devotee of the TV show. I saw some of them, but I was usually—you know, at work when she was on. But I understood where she was coming from, and I had seen enough of her to really have a tremendous admiration for her.

But I did have the concern that, regardless of how good a job she might do on the part, and I think, again, you had to assume she'd do a good job, could we—as consumers—accept Oprah Winfrey as a nineteenth-century farm woman literally haunted by her past? That's the first thing I talked to her about when we met.

CHARLIE ROSE: *And she convinced you? Or you saw something that convinced you?*

JONATHAN DEMME: Well, you know, I thought, "I'm gonna be, like, a real kind of grown-up almost businessperson and talk to my potential partner here in terms that are appropriate and say, 'Do you think that's a problem?'" And she—whatever it was—I don't even remember exactly what she said, but I know within about ninety seconds I was going, "That was a stupid question. It's no problem." She got immediately into talk on two levels—one, why she as a person felt that *Beloved* was such an important, valuable, rich kind of piece of material to make into a movie. She also talked about how she was going to attack the part and how she feels a very, very strong connection with her ancestors—not just her familial ancestors, but her racial ancestors—and how she intended in bringing Sethe to life to draw upon these forces. And I was really taken with that.

CHARLIE ROSE: *The memorabilia she has and all of the things that she—the voices she might hear about connections with slavery.*

JONATHAN DEMME: Mm-hmm [*affirmative*]. She talked at great length about Margaret Garner—who, of course, is the woman whose tragic real-life experience—

CHARLIE ROSE: *Real-life experience is the basis for* Beloved.

JONATHAN DEMME: Yeah. And incidentally I don't know if you've seen this new book called *Modern Medea*, which is a semi-scholarly but very gripping actual nice thick reportage of the Margaret Garner story itself, which I've just begun and is quite amazing.

CHARLIE ROSE: *This is a book? Not a documentary film, but a book?*

JONATHAN DEMME: Right.

CHARLIE ROSE: OK. Take a look at this. This is Oprah, talking to us last Friday about you. This is a conversation that will be on this program this week. Roll tape.

[Excerpt from interview with Oprah Winfrey]
OPRAH WINFREY: Jonathan leaves me and says, "Trust me." And the interesting thing about that, Charlie, is that there had been other directors in this ten-year period. Oh, everybody says, "Trust me." I think it's a Hollywood thing.

CHARLIE ROSE: *Yeah, right.*
OPRAH WINFREY: You leave the meeting, and they say, "Trust me, trust me, trust me."

CHARLIE ROSE: *"Trust me, it'll be OK."*
OPRAH WINFREY: "BE OK."

CHARLIE ROSE: *"I'll take care of you."*
OPRAH WINFREY: "Don't worry about it. Listen."

CHARLIE ROSE: *That's right.*
OPRAH WINFREY: "It'll be fine." And every single time that happened I would leave the meeting and I would say to Kate, my producer—I'd say, "What do you think?" "What do you think?" "I don't know. What do you think?" "I don't know. Was she OK? I don't know." And the difference is, when somebody says "trust me" and it's *right*—you don't have to ask anybody. That—Jonathan was at my house when we had that meeting, and he got up to go to the bathroom down the hall, and Kate and I were sitting at the kitchen table. And, when he left, we went [*pantomimes gleeful shouting*].

CHARLIE ROSE: *"This is it. This is it."*
OPRAH WINFREY: Yes, we danced—we call it our "Jonathan jig." He comes back in, and we're like this [*crosses her knees, placing her hands primly on the top knee*], sitting at the table. The interesting thing, too, is that he didn't say "yes" immediately, but it looked like it might be a "yes." And the next day I called Kate, and she said, "Dare we hope that life could be this good?" "Dare we hope?" I said. "I'm hoping. I'm hoping. It sounds like it's gonna be a 'yes.'" And, once he said "yes," things started moving immediately.
[End excerpt from interview with Oprah Winfrey]

CHARLIE ROSE: *Trust. Now, you said to her, "Trust me. Trust me." Meaning what?*

JONATHAN DEMME: Charlie, I think what I hope I actually said was, "You realize, Oprah, that you will *need* to trust me."

CHARLIE ROSE: *So, you were a little bit—a variation of what it is that they say too often.*

JONATHAN DEMME: I think that with someone who's taken on so many responsibilities for herself, as Oprah has and has a tremendous burden of responsibility and burden of last-wordness, I just wanted to make sure that she knew—number one—that she would need to trust her director. And I guess I wanted to reassure her that I felt she could trust me, that I wouldn't let her down.

CHARLIE ROSE: *I don't think she's done that very much. My impression is rarely does she do that. And she literally put herself in your hands because the way you evolved the film and in a sense convinced her was a little bit different than what she had in her mind, according to her. Yes?*

JONATHAN DEMME: Well, you know, it's different from what I had in *my* mind—so, I assume so. I don't know. I talked to Oprah on Sunday, yesterday, and I called her up 'cause I had gotten some phone calls the night before, heard some messages from some family and friends across the country who had seen the picture and had some things to say that moved me a lot. And I wanted to call her up to tell her—and we found ourselves just talking about how at this point there is a complete absence of the woulda, coulda, shouldas. For better or for worse, however the picture winds up doing, however far it reaches, I wanted her to know that I was completely happy and thrilled with it, and I was really happy to hear her come back and say that she wouldn't change a thing in it. So, it's great that—

CHARLIE ROSE: *It ends well.*

JONATHAN DEMME: Yeah.

CHARLIE ROSE: *Regardless of how much money it makes, regardless of how many people see it, for you and for her you made a movie that you want the audience to experience what? To know what?*

JONATHAN DEMME: Well, you know, it's funny because we were out there before coming inside and I was talking to a couple of people who had seen the new Roberto Benigni movie, and—

CHARLIE ROSE: *It's called* Life Is Beautiful, *and it's about using the Holocaust as the background for a family as a father tries to help his child come to grips with—*

JONATHAN DEMME: Right. And the gentleman I was sitting with said that he and his wife had seen it and had adored it. And I told him—I heard myself saying that I had seen the trailer for it several weeks ago, and it looked incredibly beautiful, and it looked incredibly moving to the degree that I was a little bit afraid of it.

I was afraid of the potential emotions that just the little hints I saw in the trailer—It just looks like an extraordinary movie. So, I suddenly went, "Mmm. And yet this is what I'm hoping what people's experience will be when they see *Beloved*." I want people to be tremendously moved by it—the kind of moved that maybe you *are* a little afraid to get to. It's such an incredibly powerful story that Toni Morrison was inspired by in real life and went on to tell and create this amazing piece of fiction.

And it doesn't pretend to not want to grab your heart and just pull you this way and that. And just really move you to the degree that you come out arguably feeling a little bit different about things.

CHARLIE ROSE: *It changed Oprah. Did it change you?*

JONATHAN DEMME: Very much so. Very much so. It's incredible because, again, you know, this is a great, great American book about things that are as important as anything, I think, in our country today and the world today. And what I'm referring to is, really, racial harmony versus racial exploitation. It's about humanity and man's potential inhumanity to man and man's potential showing of humanity to man. It's really about that. Now, it's dressed up in a wonderful ghost story with an even—there's a horror film in *Beloved* as well. There's a sequence—I mean, I did *Silence of the Lambs*. And there are scenes in this movie that I think are equally as horrifying. And I think the suspense in this movie gets to a point to be as intense as anything I've ever been involved with.

And it's just very, very rich, aggressive—it makes demands of an audience, and I feel that it has the ability to provide rewards consistent with the demands, but it's something that, like me with this Roberto Benigni movie, I know that I've got to kind of gear myself up, and you go and you're gonna pay money to go cry somewhere. You know, it's a strange dynamic.

CHARLIE ROSE: *When you thought about doing this, there was not anything you wanted to do—and you had been looking to make a film about race because it is so central to the American dilemma and so central to what you're concerned about.*

JONATHAN DEMME: Well, there was a time when, as a moviegoer, where I was getting fed up with the absence of African American stories and African American presence in movies. It's such a big part of our life here in America. How come it's not represented more in movies? Nothing against, you know, white-people movies. I love them, too. But I was just, as a consumer, starving for more variety and more contact, more insights, more involvement. And we, our company, looked around and tried to find some stuff. Now, meanwhile—in fact, I read the script for *Boyz N the Hood*.

CHARLIE ROSE: *Yeah.*

JONATHAN DEMME: And I read it, and I went, "Oh, my God, I would love to make this movie." And we called up—we were involved with Sony at that point, and we called up and arranged for John Singleton to come to New York to talk to us to see if he would let us—my partner and I, Ed Saxon—make *Boyz N the Hood*. But by the time John got to New York he had made his directing deal at Columbia to direct it. And he came in anyway, and we had a great time. And I reference that because John especially—I mean, Spike Lee certainly put the news out there that African Americans could make fantastic movies that could also make money and that's what gets movies made more than anything.

And I think that John Singleton kicked the door open a lot wider as well, and suddenly it seemed there was at last a really thrilling wave of African American directors—men and women—making a wonderful—everything from mindless, delightful comedies to serious stuff, the penetrating studies of what's going on today. And suddenly the screens were starting to come alive with African American imagery as well as Euro-American imagery. And I think that's great.

So, anyway, the desire to be part of that as a filmmaker I guess was there, but I wasn't really pursuing it anymore. That's why to have this script come on—I care so much about race because I feel that our country can get better and better the more we are able to transcend our tortured past and aspire aggressively towards a harmony. I think, you know, the synergy that's possible is amazing. I also think the inverse is one of our greatest, greatest threats.

CHARLIE ROSE: *And the films can play a role because of their impact on the culture? In helping us come to an understanding of how it divides us, an understanding of how, if we can get inside our hearts, maybe we can step forward and get closer together?*

JONATHAN DEMME: Yeah. And I don't think I can say it any better than that. I know myself that I have, either through books and occasionally through films, had light bulbs go on in my head. And I've been able to expand my view of others and, I guess, even of myself and of *our* potential and the funny thing is that, if you start thinking that—like, I don't think that *Beloved* can have an impact on the way the country views race or views our shameful, tragically ignored past of slavery. But I do think—and I know—that the movie can change you a little bit or someone here or there.

CHARLIE ROSE: *Or Oprah. Or you.*

JONATHAN DEMME: Well, yeah. And folks that I'm seeing coming out of the movie theaters and talking to. So, individuals can have their thoughts changed about things from movies, and I think that's why we need movies that aspire to turning on light bulbs and books that aspire to turning on—And the trick is to make 'em really entertaining in the doing.

CHARLIE ROSE: *Boy, you said it there, because there is this notion, at least—and hopefully you and Steven and others will prove them wrong—that the public doesn't want to see that. That's not what they necessarily want to see. And there is some risk in the energy and the money to make movies not knowing that that's where the public appetite is.*

JONATHAN DEMME: Mm-hmm [*affirmative*].

CHARLIE ROSE: *You felt that responsibility. Clearly Oprah said to me, "You know, I know that this is a risk. I know that they're looking to this as a test. Can we make a film that's good, that's entertaining, that in a sense touches all the points that we want to touch?"*

JONATHAN DEMME: Mm-hmm, mm-hmm [*affirmative*]. Well, you know, we're all out of school now, and we're not gonna go to the movies to pay to get educated or what have you. And we pay to get an extraordinary experience hopefully. Or either—on the one hand or another. I mean, we pay our money to have a dynamic thing happen to us in there. Either, you know, to laugh and have a certain kind of thrill like my son and I did at *Rush Hour* Friday night, which I loved. I don't know if you've seen that.

CHARLIE ROSE: *No, but I know about it.*

JONATHAN DEMME: And that is so—you know, that's the Preston Sturges *Sullivan's Travels*. There is no greater gift that a filmmaker can give an audience than a laugh. And it's true. God, we need laughter. The part where we aspire to move people and through the emotions create other consciousnesses. You know, it's funny 'cause I've had some people say to me about *Beloved*, you know, "Is this supposed to make white people feel guilty by evoking the ghosts of slavery?" And nothing could be farther from the truth for me. I think, if anything, it's an invitation to be liberated to a certain extent from the kind of denial that a lot of us are burdened with.

CHARLIE ROSE: *And it is also a way to say that slavery and other experiences in America, which we ought to better understand, can best be understood by the fact that they are a million individual experiences of what individuals went through and the passage that they had to take.*

JONATHAN DEMME: Charlie, that is so exactly what I love the most in a way about this movie. I don't know where you went to school—I went to public school on Long Island and then in Miami, Florida. And the history books that we had, when they dealt with American history, there was slavery. It didn't go into the human terms of slavery. It was a fact. It was almost kinda mythological. It was Slavery. Certain kinds of archetypal imagery.

CHARLIE ROSE: *It was this bad thing that happened in America and that was about it.*

JONATHAN DEMME: Yeah. And then Lincoln freed the slaves, and then we cut to the next—like maybe the Spanish-American War or something in 1896. And that's exciting, dynamic white army, American kind of thing. And this whole period of time, this period known as "Reconstruction," is interpreted as the country was reconstructing. But, if you see *Beloved*, you realize that human beings were reconstructing themselves emotionally, psychologically as they dared to go forward in the future.

CHARLIE ROSE: *And I think Toni's point, in part, is that those scars are very deep as you try to come to grips with the reconstruction for every individual.*

JONATHAN DEMME: They're deep and abiding. And, you know, the whole exodus of African Americans from slavery, trying without any help from anybody to carve out a life for themselves, for their children, for subsequent generations, is just such epic heroism that went on in this country and it's so underreported. And I love that *Beloved* throws a light and focuses in on these extraordinary, heroic, tormented-by-ghosts people.

CHARLIE ROSE: *You wanted to be as true to Toni's book as you could—to every detail, as much as you could. Yes?*

JONATHAN DEMME: You know, we were so collectively inspired by that book that we had to honor it, even as we knew we had to take flight from it. Because—

CHARLIE ROSE: *Because you were making a movie.*

JONATHAN DEMME: Yeah. But we all, those of us who made the movie, *love* the book. I mean, love the book. You want to hug that book and keep it with you.

And we felt that we didn't easily—we didn't change hardly anything. We couldn't use everything from the book, but we didn't make the frequent kind of little "improvements" that filmmakers often make on books—when you go, "You know, I know that they're riding up—in the book, it says they're riding up in a Chevrolet in red outfits, but wouldn't it be terrific if they arrived in a big, black Cadillac and had on tuxedos? You know, that would be much more visual, wouldn't it?" We didn't do that kind of thing. We tried to be faithful to the kind of imagery that Toni Morrison was picturing in her mind in the first place.

CHARLIE ROSE: *All right. Let me take a look. This is another excerpt from a conversation that we did with Oprah, which will appear later this week, talking about Jonathan directing her. Here it is.*

[Excerpt from interview with Oprah Winfrey]
OPRAH WINFREY: My favorite Jonathan note is one day I'm in the chair—Sethe's in the chair, and the camera comes up behind my head and Beloved's going, "Bad Sethe, bad Sethe" [lightly slapping her own face]. This is just before Denver opens the window, and she sees the food. And I was breathing in the chair [audibly breathing in and out]. So, Jonathan keeps yelling—you know, he's outside with the megaphone going, "Give me *less*. Give me *less*. It's still too much." And I finally yelled back, "Jonathan, I'm only breathing." And he says, "You know how you're doing [audibly breathing in and out]? Just do the [audibly breathing in]. No [audibly breathing out]." OK.

CHARLIE ROSE: *"A better breathe."*
OPRAH WINFREY: "A better breathe. A better breathe. A better breathe."
[End excerpt from interview with Oprah Winfrey]

CHARLIE ROSE: *How fair are you, Mr. Demme?*
JONATHAN DEMME: Well—

CHARLIE ROSE: *Let me talk a little bit about the other characters here. You have the benefit of great, great actors.*
JONATHAN DEMME: Yes, indeed.

CHARLIE ROSE: *Danny Glover—you know more about their individual names than I do—*
JONATHAN DEMME: Well, Danny Glover, Beah Richards—

CHARLIE ROSE: *Yeah, who's fabulous as—*
JONATHAN DEMME: My God. And Kimberly Elise and Thandie Newton and Lisa Gay Hamilton, who plays the younger Sethe, and Albert Hall, who played Stamp Paid, who is one of the great, great, great American actors. I don't know if you remember him in *Malcolm X*, when Malcolm goes to prison and there's a guy who kinda sets him straight and tells him to clean up his act. That's Albert Hall. He's a chameleon. He a completely different guy every time you see him in a movie.

CHARLIE ROSE: *Was this experience different from other movie experiences?*

JONATHAN DEMME: The making of the movie was different, very much so, because again we had a crew that was—it turned out to be aggressively multiracial. And everybody there on the crew, certainly in the cast, just had very strong beliefs—a belief in the potential of racial harmony, about the upside of racial harmony and we felt that we were working on something that really had an opportunity to reflect things that we all cared passionately about. And we were in touch with that on a day by day basis.

CHARLIE ROSE: *This is a clip from the film, from* Beloved, *in which Danny Glover, playing the character Paul D, suggests moving, and Sethe says, "No," and then the house starts to shake. Take a look at this clip.*

[*Excerpt from film* Beloved]

SETHE (OPRAH WINFREY): *(comforting her sobbing daughter* **DENVER***)* It's all right.

PAUL D (DANNY GLOVER): Sethe, I'm a grown man, nothing new left to see or do. But I tell you it can't be easy, a young girl living in a haunted place. Maybe you oughta move.

SETHE: No. No movin'. No leavin'. It's all right the way it is. It's all right.

PAUL D: Don't tell me it's all right, Sethe. That child's half out of her mind.

SETHE: Hush up, D. I got a tree on my back and a haint in my house, and nothin' in between but the daughter I'm holdin' in my arms. No leavin'. No runnin'. No nothing.

DENVER (KIMBERLY ELISE): Get outa—

SETHE: I will never run from another thing on this earth. Go. You can sit down and eat. Or you can be—

[*End excerpt from film* Beloved]

JONATHAN DEMME: The house is haunted.

CHARLIE ROSE: *Yeah.*

JONATHAN DEMME: There are ghosts there. I love that about the movie. I love that. I believe in ghosts. Do you?

CHARLIE ROSE: *No. Do you, really?*

JONATHAN DEMME: I believe in spirits and inhabiting—

CHARLIE ROSE: *That inhabit?*

JONATHAN DEMME: Yeah, absolutely.

CHARLIE ROSE: *Where does that come from in you?*

JONATHAN DEMME: Well, I think one thing it comes from is, as life goes on and—I mean, my grandmother, who's been dead for many years—especially when I'm interacting with my kids—she's always in the room. And I know my parents who have died—their spirits are around. And—

CHARLIE ROSE: *Maybe it's a question of definition, then, because I think all of us carry our own experiences into whatever relationship, whatever we do or wherever we go. But I don't think of that as spirits as much as I think of that as just my history.*
JONATHAN DEMME: Right. Although I know—

CHARLIE ROSE: *They don't talk to me.*
JONATHAN DEMME: Mm-hmm [*affirmative*]. They don't?

CHARLIE ROSE: *Do they talk to you?*
JONATHAN DEMME: Yeah.

CHARLIE ROSE: *I don't think so. I don't know. And I think Oprah's exactly where you are. I mean, it talks to her.*
JONATHAN DEMME: You know, I think, having spent the time I have in Haiti helped open me up because—

CHARLIE ROSE: *I can imagine.*
JONATHAN DEMME: —in Haiti as in many cultures and, in fact, right here—the original Americans, the Native Americans, have days of celebration where the presence of the spirits is acknowledged—the whole idea of Day of the Dead, where you go to the cemetery, not so much to mourn and leave flowers as we tend to do in our culture, but to go and party with the spirits.

CHARLIE ROSE: *Commune.*
JONATHAN DEMME: And celebrate.

CHARLIE ROSE: *Yeah.*
JONATHAN DEMME: Yeah, and have a *good* time. I think there's a lot to be said—Are we thinking about our ancestors because we're thinking about them? Is that some kind of psychological mechanism or what have you? Or is there something all-pervasive about the human spirit which refuses to go away?

CHARLIE ROSE: *Is it surprising that Jonathan Demme became a filmmaker?*
JONATHAN DEMME: Yeah. I became a filmmaker really through a series of flukes. I adored movies so much as a kid right away. I remember seeing my first scene from a Hopalong Cassidy movie on my first encounter with a

television set and being instantly hooked. And then seeing movies like *Treasure Island* and just going all the time and all the time. And somehow or other I'd wanted to be a veterinarian, but I bombed out of chemistry and I wound up writing movie reviews for the college paper.

CHARLIE ROSE: Yeah. But here's what they said about you—or what has been said about you—is that you kept a notebook. That you, between the first movie you saw all the way through college, every movie you kept a little personal review as to when you saw it, who you saw it with, and what the movie was about and whether you liked it or not.

JONATHAN DEMME: And a star rating, too, Charlie.

CHARLIE ROSE: *And a star rating.*

JONATHAN DEMME: You've been digging deep, haven't you?

CHARLIE ROSE: *Well, we've got some other stuff we want to talk about. So, you get out—you start making movie reviews. Your father is a publicist. Yes?*

JONATHAN DEMME: Yes, at the Fontainebleau Hotel in Miami Beach.

CHARLIE ROSE: *And then Big Joe Levine comes down there from Embassy Pictures. And your father introduces you, and then you show him a review of his film,* Zulu. *Is that a fair story?*

JONATHAN DEMME: Well, Mr. Levine told my dad, "Oh, if your son's a critic, tell him to bring his reviews to the houseboat," which was moored across the street from the hotel. And I showed up one day with my little scrapbook of clippings. And he's flipping through, and I had favorably reviewed *Zulu*. And he—literally with a cigar in hand, poking—told me, "You got good taste, kid."

CHARLIE ROSE: *"If you like my movie, you got good taste."*

JONATHAN DEMME: "You should come work with me." That's right. And I went into the service for a while, came out, and called up. And he gave me a job. And suddenly I was working in the movie business, which was ridiculous. I couldn't believe that I could actually have a job there.

CHARLIE ROSE: *But there was no dream to be a director, was there?*

JONATHAN DEMME: None whatsoever.

CHARLIE ROSE: *You were very happy to be a publicist?*

JONATHAN DEMME: Oh, yeah. I loved it. And then I met Roger Corman, and he was starting New World Pictures. And he needed scripts, and Roger said to me, "Well, Jonathan, you write these press releases and this production material. Why don't you write—"

CHARLIE ROSE: *"You could clearly write this—"*
JONATHAN DEMME: *"—a motorcycle movie?"* So, I teamed up with my friend Joe Viola, who was the greatest storyteller I had ever met, and we wrote a script, and we showed it to Roger. And he said, "This is pretty good. Joe, you direct commercials, right?" And Joe said, "Yeah." "Jonathan—I'll tell you what. Joe, you direct it. Jonathan, you can produce it."

CHARLIE ROSE: *This is great.*
JONATHAN DEMME: So, suddenly at like twenty-four years old or something like that, we're off to California to make our motorcycle movie.

CHARLIE ROSE: *Corman's great genius is he gave guys like you a chance for hands-on experience.*
JONATHAN DEMME: Well, that's one of his great geniuses. I mean, Roger is truly one of the most extraordinary, amazing, great guys that you could ever come across.

CHARLIE ROSE: *What makes him that?*
JONATHAN DEMME: You know, it's the Oprah Winfrey thing, I think, a little bit. He's got tremendous enthusiasm and also a big ego and a desire to succeed. And I love about Roger—one of the many things, 'cause he's so quotable. And one thing he always used to tell the new directors when you'd start out with him—he'd say, "You know, now listen. As a director, you're 40, 45 percent artist and 60, 55 percent businessman. Never forget that. You've got to be a businessman. People are gonna invest money in your movies, and you've got to repay that investment. And, as soon as you get—"

CHARLIE ROSE: *And that's where you learned that maxim.*
JONATHAN DEMME: And he said, "As soon as you let the arty part get carried away, you're gonna find yourself out of work."

CHARLIE ROSE: *When* Silence of the Lambs *came to you, did you have some sense that this movie was gonna become what it did? I mean, did you know because of the Hopkins performance or because of Jodie's performance, because of the script that you had there, that this had all the potential to be one of the classic American films the way it is?*
JONATHAN DEMME: I knew it had the potential to be a splendid movie. I knew that Ted Tally had written an exceptional script from a great, great, great, great book. Tom Harris is such an extraordinary writer. And I knew we had a great cast. And I knew Tak Fujimoto was gonna work his magic and everybody was gonna do their thing. I was confident we were gonna have a terrific picture. But, you know, when you're making these things, all you

know is that—all I know is the one thing that my movies have in common is I've always been really excited by their potential as movies and a belief that, if we can make a movie that winds up exciting other people as much as the potential of it excites me maybe it'll be contagious.

CHARLIE ROSE: *You'll make another sequel to that? To* Silence of the Lambs?
JONATHAN DEMME: Well, Tom—

CHARLIE ROSE: *Not "sequel." Maybe that's the wrong word, but—*
JONATHAN DEMME: Thomas Harris is writing a new book. He's been working on it a long time. I'm hoping that it's gonna be finished, you know, at some point before too long. And I'm very much hoping to have an opportunity—I know nothing about it. We believe that Dr. Lecter is a character. We believe Clarice Starling is a character. By the way, we believe that because we *want* to believe it. Thomas Harris does not talk about his work in progress. But, if he has done a new story featuring those characters, I think it's unlikely it'll be anything remotely like a straight sequel. I think he'll probably kinda go over there with it or something or other. I just can't imagine—

CHARLIE ROSE: *And you're prepared to make it?*
JONATHAN DEMME: Oh, I'm dying to make it.

CHARLIE ROSE: *Because?*
JONATHAN DEMME: Because I love those characters. And it was in its way an incredibly thrilling world to inhabit. And I love the idea of—You know, it goes back once again—sometimes people ask me, "Well, what's the common link in your movies?" or what have you. The only common link in the movies for me is that I have loved the source material, and I've loved the source material because it's been, in my view, beautifully written.

And whether that's the humor of *Married to the Mob* for me or the extraordinary human tapestry of *Beloved* or what Ron Nyswaner was wanting to say with his script for *Philadelphia* or Thomas Harris's vision of a certain kind of America here as we approach the millennium, the writing has been exceptional.

And, you know, when you make a movie, you've got to live with these things for two years if you're the director. It's a long process, and it's got to continue to feed you and got to continue to interest you in order to be able to really deliver something worthy of all that effort. So, anyway, I'd like to direct whatever Tom Harris wrote next time, whatever it is—

CHARLIE ROSE: *Hopkins is ready to go, too, isn't he?*
JONATHAN DEMME: Yeah, I believe so.

CHARLIE ROSE: *I think he is. I think he's said—*
JONATHAN DEMME: And I believe Jodie is as well. I mean, we're all in makeup. I'll put it that way, but we've learned to be patient and—

CHARLIE ROSE: *Why so much time between movies for you?* Philadelphia *was 1993.*
JONATHAN DEMME: Well, really, there's I guess two things. One—like I was just saying, the search for material that I can believe I can make into a successful movie, a movie that'll both interest me and have the opportunity to reach the kind of audience that we hope *Beloved* reaches, is one thing. And also, Charlie, I'm a late-starting daddy. I've got three kids. And, you know, what am I gonna do this afternoon? Am I gonna go to the office? Or am I gonna try to get involved with these youngsters? I've got plenty to do if I'm not making a movie. And again, you know, the search for a script is a big, big, arduous task.

CHARLIE ROSE: *Why is that so hard? There are so many stories, you would think, to tell. And the script is so crucial that what—I mean, why are there so few good scripts, I guess? And whenever you see one—frequently, not in this case—well, no. Yes, in this case, in part because Richard had to go off and make his own movie.*
JONATHAN DEMME: Right.

CHARLIE ROSE: *You had some additional work done on the script. Correct?*
JONATHAN DEMME: Oh, a lot. Adam Brooks came in. And we worked together on dozens of drafts. It's just—you're trying to shoehorn a lot into your running time. I don't know. I don't read that many books. Are there lots and lots of terrific books? Or are most of them flawed significantly in one way or the other?

CHARLIE ROSE: *I think there are more terrific books than there are movie scripts.*
JONATHAN DEMME: Right.

CHARLIE ROSE: *Evidently—you know?*
JONATHAN DEMME: But, again, you know, it's funny, I want to reference *Rush Hour* again, which I saw and enjoyed to the hilt on Friday night. It was a wonderful screenplay. Was it written for Jackie Chan and Chris Tucker? I don't know 'cause they're part—And also maybe there are a lot of great scripts that didn't have the right casting, and I know there's a lot of terrific casts out there waiting for the right script. You can see that all over the—

CHARLIE ROSE: *And a lot of talented performers.*

JONATHAN DEMME: Yeah, a lot. I mean, we've got such an incredible array of acting talent available, and these scripts are very—It's hard. And you know why? I think, also another thing is there's certainly the financial imperative involved with making these movies. You know? They're expensive. They cost, most of 'em, a million and up. And a lot of people—

CHARLIE ROSE: *Way up.*

JONATHAN DEMME: Way, way up. And a lot of people wind up getting their—their—their fingerprints all over what a script would be to reassure themselves that it's gonna make money. And that often means making it as much like previous things that have done well as possible. This is a sad old song, but it's true. So, you wind up, I think, you know—it's not as though we don't have a lot of gifted writers. We've just got an awful lot of people—

CHARLIE ROSE: *Nervous executives.*

JONATHAN DEMME: Executives, producers, filmmakers, actors, everybody.

CHARLIE ROSE: *Right, right. You also like documentaries.*

JONATHAN DEMME: I love 'em. Yeah.

CHARLIE ROSE: *You've made a documentary about Talking Heads, didn't you?*

JONATHAN DEMME: Well, I'd like to think of that as a rockumentary—

CHARLIE ROSE: *Performance, yeah. OK, a rockumentary.*

JONATHAN DEMME: It was a performance film. I've made some documentaries. I've made a couple in Haiti. I've made one about my cousin, Robert Castle, who's an Episcopalian minister and a big troublemaker up on 126th Street in New York City.

CHARLIE ROSE: *Yeah. Can you imagine not making movies? I mean, what would you do if you didn't make movies?*

JONATHAN DEMME: Open a bookstore. I could do that. Maybe even open a movie theater and show movies. But I love making films, and—

CHARLIE ROSE: *The joy is what?*

JONATHAN DEMME: One of the joys is getting together with a whole community of extraordinarily gifted people and pooling your ideas and your efforts together with a collective goal of making something extremely special for people to look at. It's very exciting—what goes on on these movie sets. I mean, it's just people who are phenomenal at what they do.

CHARLIE ROSE: *With a shared passion.*

JONATHAN DEMME: Yeah.

CHARLIE ROSE: *Yeah, it's great to have you here [crosstalk], Jonathan.*
JONATHAN DEMME: Thank you. It's wonderful to be here.

CHARLIE ROSE: *Thank you, Jonathan Demme. The movie is* Beloved. *Oprah Winfrey and an extraordinary cast of people, based on Toni Morrison's—as all of you know, Pulitzer Prize–winning novel, a story set in Cincinnati in 1873 with flashbacks to both the horror of slavery, and it is about ghosts. It's about sacrifices for love. It's about so many subjects that are common to the human experience.* Beloved, *the film; Jonathan Demme, the director.*

A Young Director Tells a Veteran How He Did It

ROB SCHMIDT AND JONATHAN DEMME / 2000

JONATHAN DEMME, the Oscar-winning director of *The Silence of the Lambs*, was at this year's Sundance Film Festival, where he saw *Crime + Punishment in Suburbia*. He was so intrigued by the film that he thought it would be interesting to talk with Rob Schmidt, the film's director.

Schmidt, thirty-four, a graduate of the American Film Institute, had previously directed *Saturn*, which premiered at the 1999 Los Angeles Independent Film Festival. *Crime + Punishment in Suburbia* is Schmidt's second feature film.

Demme, 55, who is based in New York, spoke with Schmidt in Los Angeles by phone this week. Here are some excerpts from their conversation.

JONATHAN DEMME: *What relationship does the film have to Dostoevsky's novel?*
ROB SCHMIDT: *Crime + Punishment in Suburbia* is a really loose adaptation. It doesn't have the same characters but the theme is intact. The main character kills a terrible person, conceals the crime, is consumed by it, suffers secretly, confesses, and in a spiritual way is reborn. It's just that it takes place in a California high school instead of Siberia.

DEMME: *I'm really curious about how all this started. Can you tell me anything about the life of this movie, the creative process and the casting?*
SCHMIDT: About ten years ago, Larry Gross wrote this script, and it sort of languished for a while. The idea was to make a B-movie high school flick but make it secretly about God and redemption, and it wasn't until there was the run of high school movies that people began to buy the idea of it.

From the *Los Angeles Times* (September 15, 2000), F14–15.

Then, at about that same time, Mark Waters, who directed *The House of Yes*, handed the script off to me because he had a feeling I'd like it. I loved it and I took it to Christine Vachon, one of the producers of *Boys Don't Cry*, and she agreed to produce it. Ellen Barkin, who plays the main character's mother, was the first actor to come on board and that paved the way for Michael Ironside, Monica Keena, who I'd seen when she was very young in a tiny indie [film] called *Ripe*, and Vincent Kartheiser, who astounded me in *Another Day in Paradise*. I was lucky enough to cast Jeffrey Wright before he got his roles in *Ride with the Devil* and *Shaft*. It was actually very easy to set up after ten hard years for Larry.

DEMME: *The original title of the movie was* Crime and Punishment in High School. *Why the change?*
SCHMIDT: I really loved that title and the idea was that the film would be marketed as a B high school movie. But a few weeks before we started to shoot, the Columbine massacre happened, and people's perception and sensitivity of teen violence in this country changed. Ultimately the movie was retitled because the studio wanted to take attention away from the violence, rather than explore it.

DEMME: *You've got an incredibly excruciating murder scene worthy of Alfred Hitchcock. This violence isn't "fun"—you reveal the true horror of it. The movie has an R rating, which of course makes it a marketing challenge. Do you feel there is also a moral challenge in the R rating?*
SCHMIDT: I feel that one of the main themes of the film is that kids are taught that violence is a solution, but it isn't, it devastates them. That kind of fantasizing alienates people from themselves, and I thought the movie was very responsible in the way it intrinsically portrayed violence as a bad thing. In Italy the movie was rated "14 and over." The film board made an exception because of the purpose of the film's violence. The point of the movie is that violence wreaks havoc in every direction.

DEMME: *I've seen some of your earlier work, and present in that as well as this movie is a very tough, unsentimental approach to human nature, but you also display tremendous heart and great humanity through your characters. Is that what attracted you to* Crime + Punishment in Suburbia *in the first place, a chance to bring an unflinching, humanistic vision to the table?*
SCHMIDT: I try to approach movies by loving the characters and I try to understand them as people. If they do vicious things, I want to understand why. In particular with this movie, I grew up in suburbia and I really hated it, I detested it.

I felt very alone there, particularly as a high school kid. When I read the script, I thought it was an opportunity to make a movie for disenfranchised kids, and by being hard-nosed about people in that world, I hope that kids will feel like they're witnessing something they know, not some counterfeit model of it. So really my goal was to make something for the disenfranchised teenagers of America.

DEMME: *Of all ages.*
SCHMIDT: Including myself at thirty-four.

DEMME: *And even I, another couple decades down the line. . . . I understand that there was some pressure to remove all references to God from the movie?*
SCHMIDT: At one point Larry Gross and I had a "Is God really necessary?" meeting at the studio, but they eventually decided it was OK. I don't know how we could have made Crime + Punishment in Suburbia without the concept of God, because that's the gift at the end, the blooming of faith and the chance of a new life. If the film has a gift, it is spirituality and hope.

DEMME: *Do you believe in God?*
SCHMIDT: I hope to believe more. I pray a tiny bit in the morning and I pray at night, to say thank you. That's pretty much the extent of the spirituality in my life. It's different in the movies, because you can create a world where there is no question that God exists, that's one of my favorite things about film and fiction.

DEMME: *One of the things that I loved about the picture was that I felt right from the opening sequence that here's a filmmaker, like Hitchcock, [Sam] Fuller, and Paul Thomas Anderson, who is literally experimenting with film and making it work. Do you experiment?*
SCHMIDT: I always try to work with people who love experimenting, because it's one of my favorite things in the movies when people take risks and do strange things. I've worked with two really great cinematographers, Matthew Libatique and Bobby Bukowski, and they were both ready to push and pull film, put a camera on a dolly but use it hand-held and use still photographer lenses at the risk of everything being out of focus.

This movie was the first time I got to work with sound a lot, and I discovered all these things I never realized you could do with surround sound and rumble tracks to make the audience feel the character's emotions. For example, there is a pep rally scene in the movie and we wanted to create a very frightening place out of the familiar, create a world where harm could be done to the viewer, so we underlaid elements from the Nuremberg rally, even a track of Hitler.

The Onion A.V. Club Interview: Jonathan Demme

SCOTT TOBIAS / 2002

ONE OF Roger Corman's star apprentices, Jonathan Demme was a critic and publicist before he got involved with the legendary producer's New World Pictures, where he wrote and produced such lowdown fare as 1971's *Angels Hard As They Come* and 1972's *Black Mama, White Mama*. Demme's quirky humanist touch was evident in his directorial debut, the 1974 women-in-prison classic *Caged Heat*, which brought humor, warmth, and a surprisingly progressive attitude to a sordid subgenre. But his critical and commercial breakthrough came in 1980, with the masterpiece *Melvin and Howard*, which turned the life of Howard Hughes beneficiary Melvin Dummar into a rich slice of Americana. Demme stumbled with the 1984 Hollywood comedy *Swing Shift*, which was notoriously mistreated and recut by Warner Bros., reportedly at the insistence of star Goldie Hawn. But he rebounded the same year with the groundbreaking Talking Heads concert film *Stop Making Sense*, the first of his superb performance documentaries, which also include 1987's *Swimming to Cambodia* (on Spalding Gray) and 1998's *Storefront Hitchcock* (on Robyn Hitchcock). Demme finished the eighties with two flavorful mid-budget comedies, 1986's *Something Wild* and 1988's *Married to the Mob*, but neither anticipated the scope and cultural impact of his work in the following decade. An unlikely choice to adapt Thomas Harris's grisly serial-killer thriller *The Silence of the Lambs*, Demme steered the 1991 project to enormous success, but his next major film, 1993's *Philadelphia*, invited controversy from all sides by being the first big studio movie to openly address the AIDS crisis. Demme returned to adaptation in 1998 with his faithful rendering of Toni Morrison's *Beloved*. His latest project, *The Truth about Charlie*,

From the *The Onion* (October 23, 2002). Reprinted by permission of Scott Tobias.

is a remake of *Charade*, a classically elegant 1963 thriller that paired Audrey Hepburn with Cary Grant. Thandie Newton stars as a young American in Paris who's beset by thieves and secret agents when her mysterious husband is killed, leaving a hidden fortune behind. *The Onion* A.V. Club recently spoke to Demme about the Corman years, the French New Wave, and making movies for mass consumption.

THE ONION: *How did you come to work for Roger Corman? How did you convince him to give you a chance to direct a film?*
JONATHAN DEMME: I was a publicist back in those days for United Artists, and they needed a unit publicist for a picture that Roger was going to direct called *Von Richthofen and Brown* [later known as 1971's *The Red Baron* —ed.]. I got the job, and as fate would have it, this was the exact moment in time when Roger was forming New World Pictures. This movie was being shot in Ireland, and he was desperately in need of scripts set in America. And there I was, this young American in Ireland. I remember him saying, "You write pretty good press material. Perhaps you could write a script for me." [*Laughs.*] So I teamed up with my friend Joe Viola, who was a commercial director, and we basically took *Rashomon* and rewrote it as a motorcycle movie. We showed it to Roger, who said to us, "Well, this is pretty good. Joe, you direct commercials. Jonathan, you're a bright young man. Why don't you guys come over and direct and produce it?" Three months later, I was in California, making my first movie [*Angels Hard As They Come*]. It was never something I aspired to do, but he offered me that opportunity.

O: *People always talk about the experience as attending the "Roger Corman School of Filmmaking." What were the most important things you learned from him?*
JD: He gave you kind of a visual credo—the importance of imaginative editing and imaginative camerawork in order to keep the eye involved, because if you lose the viewer's eye, you're going to lose the viewer's interest. He also stressed the importance of having as many characters as possible that are in every way just as interesting as your main characters, even if they get less screen time. He had his tried-and-true formula for audience success, which was equal parts action, sex, and comedy, with a little bit of social commentary thrown in for good measure, preferably from the left side of the coin.

O: *How do you direct actors?*
JD: I choose actors who are guaranteed to take full responsibility for their characters. Then I act as their accomplice, or guide, through the shooting of the story. I'm not a puppetmaster. I'm a collaborator. I don't like to rehearse

in advance. I like to rehearse for the first time on the set, with the cameras rolling, because I believe in the potential of first discovery being the most magical take of any particular moment. And I have a lot of fun working with actors. I love it.

O: *Does your philosophy about responsibility extend to other collaborators?*
JD: Oh, absolutely. I need to know that everyone I'm involved with on a project is smarter and more imaginative than me in their given area.

O: *Your films often have a lot of memorable faces on the fringes. Could you talk about the casting process, particularly how you cast the smaller roles?*
JD: When we cast *The Truth about Charlie*, for example, we hired a casting director in France. But instead of casting specific people for specific parts, I requested that for my first two weeks in France, I wanted the casting director to bring her favorite actors in. These actors had to be willing to come in for a general meeting, with no particular part in mind, just so I could see what a lot of people looked like and when they would be available. As I met people, I started making notes to have such-and-such an actor come back to read for such-and-such a part. In two instances, actors came in, and I liked them so much that I actually invented parts for them. The French commandant's mustachioed sidekick . . . there was no such character in the script. But I met Simon Abkarian, that actor, and I was so galvanized by his presence that I asked if he would participate in a fun experiment: If he could show up for every scene that the commandant was in, we would find a nice place for him in that scene. Over the course of the film, hopefully we could develop a very interesting character. The other made-up role was the Mysterious Woman in Black, the widow, which didn't exist in the script and which is an even more difficult character to explain. But I met Magali Noël, who is a woman of extraordinary radiance and presence, someone we recognize from many Fellini movies and from *Rififi*, and who's been a well-established stage and screen actor for about sixty years in France. So I met her and was completely enchanted by her, and felt that it would be wonderful to have a character in the story by which we could judge Thandie's progress to finding the truth about Charlie.

O: *Your work is so strongly associated with the American landscape that* The Truth about Charlie *seems like a bit of a curveball. How much did you know about Paris when you started shooting?*
JD: Probably 80 to 90 percent of my impressions of Paris entering the picture came from a lifetime of watching French movies. [*Laughs.*] In that regard, *The Truth about Charlie* is an opportunity for me to acknowledge the

incredibly important part that French movies have played in my moviegoing life. My parents, God bless 'em, took me to French movies when I was a little kid. Even at seven or eight, they'd take me to movies like *Mr. Hulot's Holiday*. During my brief moment in college, I discovered New Wave films and devoured years and years of the stuff. There was a period of my life when I was obsessed with Brigitte Bardot. I had a relationship with her. I missed Brigitte Bardot between Brigitte Bardot movies the way one misses a live person that you've got a crush on. All of these transitions of my life were marked with attachments to different kinds of French movies. So once I got over there, I was confronted with the "real" Paris of today, which is tremendously stimulating—it's as visual a city as exists anywhere. But also, the picture became a receptacle for all this love I have for French cinema and French culture and French folkways as perceived through the movies. [*Laughs.*]

O: *The film has a complicated storyline, but the style seems very on-the-fly and New Wave–influenced, as you say. Was it difficult for you to find that balance?*
JD: The way we approached shooting the picture was very much off-the-cuff in a certain sense. However, aspects of the visual side of the film, especially as it pertains to the presentation of the past, were scrupulously designed up front in concert with the cameraman, the production designer, a terrific French storyboard artist, a costume designer. . . . An enormous amount of work went into how we were going to present the past, and this fundamental choice of shooting all the past in digital, so we could make a textual distinction between people's memories of events as they might have happened and the so-called reality of the present. But we did shoot very off-the-cuff, because we wanted to have a freewheeling, New Wave style. I enjoy that as a consumer. I love that approach, and I think it's underexploited when it comes to more mainstream projects. In terms of the complicated story, one of the differences between *The Truth about Charlie* and *Charade* is that our film chooses to give more screen time to the past, and even [Newton's character's] dead husband Charlie, who in the original is only seen once as a body tumbling off the train at the very beginning. Not even at his open-casket funeral, which is one of the classic scenes. . . . It was one of the scenes in the original film that was so great, we couldn't begin to know how to redo it. That's the interesting thing about remaking a great picture: You find yourself saying, "No, we can't do that. It was too perfect. We have to do something different here." [*Laughs.*] We took a different approach to the cadaver, and we took a different approach to the orange-passing scene, which turns into a tango in our movie. Instead of seeing Cary Grant take a shower in his suit, we get to see Thandie Newton take a shower with no suit. [*Laughs.*]

O: *Both the editing and the music cues are a lot more rapid-fire than your past work.*

JD: I was really inspired by three pictures: *Run Lola Run*, Doug Liman's *Go*, and a Chinese movie called *Suzhou River*. I wanted to emulate the energy of certain pictures that had turned me on in many regards. I had the desire to tell a complicated story at a fast pace, which can be really entertaining. Also, our first cut of the film was mu-u-u-ch longer and contained a mu-u-u-ch more complicated story, told at a more traditional pace. In the editing, [editor] Carol Littleton and I would look at the movie and keep saying, "That's good, but it just ain't fast enough." We were allowing people a little too much time to think about this stuff. Finally, we arrived at what seemed to be the most exciting tempo for the movie. I also wanted it to have the feeling of a rock concert. We had an enormous amount of music, a lot of it rhythm-driven, in the movie. In the cutting room, I started to think of the story like a concert, which builds in momentum, then finds a place for a slower number, and then builds up again in intensity.

O: *Since this is a major studio film, do you still have to go through the test-screening process?*

JD: I think it would be foolish not to. This is intended to be a mass-consumption movie. It's a corporate product that's been designed, ultimately, to cater to "the masses." So we extensively tested it with preview audiences and learned a lot from that process. We did show a longer version in three situations, and it played okay, but it clearly had some areas that we liked more than the audience did. I have final cut, so in theory, I could put out any version I want. But I want a lot of people to see the movie, and one terrific way of finding out how much folks are going to like it is to show it to recruited audiences. So I embrace that part of the process very much.

O: *In your adaptations of books like* Beloved *or* The Silence of the Lambs, *how do you remain faithful to the material while still asserting your personality? Where do you get the impulse to bring these books to film?*

JD: I don't necessarily think it's the filmmaker's job to assert their personality. It's going to be reflected one way or another by how they choose to adapt it. I loved both of those books. I thought *The Silence of the Lambs* was an absolutely brilliant book. The easiest way for me to understand the huge success of the movie starts with what a great book Thomas Harris wrote to begin with. He created those characters for Jodie Foster and Anthony Hopkins and Ted Levine to bring to life. As a filmmaker, I had the delicious job of being the moviegoing audience's representative at the place where the film version was now going to happen. Of course, I had my own ideas about the strengths of the book and how best to visualize them for the screen. Same thing with *Beloved*. In *Beloved*, there was zero invention: We didn't have to fix anything in the book, no gaping holes, no problems that had to be solved. The film is very faithful to the book, because we were all so inspired by the book that we simply transferred that inspiration to the screen. *Silence of the Lambs* was essentially the same situation, except for the ending. Thomas Harris ended the book in a very meditative, poetic sort of way. This being a movie, we needed something a little bit more galvanizing as a sign-off, so we came up with the phone call and a glimpse of Dr. Lecter following Dr. Chilton off into the Caribbean sunset.

O: *In the past, you've been heavily involved in Haiti, both in appreciating its cultural richness and in exposing its human-rights abuses. Are you still active there?*
JD: I just finished cutting a documentary I've been working on for years called *The Agronomist*. It's a portrait of a great Haitian radio journalist and human-rights activist named Jean Dominique, who was assassinated on the steps of his radio station on April 3, 2000. He's a guy I met when I was making another documentary back in the eighties, and we became very good friends. When he was in exile in New York, I used to do extended video sessions with him, in which he'd tell his life story and the story of Haiti. After he was assassinated, I went back down in May of 2000 and shot a lot of footage with his family and friends, and I had been working on shaping this portrait of him while making *The Truth about Charlie*. His murder hasn't been solved yet. Incidentally, the police commandant in the film is named Jean Dominique, and the lieutenant with the mustache I told you about earlier is named Lt. Dessalines in honor of Jean-Jacques Dessalines, who was one of the great revolutionary heroes of Haiti. So my connection to Haiti remains very active. [*Laughs.*]

An Interview with Jonathan Demme

THEAGRONOMIST.COM/2004

Q: *How did you meet Jean Dominique, and when did you decide to shoot a documentary about his life?*
DEMME: I originally became interested in Haitian art and music through a store in Manhattan near my home called Haitian Corner. I decided to visit Haiti in 1986 and fell in love with the country and the Haitian people. I was so inspired by the growing democracy movement that was exploding in the wake of the collapse of the Duvalier dictatorship, that I made a documentary called *Haiti: Dreams of Democracy*. While making that film, everyone encouraged me to go to Radio Haiti Inter and talk to Jean and Michèle. I did, and some of that footage of them on the air is in *The Agronomist*.

In 1993, after the coup that toppled the democratically elected government of Jean-Bertrand Aristide, I learned that Jean and Michèle were in exile in New York. I wanted to get to know this man who I had briefly met and been so impressed with his passion and intelligence and dramatic flair. I called him and with the flimsy excuse of wanting to make a documentary about a journalist in exile, began videotaping conversations with him about Haiti, the coup, his life, the radio station, and anything else that came to his mind. We did this periodically over the course of a little more than a year, and then Jean returned to Haiti after Aristide returned. With all the complications of restoring the radio station to working order, dealing with an occupied country trying to get back on track towards democracy, and everything else in his and my life, we never finished this small film about a journalist in exile.

When Jean was assassinated April 3, 2000, the only response to the anguish and anger of losing such a dear friend and extraordinary man was

---

From TheAgronomist.com., temporary movie promotion.

to finish the film. Now it was a much bigger story about his life, his marriage and partnership with Michèle Montas, the radio station and about the country to which he dedicated his life and work and which he affected so deeply.

Q: *Could you be precise about the sources of the images? How many interviews? When did they take place, etc.? Where is the TV footage of political events coming from? Etc.*

DEMME: We interviewed Jean fifteen to twenty times between 1993 and his return in 1994. The interviews all took place in New York City and in nearby Rockland County, New York. In addition to the interviews with Jean there is material included in the film from many different archival sources including news agencies and libraries around the world as well as documentaries about Haiti and two dramatic Haitian films: *Mais, je suis belle* and *Anita*.

Q: *For you, what was most striking in Jean Dominique's attitude? His perseverance, his strong sense of justice, or something else?*

DEMME: Jean Dominique and Michèle Montas are extraordinary examples of what individuals can accomplish by sticking to their principles with bravery, perseverance, and a commitment to helping people. Jean was also extremely dramatic, smart, funny, entertaining, and wonderful to spend time with. Michèle is all of those things in her own way.

Q: *The movie is critical about U.S. government attitude towards Haiti. Have things changed? Grown better or worse?*

DEMME: I didn't set out to make a film critical of U.S. policy in Haiti. I set out to make a film about a man whose life story happens to encompass much of the recent history of Haiti. A history that is inexorably intertwined with the United States. Jean spoke bluntly about what was apparent to him as the truth.

Q: *Your filmography is extremely varied: fiction, nonfiction, musical performance films, and so on. How do you choose between these genres? Are you less interested in fiction than before?*

DEMME: I love making documentaries and I love making narrative dramatic films and I love going back and forth between fiction and nonfiction. In one form you get to create a whole world and the people in it from imagination and the collaboration of lots of other artists. In the other you get to tell a real story with the person who lived it. I can't imagine having to choose one over the other.

Q: *Since the success of Michael Moore's films, it seems that documentaries are growing in popularity. Do you agree? Would you say documentaries can, in some way, change reality?*
DEMME: I think there has always been an enthusiastic audience for documentaries. Recently there have been an awful lot of really fantastic theatrical documentaries that have been successful. I think a lot of documentaries are best suited to television and some are made with a theatrical audience in mind. When there are good theatrical films with dedicated distributors behind them, audiences find them.

Q: *Do you have a personal involvement in the human rights movement apart from your movies?*
DEMME: I tend to speak out about what I believe in and I believe in justice and human rights for all people. As an American citizen, I exercise my right to free speech along with most other Americans, and when I think that my government is doing things that are harmful to folks at home or in other countries, I feel compelled to stand up and say that I think it's wrong and that this is not what I want the government that represents me to do.

Q: *Could you write a few words about the music in the film? Who are these musicians, and what is your involvement with Haitian music?*
DEMME: If you spend any time in Haiti, it is impossible to avoid the infectious music which is such a part of everyday life for everyone. Music imbued with the beat of its African roots and steeped in the traditions of the Vodoun religion makes itself known everywhere you go. From traditional Compas to Ra-Ra to Vaccine to contemporary pop, music is as much a part of expressing yourself in Haiti as anything else.

Wyclef Jean is one of the great musical geniuses of our time, using his talent to become one of the biggest hip-hop stars in the world. He is also deeply attached and committed to his homeland of Haiti. Along with Jerry "Wonder" Duplessis, Wyclef composed an original score to the film inspired by the story and his love of Haiti. He also contributed four original songs from his upcoming Creole language album, *Welcome to Haiti*.

Q: *Did you ever feel threatened during the making of this movie?*
DEMME: No. The Haitian people are by and large very friendly and very interested in folks from other countries who come to visit theirs. There has been a lot of violence in Haiti—they have endured a disproportionate amount of abuse and exploitation and with that has come a disproportionate amount of violence, but every country contends with violence—but there is almost no history of violence against Americans. The only time that there

was a question of security was after Jean was killed: we accompanied Michèle around Port-Au-Prince, and it was necessary for her to have an armed security detail with her. That brought home to us the danger that she was in, and it was unsettling to be in the presence of so many guns, but we never felt personally threatened.

Film-makers on Film: Jonathan Demme on Jared Hess's *Napoleon Dynamite*

SHEILA JOHNSTON / 2004

"WHEN I FOUND OUT about this column, it sounded like fun," says the immensely enthusiastic Jonathan Demme. "I was racking my brains for a film to talk about and seized pretty quickly on Bernardo Bertolucci's *The Conformist*, a masterpiece which I have stolen from shamelessly again and again."

Demme wanted to watch *The Conformist* again before we met, but, like so many other classics, it proved unobtainable on video or DVD. Fortunately he had another title up his sleeve, one he has seen no fewer than four times this year. It is *Napoleon Dynamite*, a no-budget teen comedy which opens here on Friday.

Has the director gone from the sublime to the ridiculous? Crisply dismissed by the American trade paper *Variety* as "an absurdist piece about a rural community of clueless cretins . . . bottom dwellers doing stupid things that make them look even more idiotic," this film divided audiences and critics violently at its world premiere in Sundance.

"From a strictly cinematic point of view, the film is, as they say in French, nul, a void, a zero," said *Variety*'s Todd McCarthy.

"So that's what the top dwellers who write reviews had to say. How very interesting," says Demme, sixty, glimmering with sarcasm. "To me, *Napoleon Dynamite* reflects an extremely bold vision, so bold that it alienates some of our august critics. It has enriched my life and brought joy and pleasure into my household."

He was first turned on to it by Denzel Washington, the star of his own latest film, a remake of *The Manchurian Candidate*. "We were talking last summer,

---

From the *Daily Telegraph* (November 29, 2004). Reprinted by permission of Telegraph Media Group Limited.

and I asked what movie his kids liked at the moment. He said, 'They're obsessed with this film called Napoleon Something.' I said, 'My kids love that movie too.'

"I'm not sure if I would have paid it any attention—it's rated PG [in both the U.S. and U.K.], which is the kiss of death. But I found myself intrigued because Denzel's kids had gone back to it again; it's one of those repeat movies. So I went to see it and just fell in love with it."

Unconnected to Elvis Costello (who once used the name as a pseudonym), *Napoleon Dynamite* is centred on two misfits from small-town Idaho, the ginger-frizzed, buck-toothed Napoleon and his even geekier elder brother, Kip. "Their performances are so vividly etched and fully realised that you wonder, 'Was there a script?'" Demme says.

"Every shot is very simply but carefully composed. The cuts to an incoming scene often begin with a straight-on, proscenium shot of somebody set against the neighbourhood, a little in the style of Bill Owens, a photographer who went into the suburbs in the 1960s and '70s and did portraits of working-class people. Much of the film occurs in impersonal houses and these barren, unappealing landscapes with the same desolation that the characters are experiencing within themselves."

However, after some humiliating misadventures, both brothers begin relationships which transform their lives. Napoleon teams up with a new kid at school, while Kip meets the bootylicious LaFawnduh through an internet chat room. "They live in this all-white community, but the guy Napoleon befriends is Mexican and the profoundly irritating Kip just blossoms the moment LaFawnduh, a black woman, steps off the bus.

"It never stops being hilarious, it never starts being remotely sappy, but it's beautiful to watch them emerge out of their little world. I don't think it's patronising. Then, having endured their painful struggle to expand their lives, all the characters are rewarded with a blissfully funny montage of redemption.

"I love the score, too. There's wall-to-wall music of well-chosen pop and a sort of organ music for semi-hopeful moments. I can imagine someone describing it as rinky-dink but it's smartly emotional."

Directed by a twenty-four-year-old first-timer, Jared Hess, *Napoleon Dynamite* confounded reviewers by becoming a cult hit in the States. Five months after it opened there in June, it is still playing in cinemas, and a postscript has been shot for the DVD. "It takes the notion of the happy ending into the ozone," Demme says. "When you talk about the film, it all sounds so serious, but the whole point is that this is an escapist, fun movie."

It's refreshing and surprising to hear a director endorse a film so far on the fringe of the critical canon, and with such modesty. "What I loved as an audience member and was in awe of as a filmmaker was its endless originality. My own recent films have been well-budgeted, super-equipped Hollywood movies, and I've been hearing myself say for years that I would love to make a much more daring, idiosyncratic feature.

"For anyone who wishes to do something offbeat, there could be no greater challenge than *Napoleon Dynamite*, made on a shoestring. I hope I find in the next year or two that, yes, I too still have the courage and ability to make a movie like that."

Mind Control

DAVID THOMPSON / 2004

WHEN IT WAS announced that Jonathan Demme was to remake the 1962 Cold War classic *The Manchurian Candidate* many—including myself—thought it a dangerous step after his disappointing revision of Stanley Donen's elegant 1963 thriller *Charade*, *The Truth about Charlie*. Clearly intended as a homage to the French New Wave, *Charlie* (2002) received arguably the roughest critical and commercial ride of Demme's career. The original pairing of the charm-laden Will Smith with Thandie Newton might have worked, but when the need for an immediate start to filming led to Mark Wahlberg being cast in the lead, by Demme's own admission sparks failed to ignite. Would Demme succeed in updating another 1960s classic, this time an apparently unbeatable, subversive take on the American political scene?

In fact, Demme's new *The Manchurian Candidate* is his most compelling movie since *The Silence of the Lambs* (1991), a dizzying reinvention of the original set in an era stretching from the first Gulf War to the present conflict in Iraq. Richard Condon's novel and the film that came soon after (scripted by George Axelrod and directed by John Frankenheimer) dealt with a platoon, lost in the Korean War, whose men eventually return home convinced that one of their number, Sergeant Raymond Shaw, is their saviour and hero. However, their commander, Colonel Marco, is haunted by a nightmare that they are victims of a brainwashing exercise by a communist conclave, creating in Shaw a puppet who can be commanded—by uncovering the queen of diamonds in a game of solitaire—to carry out a political assassination. The entire cunning plot is revealed to be in the service of his stepfather, vice-presidential candidate Senator John Iselin, a rabid right-winger (modelled

---

From *Sight & Sound* (December 2004), pp. 14–18. Reprinted by permission of the British Film Institute.

on Joseph McCarthy), who is in turn guided by Raymond's domineering mother.

The Frankenheimer film, which opened during the Cuban missile crisis and shortly before the Kennedy assassination, made an indelible impact through its quasi-surrealist ambience and because it presented a fractured mirror image of the politics of its time. Most famously, Marco's nightmare consists of a daringly long sequence in which the platoon are sitting in a ladies' garden club that gradually morphs into a clinical demonstration of brainwashing before communist dignitaries. Marco was played by Frank Sinatra, with an air of internalised anxiety, while a haughty Laurence Harvey was well cast as the callous Raymond and a powerhouse Angela Lansbury (only three years older than Harvey) memorably incarnated his appalling mother.

Demme's version, from a script by Daniel Pyne and Dean Georgaris, follows the structure of the original but makes Marco (Denzel Washington) a more complex figure; Raymond Shaw (an oleaginous Liev Schreiber) becomes the candidate for vice-president and his mother (a diamond-sharp Meryl Streep) a full-blown senator. The soldiers have been plucked from Kuwait and subjected to mind-controlling implants; the manipulators are no longer the Red Menace but a huge, almost invisible corporation called Manchurian Global, seized on by many commentators as an obvious fictional equivalent to Halliburton or the Carlyle Group. Central to the visual and aural mix of an already multi-layered movie is the constant barrage of television coverage of political events and news reports.

With filming over by January this year, Demme worked feverishly with two editors to complete the movie in time for release before the U.S. election in November; in fact it opened much sooner, the day after John Kerry's nomination as presidential candidate for the Democrats.

DAVID THOMPSON: *The news that you were going to remake* The Manchurian Candidate *worried people who were not appreciative of your spin on* Charade, The Truth about Charlie.

JONATHAN DEMME: I wasn't seeking another 1960s classic to get in trouble with. I'd been sent Dan Pyne's script and Denzel Washington had agreed, so the film was a real project. The original was irrevocably wedded to its time, but I was taken with Dan's idea of replacing communism as the great global threat to mankind with what is arguably the biggest threat to humanity today: the multinational corporations who profit from war. I also liked the way the script turned the piece back towards the book, playing it more as a psychological thriller and providing the opportunity to engage more fully with the characters.

DT: *You've said in the past that* The Silence of the Lambs *was a major influence.*
JD: I loved making that movie and I'd always assumed I'd be back with Clarice and Dr. Lecter at some future date, but when ten years later Thomas Harris finished his new book, *Hannibal*, he'd taken the characters in a direction I couldn't relate to. So I passed, but I still had the desire to do a film like it.

And this was the one—an American movie in which the characters are very well written. The only thing that worried me was that there was still too much residue from the original—they were still using the cards and the extended dream scene. The 1962 movie got away with that because it was the first of a kind, but here we felt that a scene with Raymond strangling somebody surrounded by a lot of technology is enough to haunt a guy for a long time.

Also the ending was just as utterly bleak as in the original version, with Marco saying "Hell, hell," but under different circumstances. I had the feeling I couldn't go into this arena and end with a sense of utter hopelessness. I thought it was important to close on a disturbing and haunted note, but we couldn't watch Denzel go through all this and end up with him behind barbed wire in a desert. So we worked on finding an ending that would allow him to survive, and at the same time give us the opportunity to comment on war and what soldiers are forced to do.

DT: *A major change was making Eleanor Shaw a senator rather than a Lady Macbeth figure, with her son as the political candidate.*
JD: That kind of fundamental change helped me deal with my fear that people who loved the original would just sit there and watch the new movie unfold as a straightforward remake. Once you cut out John Iselin and make Raymond the candidate it's a whole new ball game.

DT: *You also give Rosie a new dimension—she's no longer a marginal figure but is directly involved in the course of the investigation.*
JD: Dan's idea was that if Marco is going to have a much more difficult journey, then someone has to function the way Marco does in the original film and be the force of good riding to the rescue. So this became Rosie's role.

DT: *Given that brainwashing was the theme of the original, how did you come up with the idea of brain implants for the new film?*
JD: Dan did a lot of research into experiments with implants being done, arguably for dark reasons, by scientific outfits with huge government contracts as well as to help people. The two assistants working alongside Simon McBurney when he performs the operation are actual neurosurgeons, and what we depict is accurate in every way, including—absurdly—the drill. I was hoping we could achieve a sense of the film being just in the future,

which is how we found ourselves reading about genomic reconstruction. Currently—as best we know—this is being done only on an embryonic level, but a guy like Dr. Noyle would be too impatient to wait for genomic reconfiguration in twenty or thirty years: he'd want to get into adults and try to reconfigure them, so he's using a combination of disciplines to create this Manchurian candidate.

DT: *I enjoyed the yin and yang of the rogue scientists. What led you to cast two distinguished European theatre actors?*
JD: I felt it was important to have someone other than the usual American reliables one might turn to. So I came to London for a few days of casting and met Simon McBurney, whom I was not familiar with. In his work for Theatre de Complicite Simon is clearly very involved with the workings of the mind, with perception and reality, and he seemed obsessed with that stuff. I thought to myself, "This is what it would be like to talk to Dr. Noyle," so I was taken with him immediately.

We don't really know where the other scientist, Delp, comes from, or where he goes—though I have my ideas about that. His job in the movie is to provide a lot of disturbing information, and he's the one Marco turns to in his desperate choice to have some investigations of his own done. I thought we needed someone who could bring a whole life story into the movie, that old-European gravitas, so I decided to try Bruno Ganz, who was just finishing playing Hitler in *The Downfall*. Denzel is a very demanding actor, and every time we got together to prepare this movie he would say, "Get me actors, Jon, get me people to work with who are going to give me stuff." To be in the same room with Denzel Washington and Bruno Ganz was very stimulating.

DT: *Watching Meryl Streep's performance, I found it hard not to think of Hillary Clinton.*
JD: Meryl's original ideas of what she wanted to look like were far removed from the Eleanor we ended up with. We tested a few flamboyant looks, but I felt very strongly I didn't want Eleanor to be simply a one-dimensional villain or a dragon lady. Arguably there's no character Meryl has ever played who is so completely removed from who she is as a person, yet we were able to capitalise on some of her real-life characteristics: how rampantly smart she is, and how sexy and charismatic. When Meryl Streep enters a room everybody quiets down a little, so we went back more and more to a relatively natural look. Meryl has said she has studied male power figures a lot, and she was using what she's observed of people in high office or with tremendous wealth. A lot of energy also went into being a mother who adores her child to a damaging degree.

DT: *The one scene that seems very close to the original is when Eleanor kisses Raymond.*

JD: I started watching Frankenheimer's film again when I first got involved in the remake but after about twenty minutes I stopped because I found it was confusing me. But I do remember from when I last saw the movie about eight years ago how shocked I was by that kiss.

DT: *Perhaps the way it was shot was lurking somewhere in your subconscious?*

JD: I guess so. I don't know. I think my contribution was to get them in the bathroom dressed only in robes and towels and to make it very bright and to let them do their stuff. When a mother moves in for too lingering a kiss with her grown-up child we're in a zone that people are bound to find disturbing. You should hear American audiences during that scene—it's unbelievable.

DT: *A strong component of the film is the constant noise of the media invading the minds of the characters.*

JD: American media are like that. We wanted to present the political material like sports coverage, and we hoped to be nicely over the top—for instance, by having all the firemen, soldiers, and jet pilots up on stage at the victory party—though the recent conventions show us we're closer to reality. Living in New York, we are terrified of attacks so we hate to hear the news, yet we're always listening to it. So it seemed we couldn't provide a moment's relief from the media onslaught of disturbing information. I'm sure the reason Richard Condon wrote the book was his outrage at the way the powers-that-be back in the 1950s were using fear to brainwash the population into submissiveness. And we have a very similar thing going on today, if anything broader and cruder. We were changing the newscasts right up to the final mix, desperately trying to stay in the moment, having long abandoned hope of being ahead of the curve.

DT: *You never mention whether Raymond is a Democrat or a Republican.*

JD: The last thing we wanted was to endorse one of the big parties. In America there's a strong feeling of frustration that this two-party system is in fact more like one big fat party with two different sides. So we didn't want to show the movie's disrespect for the establishment as coming from any party line.

DT: *But many have read Shaw as a Democrat.*

JD: Eleanor is clearly extremely conservative, and it would appear that Raymond is treading in the populist footsteps of his late father. At the same time, he is being used as a pawn to play into the fear that will make people swing with Eleanor's more conservative view. So in his big convention speech he presents himself as someone who has faced the enemy first hand, living proof that he can triumph.

We didn't at the time know that there would be such a fuss over John Kerry's war record. But what heightened our sense of responsibility was that within weeks of finishing filming Iraq was invaded. That really ratcheted up our sense of needing to make a film that portrayed soldiers in a way that was meaningful today.

DT: *The main criticism of the film seems to be that since everyone knows business interests control politicians, where's the conspiracy?*

JD: There's a moment where Jon Voight as Senator Jordan says Raymond is being groomed to be the first fully owned and operated vice-president in the U.S. It always makes me want to shout out: "What do you mean? We have that already." For me, the movie plugs most into Dick Cheney, someone who made millions by being at the top of a multinational corporation that profits from war, then left to take up the second-highest office in the land. He enters this new office with a ferocious war agenda and helps lead the country and the world into a horrendous war from which the company he was involved in profits at untold levels. In this movie, I've tried to ask the questions: "Is this OK? Is there something morally wrong with this?" And I firmly believe there is something profoundly wrong with this—it takes the notion of conflict of interest into an Armageddon dimension—but infuriatingly no one is talking about it. It's one of the things the movie wants to be provocative about, along with the exploitation of soldiers—bodies for billions.

The level of debate in the U.S. media is unbelievably low, and we enjoyed showing the free press—the cornerstone of democracy—as an entertainment industry. One of my favourite lines is when the counter-conspiracy has lobbed a couple of smart bombs into the corridors of Manchurian Global using former employees as assassins. The newscaster says that another former employee was arrested, and the authorities are pursuing any other links that might exist. In other words, it's not the media who is pursuing it—they'll report what the authorities tell them. So our anger isn't a copycat, recycled anger from Richard Condon's book or Frankenheimer's movie: there's a lot to be enraged and frightened about today, and our film has plugged into that. I think we've made a good time-capsule movie, in the same way as the earlier film was a time capsule of the 1960s.

DT: *Do you regard your film as a close relative of* Fahrenheit 9/11?

JD: I'd like to think we're cousins. I have a huge respect for and gratitude to Michael Moore, and whether or not he gets every single fact straight, I think his film is a profoundly important piece of work. But what's missing is a *Fahrenheit 9/11* about Kerry—I'm not sure exactly what it would be, but I wish it was in circulation too.

DT: *Has* The Manchurian Candidate *had any appreciable political impact?*

JD: It's made it off the entertainment pages, and I've received letters from students saying they now see things differently. I know movies can change how a person feels because of the way my own perspective altered when I went to see *Far from Vietnam* in 1967. I entered the theatre a young American guy terrified of being drafted but ready to go if my country called me, and after the Alain Resnais section I came out thinking the war was all wrong. One week later I was down in Washington at the protest. Of course, *The Manchurian Candidate* is a thriller—Paramount made it because they hoped it would be a really frightening Denzel Washington psychological thriller—but if it provides some food for thought as well, that's terrific. It opened in the U.S. in the summer, and I believe it's going to play through election day, which should be in its favour.

Interview: Singer Neil Young and Director Jonathan Demme

TERRY GROSS/2006

TERRY GROSS: *This is* Fresh Air. *I'm Terry Gross.*

My guest, Neil Young, gives a very moving performance in a new concert film directed by Jonathan Demme, who's also with us. It was filmed in Nashville at the Ryman Auditorium, the former home of the Grand Ole Opry, with a band of old friends. The music is pretty remarkable, so is the story behind it. The new songs Young performs were written and recorded in the period when he was diagnosed with and treated for a brain aneurysm. Those songs were first recorded on his album Prairie Wind *which was released over the summer. In the film, Young also performed some of his classics like "Old Man," "I Am a Child" and "Heart of Gold." The film was called* Neil Young: Heart of Gold. *The director Jonathan Demme also made the 2004 version of* The Manchurian Candidate, Philadelphia, Silence of the Lambs, *and* Something Wild. Heart of Gold *opens in select theaters this Friday, but the soundtrack won't be released until the spring. So the versions of Young's new songs that we'll hear are from his album* Prairie Wind. *Let's start with "It's a Dream."*

[*Soundbite of Neil Young's "It's a Dream"*]

GROSS: *I asked Jonathan Demme what it was like to approach Neil Young about making a film at a time when Young was dealing with a brain aneurysm.*

JONATHAN DEMME: The turning point I thought I was contacting him at was that he had just created what was arguably one of the major masterworks in this master's artistic life. I just heard these songs that he was sending up from

Nashville and thought, "My God, to capture this stuff somehow or other on film could be really amazing." I responded to the emotional dimension. I responded to my own emotions. I got very emotional as I heard this stuff, and it just gave me a lot of confidence to pursue the idea that—if we were able to stage a concert in Neil's ideal location, that would be the Ryman Auditorium in Nashville, Tennessee, with his ideal group of musicians—that we would probably wind up with something that would be incredibly singular amongst music on film and the music on film category, and something that I know I would feel very privileged to be a part of.

GROSS: *Neil Young, this is, to me, just an incredible part of the story. The way I understand it, you find out you have this aneurysm on your brain, and in a couple of weeks, you are going to get a procedure to fix it or do away with it or whatever the medical term is, and so you decided to book a studio in Nashville and record a new album except you haven't written the songs yet. So you go to Nashville with the intent of writing these songs before the procedure is done. Do I have that story right?*

NEIL YOUNG: Well, it's kind of right.

GROSS: *You tell it. You tell it.*

YOUNG: Really, really what happened, I was at the Rock and Roll Hall of Fame inducting Chrissy Hind and the Pretenders into the Hall of Fame and visiting, and I was planning to go to Nashville the next day to record, and I had one complete song and it was enough to go in, and I kind of had confidence that if I was going to go in there and get started, that it would start things going, and I would probably write more because I'd be in a situation where if I wrote it, I could put it down right away. And so the Hall of Fame came along, and I did my presentation to Chrissy and the Pretenders, and then I went home, and then the next morning I woke up and I was shaving and I looked out the window, and there was this—you know how you get something caught in your eye sometimes and it looks like one of those micro-being things, a little, you know, long, looks like DNA or something floating around on your eye, and you're going, "Wow," you know, "look at that, it's a science project." So I was—I had one of those, but it looked different to me. I said, "That's a big one, I've never seen one like this." Then I closed my eyes, and it was still there. So then I started pushing on my eye, trying to move it around like you usually would be able to, and it just didn't move. So I said to myself, "Well, you've got—this is something on your brain, not on your eye." So that became a little bit—by then it had grown to cover half of my field of vision, and everything to the left of it was, just kind of looked like a mercury, silvery kind of a thing moving around like reflections on water, and everything to the right of it was clear as a bell. There was this line, a shard of glass or something, right through the middle of it that was really vibrating. So I was experiencing this, and it was becoming a little disorienting because just having so much of your vision kind of out to lunch was—the whole thing was disorienting. So I decided at that time that I was going to get it checked out, and I had a doctor friend that I had just seen the day before for an unrelated thing, and so I called him, and he said come on in. So I went down there, and by then, it had gone away. It only lasted about twenty-five minutes. So when I went down there, Dr. Positano took me to all of the experts in fields that were related to this. And so I saw five doctors, and they did a bunch of tests and things on me, and they're trying to figure out what it was, and they never came to a conclusion of what it was, but during the searching, they found this aneurysm which was completely unrelated to the . . .

GROSS: *It was unrelated?*
YOUNG: Yes. It was unrelated. It was kind of an accident that they found it. And the visual disturbance turned out to be a visual migraine, and now I just simply take a little aspirin, and that doesn't happen anymore. Of course, you know, I guess someday I will have to take a little more aspirin or something. I don't know. Hopefully, everything will be OK there, but the aneurysm had nothing to do with it.

GROSS: *Oh, you're lucky.*
YOUNG: Yeah. So I was fortunate to have a great neurologist who I'd met and his name is Dexter Sun. And he is there in New York, and he told me in his Chinese way that I had had this aneurysm for a hundred years and is showing me on the big, you know, readout, that they had this big piece of film, and you could see the thing kind of looked like Florida hanging off of the United States. And I was looking at it, and it kind of scared me at first, and then he said, "Neil," he said, "you've had this for a hundred years. There is nothing to worry about. For you, it's nothing to worry about. For me, I have to get rid of it as soon as possible. It has to go. We have to get rid of it. It has to be gone from your head." And I said, "Well, how do we do that?" And he said, "Well, I need to make some calls and we're going to set up an appointment for you with this surgeon, Dr. Gobin, at New York Presbyterian." So they did that, and I went. Dr. Gobin wasn't going to be in for a couple of days, so I had three or four days between when he was coming in, and then so rather than sit around, knowing that I had an aneurysm and just sitting in New York with my aneurysm, I decided to go to Nashville and do what I was going to do in the first place and then fly back. So I went in there, and

I recorded "The Painter," and then I recorded—the next song I wrote was "I Wonder." The next day I wrote that, the evening after "The Painter" and the morning, the following morning I wrote that and then we recorded it, and then I wrote "Falling Off the Face of the Earth" that night and the next morning and we recorded it, and then I went back to New York and met Dr. Gobin, and we scheduled the procedure for ten days from that point, and then I went back to Nashville and finished the record.

GROSS: *So, was your life in jeopardy at this point?*

YOUNG: Well, it's one of those things where your life is in jeopardy if you have this thing. And on one hand one doctor was telling me everything was OK, you know, I can fly, "You can do whatever you want to do. You've had this for a long time, there is no reason to change what you are doing and just go on with your life, and we will take care of it here in a week or two, and everything will be fine." And other doctors were telling me, "Don't lean down to tie your shoes. Have someone else tie your shoes for you. Don't put your head down," because, you know, if you put your head down really fast and then bring it back up, there is a lot of pressure happens there or something. So, this is kind of turning into a medical show, but that's OK.

DEMME: The great American actor Trey Wilson, who played Nathan Arizona in *Raising Arizona*, and I got to work with him in *Married to the Mob*, he was perfectly healthy, and he was in a restaurant one night and his aneurysm exploded on him, and that was it.

GROSS: *Oh, really.*

YOUNG: Yeah. It's like, you know, if it goes off, you're finished. So, and this was an ugly one. It's a series of bubbles that form, like if you think of one of your arteries as like a bicycle tube . . .

DEMME: I'd rather not.

YOUNG: . . . which is easy for me to do. So, I have a Schwinn brain. So, anyway, I was riding along on my balloon tires, and, suddenly, I realized there was this huge bump on my tire. And then, you know what happens is, that's a weakness in the wall of the vein, and so the pressure makes this bubble come out. And I had a series of six or seven bubbles on top of bubbles.

GROSS: *Gee!*

YOUNG: It was getting thinner every time it happened. So it was obvious that Florida had to go, you know. We had to get rid of that state.

GROSS: *You know that classic movie plot, you go to the doctor, you find out you only have two weeks to live or six months to live and the rest of the movie is like, "What are you going to do with that time?" And it's like you find out, it's conceiv-*

able that you only have a couple of weeks to live, you know. And what do you do? You go into the studio and you write songs. I mean, if given your choice, would that have been the thing that you most want to do if you felt that your time might actually be limited?

YOUNG: Well, you know, there was really no way of knowing how long this thing would go on, and it had gone on maybe my whole life, building to where it is now. We don't know how long it took to get to where it was, but something told me that the thing to do was do what you do. Just do what you were doing before and just keep on going. So when I'm making music and writing songs, and, you know, I had my wife with me, Pegi was there, and she was helping on the record. So everything was good. We were together, and we were doing what we love to do, so we decided that's how we're going to spend our time.

DEMME: I heard that when you were down in Nashville cutting the record, in the midst of all of this, that you were eating barbecue every night and just really, really chowing down.

YOUNG: No. There's no truth to that. That's one of those Internet rumors.

GROSS: *I want to play the song "Falling Off the Face of the Earth." You mentioned this is one of the songs you wrote right before the procedure, and it's just such a beautiful song and it's about, like an older person's love, not like new romantic "I've just fallen in love" love, but the kind of love that you have with somebody who you've been with for a very long time. It's a very beautiful song. Would you say a little bit about writing this song, Neil Young?*

YOUNG: Well, writing "Falling Off the Face of the Earth" is really a case of, I had a melody that I was writing that I had just come up with that night, and then I was going to bed and I couldn't come up with the lyrics, but I had a melody and chord changes. So I thought, "Well, I'll just go to sleep and I will wake up in the morning and start playing the changes and the words will be there." So, I checked my voice mail, and I had a message from Jim Jarmusch, who did my film, *Year of the Horse*.

GROSS: *An earlier concert film?*

YOUNG: An earlier concert film of Crazy Horse which is almost the polar opposite of this film in some ways because of the musical content. But, anyway, Jim and I are good friends and he left a voice mail, and it seemed, I'm not sure if he knew I had this aneurysm or if he didn't—I think he did—but he was just thinking about me, and so he left me a message and some of the phrases that are in the message, I played it again and I wrote down some of the phrases that he used. And then, you know, in the morning, I had the song all done because some of the phrases that he used in the voice mail were in the—I just used them out of context in the song and kind of opened up the door for everything else, so the chorus and everything all just fell out.

GROSS: *Did he say something like feeling like he's falling off the face of the earth?*
YOUNG: No. He said, I just wanted to thank you for all the things we've done. We've done some special things together, you know. It may sound simple but things like that, little phrases that are in the song.

GROSS: *Well, it's a beautiful song. Let's hear it. And this is the version from Neil Young's CD* Prairie Wind. *He also performs it in the new concert film which is called* Neil Young: Heart of Gold.

[*Soundbite of Neil Young's "Falling Off the Face of the Earth"*]
GROSS: *That's Neil Young singing his song "Falling Off the Face of the Earth." We heard the version on his CD* Prairie Wind. *He also performs it in the new concert movie,* Neil Young: Heart of Gold, *which is directed by Jonathan Demme, who is also with us.*

Neil Young, I think of that as a song—although you said that the song, the idea after the song, came from a Jim Jarmusch phone call—in my mind, it's a song for your wife. I don't know if there's any truth to that, but that's how I hear it, when I hear it.
YOUNG: I agree, I agree. I think that—you know, that's the magic of songs. That's what it's all about. Everything is connected in one way or another and the feelings that one person may have, maybe when you write them down and when you sing them, it becomes a completely different thing. So, you know, that's the magic of art. That's the magic of taking a picture of something and putting it in a different context with other pictures, and, suddenly, it means something completely different. And that's what Jonathan and I do. So that's just the way that happened. It *is* a song for my wife. Obviously, I'm deeply in love with my wife, and she's the most important person to me, and I was talking to her in the song, but I was using Jim's words in some cases and couching them in a different framework.

GROSS: *Then she sings back up in the concert and on the CD. Jonathan Demme, since you have Neil Young singing and his wife being one of the backup singers on this, how much did you want to make of that when you were shooting? I mean, you could, like there's a couple of very meaningful glances they give each other, but you could have like really made a lot out of this. Do you know what I mean? How did you decide how much to notice that?*
DEMME: Well, a couple of things. One is that, as far as Pegi Young goes in the film, one of the things that I really love about the movie is that for the first several songs, Pegi is part of this preposterously overqualified genius backup

legion including Emmylou Harris, Diana DeWitt, and that's just on the female side. And then at a certain point in the movie, later in the movie when it starts opening up, Pegi comes forward and joins Neil side by side for a couple of songs there towards the end, and I can't explain why, but there is just something very beautiful about the movement of Pegi in that context, and it's kind of thrilling, I think, to see these two side by side with their guitars, singing these beautiful songs together and certainly exchanging glances with each other, but they're exchanging glances with everybody else on stage, too.

When Neil and I first started talking very seriously about doing this film, which we just always described as a performance film and not a concert film because we didn't go down there to film a concert, we staged a concert in order to film it. And one of the things that Neil talked constantly about in our early conversations on the telephone was just his tremendous regard and love for the other musicians, Pegi and Emmylou and Ben Keith and everybody. He spoke individually about every single person, and he would pepper our conversations with—you know Anthony Crawford comes up on that song and you know that's the song that Grant Boatwright plays the electric guitar on. And I would be scribbling all this stuff down and just really getting very excited about the possibility of capturing all these strong bonds that exists between these brilliant musicians on film and making that part of the texture of the movie.

GROSS: *This is* Fresh Air. *I'm Terry Gross. We are talking with Neil Young and director Jonathan Demme about their new performance film,* Neil Young: Heart of Gold. *Most of the songs on it were written last year after Young was diagnosed with a brain aneurysm, which has since been successfully treated. The new songs in the film were first recorded on Young's album,* Prairie Wind. *From that CD, here is Young's song "The Painter."*

[Soundbite of Neil Young's "The Painter"]

GROSS: *Let's get back to our interview with Neil Young and Jonathan Demme who directed Young's new performance film. Demme also made* Silence of the Lambs, Philadelphia, *and the 2004 version of* The Manchurian Candidate.

One of the things I like about the way you shot this, Jonathan Demme, is that it's so much about the music and about the emotion behind the music. I think there really are a lot of performance films that are about how hip a band is, about how cool and fashionable they are, about what a good time the audience in the concert hall was having.

DEMME: You can forget that.

GROSS: *Do you know what I mean? And it's not just about the music itself, and a lot of camera work is so restless at these things, making you think that unless the camera is constantly moving and unless there is an edit every second, that you're going to be bored, and a lot of that sometimes distracts your attention from the music, and I feel like all the camera work, everything's done in service to the music and the emotion.*

DEMME: Well, to put even more of a point on it, one of the bottom line missions here was to make sure that every single lyric, every word of every song, which in our film kind of functions a little bit like stories—Neil is a story teller with his songs—we wanted every single word to be just so easily accessed that nothing would intrude, just a complete intimate relationship between the audience and the message that Neil was singing about. And the other thing was I wanted to make sure that we were up very, very close a lot of the time on Neil as he was singing these songs so that his emotional state, as he presented the stuff, was something that we could be very, very akin to. And I definitely felt that, you're right, stylish camera moves and dolly shots and crane shots and kinetic editing, all of which I love, and have been used exceptionally well time and again with music and drama and what have you, but certainly in the music world. I felt that, you know, none of that stuff would serve us nearly as well as beautifully composed, beautifully lit—we had Ellen Kuras doing the lighting, she invented new colors in her artistic interpretation of what the songs meant to her—nothing could serve us better than those kind of shots. I really aspired to find ways and hoped that our shots played a long time and were not interrupted by an edit to another shot, unless we had something *really* worth going to, operating on the premise that we're providing the best seat in the house so we don't need to be cutting around all the time. So, what it all added up to in a way was I felt, you know, this is kind of bold. It's almost in this day and age where the camera is always moving, who knows, maybe the fact that we're kind of settled in a little bit more and don't cut as much might feel kind of avant garde at this stage of the game.

GROSS: *Neil Young, when you went back to the recording studio, after the procedure to remove the aneurysm, were you in the same mood that you were before? You know you had had this terrible revelation about the aneurysm, you had the procedure, you got through it, it seemed to be successful. Were you in the same frame of mind that you were when you had started writing and recording those songs?*

YOUNG: Well, now when I shake my head—you know, they put some coils inside my brain—and now when I shake my head it . . . [*sound of rattling*] . . . sounds like, you know—just kidding.

GROSS: *[Laughter] But you're not kidding about them putting . . .*
YOUNG: Cheap shot. I shouldn't do that, huh?
DEMME: This is radio, isn't it?
YOUNG: Cheap shot.
DEMME: Hey, come on. It's radio, Bob and Ray.

GROSS: *But you are not kidding about coils inside your brain, right?*
YOUNG: No, they're little platinum slinkies.
DEMME: He was actually shaking his head just then. That was the darndest thing.

GROSS: *But what did they put inside your brain?*
YOUNG: It's a pretty cheap shot, you know.

GROSS: *What did they put inside?*
YOUNG: Little platinum slinkies.

GROSS: *And what's the purpose?*
YOUNG: Tiny little slinkies. Well, they're flexible, and they're springs, kind of, and they're made out of the thinnest, smallest, most delicate platinum, and they stuffed this thing full of them. They went in with this, you know, radiology thing or whatever, they watched it in on TV and they sent this thing up through, you know, from my leg up through and into my head and packed this little aneurysm full of these slinkies.

GROSS: *And that does what?*
YOUNG: Fooled me. Fooled my body completely. My body thought I had a bunch of scar tissue going in there, so scar tissue gets more scar tissues, so I think my body filled up the whole aneurysm with scar tissue, and now it's full of scar tissue, and there is nothing there. The blood just goes flying by like nothing's wrong.

GROSS: *That's really amazing. So . . .*

[Soundbite of rattling]

GROSS: *Be still!*
DEMME: He just scratched his head.

GROSS: *But I want to play another really beautiful song from* Prairie Wind, *one of the songs you do in the performance from* Heart of Gold. *And this is a song that was written for your daughter. It's called "I'm Here for You." Would you talk about writing this one?*

YOUNG: Well, this is probably the second to last song that I did before going back to New York, and it's a song about about my daughter. She's twenty-one and she's moving on, you know. She's in college, she's graduating, and I'm really proud of her and how well she is doing. She's an artist, and of course, I miss her all the time but I really don't want to intrude so I was just trying to communicate to her that she had a place to go, but it wasn't a place she had to go. If she needed me, I was there, that myself and her mother would be there for her if she ever needed us and that she was free to go and free to stay. And that we were behind her all the way, you know. So it is just that kind of a song, a kind of letting go without letting go kind of.

GROSS: *Well, it's a great song. Here it is. It's "I'm Here for You."*

[*Soundbite of "I'm Here for You"*]

GROSS: *That's "I'm Here for You," a song from Neil Young's latest CD* Prairie Wind, *and he also sings the songs from the CD on his new performance film which is called* Neil Young: Heart of Gold, *and the film is directed by Jonathan Demme, who is also with us.*

You know, the two songs that we just played, this one and the one called "Falling Off the Face of the Earth," I hear them, and I might be being overly dramatic here, but they sound to me like the songs that you might have written as messages to leave behind for the people you love just in case something happened to you. Am I reading too much into it?

YOUNG: Well, these songs are meant to be for anything. They're meant to be for if I'm here or if I'm not here. But all my songs are like that. So, I really try to write songs like that. I wrote a song years and years ago called "I Feel Like Going Back," and it could have been one of these songs, and it's all about not one particular time or place or situation but the whole thing. I try to make it so that it will work, you know, that's where I'm coming from, so it will work no matter what happens.

DEMME: This movie ends with "One of These Days" which Neil wrote years ago and reinterpreted for the movie, but that's as rich and emotionally powerful a summing up song as any other song on the *Prairie Wind* album, I think.

GROSS: *Are there things that you think were easier to say in a song than in conversation?*

YOUNG: Oh, yeah. Yeah, on practically everything. Actually, yeah, but, you know, I'm glad that I can write songs because I would've probably gone crazy by now if I couldn't have put some of these ideas down in a way that is obscure enough so you can say them at any time, and yet, when you hear it, if you are thinking about it and you are wide open to it, then you can go a lot farther than the current conversation.

GROSS: *How did you both decide which songs to include in the performance film? Obviously, you have the songs from* Prairie Wind, *but there are also earlier songs, early Neil Young songs on there and you obviously had a lot of songs to choose from. So, how did you decide which ones you wanted to include?*

DEMME: Well, *Prairie Wind* was all I cared about when we started making the movie. It was it. Just that suite of songs was, as far as I'm concerned, just a perfect amazing body of work unto itself. And we were pretty far down the line. We knew we were going to go to the Ryman. We knew that Manuel was going to do the costumes. We knew that Michael Zansky was going to do the backdrops. We knew that Andy Keir was going to cut it and Ellen was going to shoot it.

And then I was in my kitchen one day, and I suddenly went, "Wait a minute, we're going to have a fifty-five-minute movie." So I called Neil up and said, really pretty crude, I just said, "You know, if we only have fifty-five minutes and we're hoping that we can get this film into movie theaters, would it be possible to add an encore dimension to kind of rough out the running time, to flesh out the running time?" And Neil right away said—I felt funny asking him that, but I did—and then he said right away, "Sure, let me think about it. Obviously, I'll have to draw from my Nashville body of work pretty much." And he also said he wanted to think about it and select songs that would be thematically compatible with the songs of *Prairie Wind*.

So off he went. And then we saw each other a little while later, and Neil had created a list of songs. And he showed them to me, and it was basically the songs that are in the movie and a couple of others. And it is such a treasure trove.

But the funny thing for me is that I was so focused on *Prairie Wind* and my love for *those* songs that—and I thought that's terrific that our film will end with some wonderful performances of the earlier songs. But I had no idea that those earlier songs were going to wind up packing such a tremendously strong emotional wallop.

GROSS: *Well, the effect that you have with some of the old songs, the effect I think that it registers on me, anyway, and the audience is that here you have some of the songs, Neil Young, that you wrote and recorded when you were a young man, and some of these are about age. And now you're singing them as someone who isn't a young man. I think, what, you're around sixty now?*

YOUNG: Yeah.

GROSS: *And so the songs . . .*
DEMME: What's so old about that?

GROSS: *And so the songs, they have a different resonance. They have a different meaning. And the audience, like you, feel you almost reflecting on the songs and how the sound of the songs have changed. Do you . . .*
YOUNG: Well, there's a trick in there.

GROSS: *Yeah.*
YOUNG: To interrupt. Sorry to interrupt you. But what really happens with these songs is that the whole beginning of the film we're singing songs that have never been heard by the audience that we're singing them for. And they are all brand-new, so they are first-time presentations of the songs, which makes you listen and you open up and start listening to something because you don't know what it is. And you're seeing it in a way that you've never seen anything from me before. So you're seeing it in a new way and you're listening to new songs that are being done for the first time. So it really opens you up. So what happens when we get to the second half is that the audience is totally open to new material and listening to the words and trying to pick up on everything that these songs are saying because you only had one shot to pick up on it.

And when we go into the second part of it, it's basically a chronological trip through my music, with a few departures from chronology. But it is starting back in Buffalo Springfield and going through to, I guess, "Harvest Moon." So it goes through that. But the thing is, you listen to it a lot more than you—Instead of celebrating, "Hey, there's another old song and he's doing these songs that I like," you're not doing that. You're still listening because you've been tuned into listening in the beginning and listening for the words. So they become part of the story because you're trained and you have trained yourself to listen instead of just watching and celebrating these old tunes that you've heard before. You're listening to them like they're new tunes. And so I think that opens the door for people to go on the journey with the songs.

GROSS: *The songs in the movie, the takes are all so good that you almost feel like, "God, it must have been post-dubbed or something because no concert goes this smoothly." You know that with like note-to-note perfection.*

Jonathan Demme, how many takes were there for each of the songs? How did you manage to get such good takes?
DEMME: Well, we didn't do takes per se. The concert was performed on two nights in a row, August 19 and August 20. And the curtain parted and the

music was there. In fact, the music started before the curtain parted. And we didn't redo any of the songs. We filmed them on both nights, and then later we were able to either select which night seemed to be the better of the two excellent performances. Because, frankly, each night was unbelievably great. And every once in awhile, we did some combination of the two nights.

And in one instance, in "Old King," which is a song I love, I got so carried away that, with Neil's permission, we actually made that longer and stretched out the instrumental part of that so we could really just let the audience just—something about everybody up there doing that kind of what I call a hoedown. And Emmylou Harris strumming amazing guitar, and Neil rocking out on the banjo and what have you.

And so that was it. We didn't do any retakes. You have to realize the amount of preparation for Neil and his fellow band members that preceded the show; they rehearsed for ten solid days straight ahead. Like Neil said earlier, everybody knew that they were introducing the *Prairie Wind* songs for the very first time. No one out there ever would have heard these. The CD hasn't come out yet. It was going to be a brand-new experience. And they had the unique thrill of presenting it for the first time on the stage at the Ryman Auditorium in Nashville to an audience that had been largely invited and was made up of songwriters and musicians and people who just adore the kind of music they were about to hear.

So everybody was just at their peak form. And we just got the cameras in focus, and they let it rip. And it was quite an exquisite night of music.

GROSS: *Neil Young, one of the things that adds to the emotional depth of the movie is that onstage, before introducing one of the songs that has to do with your father, you talk about how he had recently died after having dementia for ten years. And you talk about how interesting it was to watch him living in the moment. And I thought that's a kind of positive thing to find about somebody who has dementia, that they're living in the moment. Did you hold on to that as a way of seeing something positive about his dementia and his inability to remember the past?*

YOUNG: Well, I just focused on what his life was about now and not what it used to be about. Just more, because the love is still there and everything, but I couldn't think of any other way to describe it.

GROSS: *Mm-hmm.*

YOUNG: Because that's really all that I think was left. I just—I don't know. Perhaps it was easier for him to remember things than it was for him to speak about what he remembered. So I don't know the connection. I don't know whether people with dementia actually can't remember anything or whether they can't put the words together to explain what it is. Because just putting a sentence together takes an incredible amount of reasoning power in the present. And it really, we take it for granted, and we speak along and it's quite a creation, the human body, that enables us to think and talk and do all of these things at the same time. So as it slowly breaks down and the connections get lost, it's kind of hard to say exactly where things are and what's happening. But I know that my dad was living in the moment so I use that phrase to describe what was going on. That's the best I could do.

GROSS: *There's something very cathartic about the performance film. Do you feel like you've come through the other end of something by having lived through the whole aneurysm thing, written the songs you wanted to write, recorded the CD, done the performance film? They are both really emotional kind of experiences. Do you feel like you're out the other end of something?*
YOUNG: I feel like I'm at the beginning of something else now.

GROSS: *Of what, do you know?*
YOUNG: No. But I know I'm at the beginning of something. And nothing ever really ends with music. It just keeps on going on. It's like it's an eternal exhaust out of some interplanetary spaceship. It just keeps going, you know. It's just out there. All that you put out just keeps on happening. People could listen to this music in a hundred, two hundred, three hundred years from now as far as I know. So what we do now lasts forever. And what we're going to do next is what matters.

GROSS: *Jonathan Demme, one last question for you. When you were making this movie, did you dream these songs every night? Were you hearing them so much and thinking about them so much that they just like stuck with you even when you should have not been thinking about them, like when you should have been sleeping?*
DEMME: I'll tell you, all my three children worked on the movie with me, each in different capacities. And my wife Joanne was there. And all I can tell you is that everybody is obsessed with these songs, and we'd no sooner come home from twelve- to fourteen-hour rehearsal sessions, and we'd come home and somebody or other would put the CD on. So we lived *Prairie Wind* throughout the shooting and driving in the cars on the weekends playing it. And, finally, we all were able to sing all the lyrics to all the songs. So it got very obsessive. Yes.

GROSS: Well, I want to thank you both so much for talking with us. Thank you.
DEMME: It was fun, Terry. Thank you.
YOUNG: Thank you.

[*Soundbite of rattling*]

DEMME: That was Neil getting up.

GROSS: Neil Young's new performance film, Heart of Gold, was directed by Jonathan Demme. It opens Friday in select cities and in more cities next week. I'm Terry Gross. We'll close with another song from Prairie Wind that's also featured in Neil Young's new film.

[*Soundbite of Neil Young singing "When God Made Me"*]

INDEX

Abkarian, Simon, 143
Academy Awards, 15, 17, 35, 79, 84, 85–86, 94, 120
Accused, The, 72
ActionAIDS, 81
African American filmmakers, 116, 126
African American subject matter, xvi, 115–17, 125–26. *See also* Race relations, Demme's interest in
Agronomist, The, xviii–xix, 146, 147–50
AIDS, xv, 59, 78–79, 81, 84, 86–87, 93, 95, 109, 113, 117
AIDS discrimination, 82, 89, 109
Allen, Irving, 36, 106
American dream, 14, 17, 25, 37, 48, 55, 70
Americana, 7, 25, 32, 34, 37–38, 49, 58, 115, 141
Anderson, Laurie, xi, 33
Anderson, Paul Thomas, 108, 140
Angels Hard as They Come, 18–19, 44, 67, 85, 133, 142
Anita (1982), 148
Apocalypse Now, 97
Aristide, Jean-Bertrand, 147
Armitage, George, 19, 57, 69
Ashby, Hal, 25, 97
Attack, 66
Audience: concern for, 22, 54, 56, 62, 68, 87–88, 92, 127, 145; and Roger Corman's rules, 19–20, 142
Avco Embassy, 4, 18
Aznavour, Charles, xviii, 42

B movies. *See* Exploitation films, and Demme's early career
Bailey, John, 52
Banderas, Antonio, 79, 86, 88, 93
Banks, Russell, 37, 55
Bardot, Brigitte, 144
Barkin, Ellen, 139
Bartel, Paul, 19, 35
Beloved, xvi–xvii, 104–5, 108–10, 115–19, 120–30, 137; faithfulness to book, 128–29, 141, 145–46; as ghost story, 105, 130; as historical drama, 117, 127–28; horror in, 125; multiracial crew, 130; music, 107; screenplay, 117–18, 120–21, 135
Beloved (Toni Morrison), 117–19, 120, 125, 128–29, 134, 137, 141, 146
Bertolucci, Bernardo, 151
Black Orpheus (Orfeu negro), 42
Black Panther Party, 76
Bloom, Murray, 10
Boatwright, Grant, 167
Boetticher, Budd, 24
Book adaptations: *Beloved*, 117–18, 146; *Last Embrace (The Thirteenth Man)*, 10; *The Silence of the Lambs*, 112–13, 145–46
Botas, Juan, 86–87
Box-office success, 65, 93, 103–4
Boyz N the Hood, 126
Bozman, Ron, 80, 82
Branch, Taylor, 95
Brickman, Paul, 5, 7–8, 20, 47

178 INDEX

Brooks, Adam, 118, 135
Budgets: *Angels Hard as They Come*, 44; concern for, viii, 89–90; low-budget productions, xv, 16, 56, 95; *Swing Shift*, 53
Buena Vista, 108
Busia, Akosua, 118
Byrne, David, xi, xii, 26, 27, 33, 50–51, 59, 98–99, 107

Caged Heat, 4, 19, 35, 36, 44, 71, 85, 90, 141
Cale, John, 36
Cangaceiro, O (1970), 44
Carr, David, xix
Castle, Robert, 59, 76–77, 136; role in *Philadelphia*, 80
Catharsis, 75
Character: concern for, 6, 15, 22, 48, 85; and Roger Corman's rules, 19–20, 142
Charade, 142, 144, 154
Cheney, Dick, 159
Child abuse, 73–74
Chinatown, 10
Cinematographers, 46
Cinematography: camera movement, 6, 19, 89, 168; close-ups, 63, 67, 168; crane shots, 12; digital camerawork, 144; lighting, 13, 27, 52, 64, 98, 168; multiple cameras, 28, 51; subjective camera, 21, 60, 63
Citizens Band. See *Handle with Care*
Clarke, Shirley, 20, 44
Clinica Estetico, 86, 108
Clinton, Bill, 93
Cole, Nat King, 36
Collaboration in filmmaking, 47, 52, 64, 92, 109, 143; with actors, 47–48, 89, 105–6, 142–43; with cinematographers, 63–64; with composers and musicians, 107 (see also *Complex Sessions, The*; Music videos; *Neil Young: Heart of Gold*; Performance films; *Stop Making Sense*; *Storefront Hitchcock*); with editors, 110; with screenwriters, 8, 10, 20–21, 23, 47, 69
Collaborators, praise for, viii, xii, 5, 46, 50, 100
Columbine massacre, 139
Columbo: Murder under Glass, 21, 28
Commercials, directed by Demme, 15–16
Complex Sessions, The, xvi, xvii, 99

Concert films. See Performance films
Condon, Richard, 154, 158, 159
Conformist, The (*Il conformista*), 151
Continental Drift (Russell Banks), 37, 55
Coppola, Carmine, 51
Coppola, Francis Ford, 20, 41, 68
Corman, Julie, 44, 45
Corman, Roger, viii, 6, 8, 18–20, 22, 44–45, 47, 58; and business of filmmaking, 89, 96, 103; Demme as protégé of, 4–5, 18, 35, 43–44, 71, 85, 94, 132–33, 142; role in *The Silence of the Lambs*, 68–69; role in *Swing Shift*, 19, 69; rules of filmmaking, 19–20, 40–41, 49, 71–72, 89–90, 96, 99, 142; social issues and, 19, 20, 90
Cousin Bobby, xiv, 59, 76–77, 136
Crawford, Anthony, 167
Crazy Horse (band), 165
Crazy Mama, 4, 6, 7, 9, 20, 35, 44–46; DVD commentary track (Demme and Roger Corman), viii
Crime + Punishment in Suburbia, 138–40
Critical acclaim, 17, 25, 35, 40, 97, 103
Cronenweth, Jordan, 5, 27–28, 98

Dailies (rushes), 27, 56, 107–8
Daniels, Jeff, 30–31, 64
Dante, Joe, 35
Daves, Delmer, 12
Dead, The, 41
Demme, Jonathan: childhood and youth, 18, 34, 36, 42–43, 58, 84, 131–32; family life, 80–81, 95, 103, 135; father, 18, 34, 42–43, 84, 94, 132; favorite films and filmmakers, 19, 24, 41, 42–43, 48–49, 51, 144, 151; favorite part of filmmaking, 56; as film critic, 4, 18, 34, 43, 84, 93, 132; music, love of, xi, 36, 98; parents, 42, 144; politics, views on, vii, xiv–xv, 16, 52, 54, 59, 76–77, 87, 148–49, 154–55, 158–60; protégé of Roger Corman, 4–5, 18, 35, 43–44, 71, 85, 94, 132–33, 142; as publicist, 4, 18, 35, 43, 58, 71, 85, 132, 142; as rock journalist, xi, 36, 106–7; social issues, interest in, xiv, xv–xvii, 23, 54, 59, 76–77, 86, 90, 95, 149; start in film business, 4, 18, 34–35, 43, 84, 93–94, 132; young filmmakers, support for, xix
Dessalines, Jean-Jacques, 146
DeWitt, Diana, 167

Directing, 47, 61–62; actors, 47–48, 89, 105–6, 142–43; casting, 89, 143; influences, 19, 24, 145, 151. *See also* Collaboration; Cinematography
Documentaries, xv, xviii, 65, 86, 95, 98, 136, 149; *The Agronomist*, xviii–xix, 146, 147–50; contrasted with fiction films, xix, 54, 102–3, 148; *Cousin Bobby*, xiv, 59, 76–77, 136; *Haiti: Dreams of Democracy*, xii, 37, 52–53, 86, 95, 147. *See also* Performance films; *titles of individual films*
Dominique, Jean, 146, 147–50
Donen, Stanley, 154
Dostoevsky, Fyodor, 138
Dowd, Nancy, 22–23
Dummar, Melvin, 7, 11–13, 14, 17, 23, 25, 33, 48, 70, 85, 141
Duplessis, Jerry, 149

Easy Riders, Raging Bulls (Peter Biskind), 97
Edelstein, David, vii
Editing, 110, 168
Elise, Kimberly, 119, 129
Engleberg, Mort, 4
Exploitation films, and Demme's early career, 4, 14, 18–20, 35, 43–46, 58, 85, 96–97, 133, 141, 142
Eyewitness (*Sudden Terror*), 36, 106–7

Fahrenheit 9/11, 159–60
Falk, Peter, 21
Far from Vietnam (*Loin du Vietnam*), 41, 160
Feminism, 44, 71–73, 97
Ferro, Pablo, 5
Fields, Freddie, 7, 20
Fields, Shep, 5
Fighting Mad, 4, 20, 35, 44–45, 46, 67
Film critic, Demme as, 4, 18, 34, 43, 84, 93, 132
Film noir, 10, 21, 33
Film Society of Lincoln Center, viii–ix
Final cut, 109, 145; in *Swing Shift*, quarrel over, x, 25–26, 35, 53, 58–59, 85, 91–92, 97–98, 100–2, 141
Flannery, Bruce, 81
Flashbacks, 13, 43; in *Beloved*, 118–19
Fonda, Peter, 35
Forte, Kate, 105, 123
Foster, Jodie, 60, 72–73, 85, 133, 135
Fraker, William A., 102

France, Demme filming in, 143–44
Frankenheimer, John, 154, 155, 159
French films, influence on Demme, 143–44
French New Wave, xvii–xviii, 144, 154
Frye, E. Max, 61
Fujimoto, Tak, 11, 13, 45–46, 63–64, 102, 107, 133
Fuller, Sam, 140
Fusion, xi, 4, 36

Gangster films, 48–49, 85
Ganz, Bruno, 157
Garner, Margaret, 122
Gay characters, 86–89, 93, 113–14
Gay reaction to Demme films: *Philadelphia*, xv, 86, 88–89; *The Silence of the Lambs*, xv, 74, 86, 88
Genres, 48–49, 54–55, 71, 121
Georgaris, Dean, 155
Getaway, The, 66
Ghosts, Demme's belief in, 130–31
Glenn, Scott, 67
Glover, Danny, 129, 130
Go (film), 145
Godfather films, 20, 68
Goetzman, Gary, 57, 98, 105, 113
Goldman, Bo, 11, 17, 22, 35, 56, 70
Goldstein, Richard, 7
Good Morning, Steve, 4, 18
Grant, Cary, 142, 144
Gray, Spalding, 33, 51–52, 85, 92
Greater Philadelphia Film Office, 79–80
Griffith, Melanie, 30–31, 64
Gross, Larry, 138, 140
Guinness, Alec, 112

Hackman, Gene, 72
Haiti, Demme's interest in, xii, xix, 52, 59, 69, 131, 146, 147
Haiti: Dreams of Democracy, xii, 37, 52–53, 86, 95, 147
Hall, Albert, 129
Hamilton, Lisa Gay, 129
Hammer, Joshua, xi
Handle with Care (*Citizens Band*), viii, 3–5, 6–9, 14, 17, 20–21, 25, 35, 40, 46–48, 85; awards, 7, 35; box-office failure, 3, 9, 17, 21, 25, 35, 46–47; screenplay, 7–8, 20–21, 46
Hanks, Tom, 79–81, 86, 87–88, 92, 93, 113–14, 117

Hannibal (Thomas Harris), 111, 113, 134–35, 156
Hansen, Brian, 15
Harris, Ed, 101–2
Harris, Emmylou, 167, 173
Harris, Thomas, 61, 67, 85, 111–13, 133–34, 145–46, 156
Harvey, Laurence, 155
Hawn, Goldie, 15, 16, 22–23, 35, 53, 58–59, 85, 97, 101, 141
Hepburn, Audrey, 142
Hess, Jared, 152
High school movies, 138
Hitchcock, Alfred, 139, 140; influence of, 10, 21, 54
Hitchcock, Robyn, 98, 99–100, 111
Hitler, Adolf, 48
Homophobia, 74, 84, 89, 113, 117
Hopkins, Anthony, 62, 67, 72, 85–86, 112, 133, 134–35
Horror films, 75, 121, 125
Hot Box, The, 44
Howard, Joanne (second wife), 80, 86, 174
Hughes, Howard, 7, 11, 13, 23, 48, 49, 70, 85
Human rights movement, 149
Humor, 6, 15, 25, 64, 90, 116, 141, 152; in *Married to the Mob*, 48–49, 55; in *Philadelphia*, 79, 113; in *Something Wild*, 31; in *Stop Making Sense*, 26; in *Swimming to Cambodia*, 85

Intolerance, 41
Iraq war, 159
Ironside, Michael, 139

Jamison, Peter, 46
Jarmusch, Jim, 165–66
Jean, Wyclef, 149
Jimmy Carter Man from Plains, xviii–xix

Kael, Pauline, xii–xiii, 7, 39–41
Kaleidoscope (band), 106–7
Kaplan, Jonathan, 35, 72
Kaplan, Mike, 4
Kartheiser, Vincent, 139
Keena, Monica, 139
Keir, Andy, 171
Keith, Ben, 167
Kerry, John, 155, 159, 160
Killing Fields, The, 52, 85
King, Martin Luther, 95

Kitsch, xii, 34, 40, 49–50, 59, 65, 75
Kramer, Larry, 86, 88
KRS-One, 77
Kuras, Ellen, 168, 171

LaGravenese, Richard, 117–18, 135
Lang, Fritz, 42
Lansbury, Angela, 155
Last Embrace, 6, 9–11, 21, 53, 54
Last Waltz, The, 27, 51
Le Carré, John, 112
Le Mat, Paul, 11, 13, 22
Leachman, Cloris, 35, 45
Lear, Norman, 15–16
Lee, Spike, 126
Levine, Joseph E., 4, 18, 34–35, 43, 84, 94, 132
Levine, Ted, 67–68
Life and Times of Rosie the Riveter, The, 23, 91
Life Is Beautiful (La Vita è bella), 124–25
Linson, Art, 11
Littleton, Carol, 52, 145
Logan, Bruce, 46
Los Angeles Independent Film Festival, 138
Lupino, Ida, 49

Mais, je suis belle, 148
Malcolm X, 129
Malley, Bill, 5
Manchurian Candidate, The (1962), 154–55, 156–57, 158
Manchurian Candidate, The (2004), xviii, 154–60; differences from original film, 156–57
Manchurian Candidate, The (Richard Condon), 154, 155, 158
Mandela, 103
Manhunter, 62, 67, 111
Manuel (costume designer), 171
Married to the Mob, 32–34, 40, 48–50, 55–56, 65, 85, 90–91; dance scene, 33, 37–38; humor in, 48–49, 55; music, 33, 38, 51, 59, 107; screenplay, 134; violence in, 66
Masculinity, 61
Maslin, Janet, viii
May, Elaine, 101
McBurney, Simon, 156–57
McCarthy, Joseph, 155
McCarthy, Todd, 151
McGill, Bruce, 47

INDEX 181

McKay, Craig, 110
Medavoy, Mike, 94
Melvin and Howard, ix, 7, 11–13, 14, 17, 23, 25, 33, 35, 48, 70, 94, 141; awards, ix, 15, 17, 25, 35; screenplay, 15, 21–22, 56, 70
Menell, Jo, 37, 52, 103
Miami Blues, 57, 69
Middle America, ix, xii, 6–9, 14–15, 33–35, 49, 58
Mise-en-scène, 34, 37, 40, 48
Modern Medea (Steven Weisenburger), 122
Modine, Matthew, 32, 37–38, 55
Montas, Michèle, 147–48, 150
Moore, Michael, 149, 159–60
Moriceau, Norma, 50
Morricone, Ennio, 51
Morrison, Toni, 104–5, 108–9, 115–16, 125, 128–29
Mount, Thom, 21–22, 94
Mr. Hulot's Holiday (*Les vacances de Monsieur Hulot*), 144
Muhammad Ali, 16
Mulvey, Laura, 72
Museum of Modern Art (New York City), 4
Music: avant-garde, xi; in *Beloved*, 107; Demme's love of, xi, 36, 98; effect on audience, 92; Haitian, 52, 59, 149; in *Married to the Mob*, 33, 38, 51, 59, 107; in *Philadelphia*, 92–93, 94–95; in *Something Wild*, 36, 59; source music in films, 53. See also *Complex Sessions, The*; *Neil Young: Heart of Gold*; Performance films; *Stop Making Sense*; *Storefront Hitchcock*
Music videos, 36, 59, 65, 72
Musicians, street, 53

Napier, Charles, 7, 35, 68
Napoleon Dynamite, 151–53
National Book Award, 116
National Society of Film Critics Awards, 25, 35, 85
Neil Young: Heart of Gold, xviii, 161–75; film style and technique in, 167–68
New Order, 36, 99
New Wave, French, xvii–xviii, 144, 154
New World Pictures, 4, 18, 35, 43–44, 85, 94, 132, 141, 142
New York City, x–xii, 10, 18, 99–100, 158; Demme filming in, 16, 30–31, 32–34, 37–38, 85

New York Film Critics Circle Awards, 7, 25
New York Film Festival, viii–ix, 3, 5, 7, 17, 35
New York Times, vii, viii, xix, 116
New Yorker, 39–40
Newton, Thandie, 129, 142, 154
Nichols, Mike, 11, 22, 35, 56, 94
Noël, Magali, 143
Nyswaner, Ron, 22–23, 79, 87, 109, 134

Offbeat subject matter, 6–7, 31, 33–34, 58–59, 65, 115, 153
One Foot on a Banana Peel, the Other Foot in the Grave, 86, 95
Opportunists, The, 108
Optimism, xi, 3, 37
Orion Pictures, 10, 31, 33, 34, 37, 53, 60, 72–73, 100, 109
Oscars, 15, 17, 35, 79, 84, 85–86, 94, 120
Owens, Bill (photographer), 152

Panama, Steve, 4
Paramount Pictures, 3, 8, 9, 20, 25, 40, 46, 108, 160
Paris, France, Demme filming in, 143–44
Parting the Waters (Taylor Branch), 95
Pathé Contemporary, 4, 18, 35
PBS (Public Broadcasting Service), 14, 16, 53, 56, 59
Pé de Boi, 33, 38
People for the American Way Foundation, 15–16
People Magazine, xi
Performance films, xi, xvi, xvii, 26–27, 36, 92, 98–99, 136, 141, 167; live audience in, xi, 27, 28, 172–73. See also *Complex Sessions, The*; Documentaries; Music videos; *Neil Young: Heart of Gold*; *Stop Making Sense*; *Storefront Hitchcock*; *Swimming to Cambodia*
Perillo, Joey, 82
Pfeiffer, Michelle, 32, 37–38, 55, 85, 90
Philadelphia, xv, 78–83, 86–89, 90, 92–93, 117, 141; awards, 84, 86, 94; box-office success, 84, 103–4; casting, 113–14; gay reaction to, xv, 86, 88–89; humor in, 79, 113; opera scene, 92–93; screenplay, 87, 134; songs composed for, 94–95
Philadelphia, Pa., Demme filming in, 78–83
Phillips, Don, 11
Picker, David, 8
Pinkenson, Sharon, 79–80

Politics, Demme's views on, vii, xiv–xv, xviii, 16, 52, 54, 59, 76–77, 87, 148–49, 154–55, 158–60
Pollack, Sydney, 24
Porter, Cole, 59
Portman, Rachel, 107
Prairie Wind (album), 161–62, 164–67, 169–71, 173–75
Prelude to a Kiss, 88
Prizzi's Honor, 48
Producing, 44, 105; and Demme, xvi, xviii, 18–19, 43–44, 57, 69, 86, 133, 142
Production design, 37–38, 49–50, 62, 144
Production numbers, 37–38
Public Broadcasting Service. See PBS
Publicist, Demme as, 4, 18, 35, 43, 58, 71, 85, 132, 142
Purcell, Evelyn (first wife), 4
Pyne, Daniel, 155–56

Quirky subject matter, 6–7, 31, 33–34, 58–59, 65, 115, 153

Race relations, Demme's interest in, xiv, xvi–xvii, 61, 65, 77, 109–10, 115, 125. See also African American subject matter
Rachel Getting Married, xviii
Radio Haiti Inter, 146, 147
Rafelson, Toby, 50, 56
Rashomon, adapted as motorcycle movie, 19, 35, 43, 85, 142
Reconstruction, 105, 118, 128
Red, Hot + Blue, 59
Red Baron, The (Von Richthofen and Brown), 18, 142
Red Dragon (Thomas Harris), 62
Rehearsing on film, 106
Remakes. See *Manchurian Candidate, The*; *Truth about Charlie, The*
Rendell, Ed, 79–80
Resnais, Alain, 41, 160
Richards, Beah, 129
Right to Return, xviii
Ritt, Martin, 24
Robards, Jason, 13, 22, 79
Rock journalist, Demme as, xi, 36, 106–7
Rodd, Marcia, 6–7
Romero, George A., 68
Rosemary's Baby, 64, 75
Roth, Joe, 109

Rowe, Bill, 78, 82
Rowley, Isaiah, 76–77
Rozsa, Miklos, 10–11, 54
Rudolph, Alan, 53
Run Lola Run (Lola rennt), 145
Rush Hour, 127, 135
Rushes (dailies), 27, 56, 107–8
Russell, Kurt, 53, 97
Ryman Auditorium, Nashville, Tenn., 161–62, 173

Sarandon, Susan, 16, 56
Saturn, 138
Savage Seven, The, 19
Saxon, Edward, 79, 81–82, 87, 103, 105, 109, 126
Scheider, Roy, 10, 21, 54
Schmidt, Rob, 138–40
Schreiber, Liev, 155
Scorsese, Martin, 41, 51, 53, 58
Screenplays, 15, 46, 61, 134–36
Screenwriter, Demme as, 18–19, 20, 43, 132–33, 142. See also Collaboration in filmmaking: with screenwriters
Screwball comedy, 33, 55
Shaber, David, 10, 21
Shoot the Piano Player (Tirez sur le pianiste), 42
Sight and Sound, 110–11
Silence of the Lambs, The, xiii–xiv, 59–64, 67–69, 71–75, 94, 112–13, 125, 133–34, 141; awards, xiii, 79, 85, 120; box-office success, 86, 93, 103–4; faithfulness to book, 112; gay reaction to, xv, 74, 86, 88; screenplay, 133
Silence of the Lambs, The (Thomas Harris), 72–73, 75, 112, 134, 141, 145–46; sequel to (*Hannibal*), 111, 113, 134–35, 156
Sinatra, Frank, 155
Since You Went Away, 23
Singleton, John, 126
Slavery, 104–5, 115, 118, 122, 126, 127–28
Small-town America. See Middle America
Social issues, Demme's interest in, xiv, xv–xvii, 23, 54, 59, 76–77, 86, 90, 95, 149
Something Wild, 30–31, 33–34, 54–55, 59, 64–65, 72, 85, 92, 109; high-school reunion scene, 37, 40, 64; humor in, 31; music, 36, 59; screenplay, 61; violence in, 41, 66–67, 91
Sony Pictures, 113, 126

Sothern, Ann, 45
Sound of Trumpets, The (Il posto), 9
Spinell, Joe, 55
Springsteen, Bruce, 94–95
Squat Theatre, 99–100
Stallone, Sylvester, 90
Steenburgen, Mary, 17, 22, 35, 79
Stockwell, Dean, 32, 48, 66
Stop Making Sense, x–xi, 26–29, 36, 51, 91–92, 98–99, 101–2; award (National Society of Film Critics), 85; humor in, 26
Storefront Hitchcock, xvii, 99–100, 111, 114
Streep, Meryl, 155, 157
Sturges, Preston, 49, 127
Sudden Terror (Eyewitness), 36, 106–7
Sullivan's Travels, 49, 110, 127
Summerour, Lisa, 82
Sun City (music video), 59
Sundance Film Festival, 138, 151
Suzhou River (Suzhou he), 145
Swimming to Cambodia, 51–52, 59, 85, 92; humor in, 85
Swing Shift, ix–x, 15, 17, 19, 22–24, 91; director's cut destroyed, 91, 110–11; final cut, quarrel over, x, 25–26, 35, 53, 58–59, 85, 91–92, 97–98, 100–2, 141; script, 22–23, 87
Sylbert, Richard, 8

Take One, 25
Talking Heads, 26, 28, 36, 51, 85, 92, 98, 99, 136
Tally, Ted, 59, 62, 72, 112, 133
Taylor, Mike, 9–10, 21
Test screenings, 145
Texas Chainsaw Massacre, 75
Thirteenth Man, The (Murray Bloom), 10
Touchstone Pictures, 117
Transvestitism, 68
TriStar Pictures, 79, 83, 86
True Stories, 50–51, 59
Truffaut, François, 17–18
Truth about Charlie, The, xvii, 141–42, 143–45, 154; differences from *Charade*, 144
Trying Times, 59
Twentieth Century Fox, 10

Unbearable Lightness of Being, The, 41
United Artists (UA), 4, 9–10, 21, 35, 142
Universal Pictures, 11, 21, 94, 108
Utt, Kenneth, 79–80, 82, 83

Vachon, Christine, 139
Van der Graaf Generator (band), 106–7
Venice Film Festival, xix
Viola, Joe, 18–19, 43, 94, 133, 142
Violence in cinema, 9, 65–67, 139; in *Married to the Mob*, 66; in *Something Wild*, 41, 66–67, 91
Voight, Jon, 159
Von Richthofen and Brown (The Red Baron), 18, 142
Vonnegut, Kurt, 14, 16, 56

Wahlberg, Mark, 154
Walken, Christopher, 108
Walker Art Center, 14, 39
Walsh, Raoul, 19, 24
Walt Disney Company, 108–9
Walter, Tracey, 68
Ward, Fred, 57
Warner Brothers, 35, 91, 98, 100–2, 111, 141
Washington, Denzel, 88, 113, 151–52, 157; in *The Manchurian Candidate*, 151, 155, 156, 157, 160; in *Philadelphia*, 78–79, 86, 89, 92, 93
Wedgeworth, Ann, 6–7, 35
Westerns, 121
White slavery, 10, 54
Who Am I This Time?, 14, 16, 56, 58
Wigutow, Dan, 9–10, 21
Wild Angels, The, 43
Wilford, Charles, 57
Wilson, Trey, 164
Winfrey, Oprah, 108–9, 115–16, 120, 121–24, 125, 127, 131; as actress, 105, 121–22, 129–30, 137
Woman's pictures, 60, 61
Women's roles, in Demme's films, x, xiv, 23, 60, 72–73, 90–91
Woodward, Joanne, 79
Wright, Jeffrey, 139

Year of the Horse, 165
Young, Neil, 94–95, 99, 161–75; brain aneurysm, 161–65, 168–69, 174; Nashville songs, 171, 172; *Prairie Wind* songs, 161–62, 165–67, 169–71, 173–75
Young, Pegi, 165, 166–67

Zansky, Michael, 171
Zea, Kristi, 50, 62, 64
Zulu, 4, 18, 34, 43, 84, 132

www.ingramcontent.com/pod-product-compliance
Lightning Source LLC
Chambersburg PA
CBHW021840220426
43663CB00005B/330